PROSPERITY AND POVERTY

PROSPERITY AND POVERTY

The Compassionate Use of Resources in a World of Scarcity

E. Calvin Beisner

Wipf and Stock Publishers
150 West Broadway • Eugene OR 97401
2001

Prosperity and Poverty

The Compassionate Use of Resources in a World of Scarcity
By Beisner, E. Calvin
Copyright©1988 by Beisner, E. Calvin
ISBN: 1-57910-808-3

Reprinted by *Wipf and Stock Publishers*
150 West Broadway • Eugene OR 97401

Previously published by Crossway Books, 1988.

To Susan

May she be among the meek
who inherit Heaven and Earth

TABLE OF

CONTENTS

ACKNOWLEDGMENTS

*D*r. Herbert Schlossberg and Dr. Marvin Olasky gave me the initial idea for this book and made helpful suggestions for its organization. Marvin carefully read and criticized the initial draft of every chapter; his thoughts, often challenging ill-formed ideas, provided invaluable guides for revision. My wife, Deborah Melvin Beisner, also read initial drafts of all the chapters, catching many weaknesses and errors of emphasis and mapping out ways to correct them. Dr. Russell Kirk, my mentor several years ago in an intensive study of economic ethics, has had much to do with shaping my thought, and his influence on this work will be seen by anyone familiar with his writings. None of them, of course, is responsible for any errors the book might have.

Members of Gateway Chapel supported me constantly and fervently in prayer, making me feel like their missionary! Thanks also go to Howard Ahmanson and the Fieldstead Institute for financial backing, without which I could not have taken the time to write this book.

Special thanks go to my wife Debby and my children David, Susan, and Kilby for their patience while I have exiled myself to the study day after day and night after night. They are my daily joy.

E. Calvin Beisner
Pea Ridge, Arkansas

Soli Deo Gloria!

*I*n a world with multiplied millions of hungry people and a nation with thousands of homeless poor, evangelicals must combine warm hearts and cool heads to discover and explain the Bible's responses to poverty. We cannot afford to promote prescriptions for the cure to poverty that are worse than the disease. As one economist puts it, "... truly compassionate policy requires dispassionate analysis."[1] The purpose of this book is to explore Biblical principles and methods of stewardship essential to effective, compassionate ministry to needy people—poor, middle-class, and rich alike. Understanding these principles and methods can help us perform the dispassionate analysis that must precede our choice of just and compassionate policies.

The stakes are high. The choices mean the difference between starvation and plenty, between liberty and oppression, for tens of millions of people. We must avoid pursuing destructive policies with compassionate motives; instead we must pursue constructive policies with compassionate motives. Our goal as responsible stewards, accountable to God, is to identify Biblical and effective ways of allocating the world's scarce resources to the production, distribution, and consumption of goods and services so that true justice prevails and human needs are met in every nook and cranny of society.

STEWARDSHIP AND ECONOMICS

Biblical stewardship views God as Owner of all things (Psalm 24:1) and man—individually and collectively—as His steward. Every person is accountable to God for the use of whatever he has (Genesis 1:26-30; 2:15). Every person's responsibility as a steward is to maximize the Owner's return on His investment by using it to serve others (Matthew 25:14-30). How best to do that is the central question of this book.

"Stewardship" and "economics" are almost interchangeable words. This is not to deny that there is more to stewardship than what most people think of as economics (money and business affairs). Instead it is to say that there is more to economics than most people think. (Just as there's more to stewardship than church fund-raising drives.) Great economists have always recognized that economics encompasses all of life. Economics—or stewardship—is fundamentally the study and practice of allocating scarce resources to various uses. It includes choices about how much time to spend in prayer, at work, at play; how many tons of corn to use feeding people or cattle; how much physical energy to spend building roads or preaching the gospel; how much emotional energy to spend on anger, love, or grief, and so on.[2]

Biblical stewardship, like economics, is concerned with finding the most just and beneficial ways of allocating the world's scarce resources for the production, distribution, and consumption of wealth—food, clothing, shelter, transportation, knowledge, relationships (including man's relationship with God), anything people value, so long as it is not inherently immoral.[3] The word "economics" is, in fact, derived from Greek words for stewards and stewardship.[4] Hence the near interchangeability of the words is rooted solidly in Biblical usage.

"Stewardship" does, however, convey more than "economics," and this is a matter of fundamental importance to this book. It is possible to imagine practicing economics without having to answer to a higher authority.[5] But autonomy is impossible for a steward, who manages the affairs of a household on behalf of its owner. Christian stewardship, then, means managing all the affairs of the world, small and large, on behalf of its Owner. Accountability is essential to stewardship.

TOWARD JUSTICE AND COMPASSION

This book seeks to explain Biblical principles of stewardship for individuals, families, churches, and whole societies and states. Only as those principles are properly understood and applied can people build and maintain just, compassionate societies in which everyone's real needs are met.

To that end, Part One sets forth some principles of Christian spirituality that equip believers for proper understanding and action as stewards. Part Two analyzes the Biblical understanding of justice and its implications for stewardship and economics. Some of my conclusions, based on careful study of Biblical texts, some of them controversial, are strongly opposed to views promoted by many recent evangelical books on the subject. All the rest of the book, including frequent analyses of current and proposed policies, stands on the spiritual and ethical foundation laid in these first two parts.

Part Three discusses basic economic principles without which it is impossible to define or formulate just, humane, productive policy, whether for economies in general or for the poor specifically. Part Four explores a Biblical understanding of the nature and functions of civil government, particularly in terms of Biblical justice, and then applies that understanding to important questions about government's relationship to the economy. In particular, Chapters Twelve and Thirteen test numerous economic regulations—most intended to help the poor—by the twin standards of Biblical justice and economic efficiency. These two standards always yield the same results because God made spiritual and material reality consistent with each other. Anything unjust is ultimately economically inefficient, and anything just is ultimately economically efficient (though it may appear otherwise in the short run).

Part Five brings Biblical principles of stewardship and justice to bear on the question of how best to minister to the poor. Particular attention goes to defining poverty Biblically, since many modern approaches to poverty assume an un-Biblical definition of the poor. That done, it is possible to determine the real extent of the problem; the policies, resources, and actions necessary for its solution; and how those three factors can best be brought to bear on helping the poor. I conclude that the problem is manageable: by properly applying Biblical principles of stewardship, we can minister effectively to all of the poor and see major reductions in the amount of poverty in our nation and the world.

BIBLICAL AND ECONOMIC ANALYSIS

Scores of books have been published recently addressing stewardship and responses to poverty. Unfortunately, many suffer from one or both of two serious weaknesses: lack of understanding of basic economic principles, and improper handling of key Biblical texts. The former frequently embrace policies that, when implemented (and many have been), have precisely the opposite effects from those intended. The latter frequently conclude that Biblical texts require some policy or action when, in fact, they require something quite different. While I hope this book rests on accurate understanding of economic principles and sound Biblical interpretation, I know my falli- bility. Thus I welcome corrections from my brothers and sis- ters in Christ, whether of exegesis or of economic analysis.

In Philippians 2:3 Paul wrote, "Do nothing out of selfish ambition or vain conceit, but in humility *consider others bet- ter than yourselves" (NIV)*. Often I take issue with some fel- low Christians on Biblical interpretation, economic policy, and ethical questions. Following Paul's admonition, I assume, when I criticize a position or argument, that whoever holds it at least does so for noble motives. I hope readers will correct me wherever they think I have been ungracious.

ENVIRONMENT, DEVELOPMENT, AND LIBERATION
For the sake of unity and brevity, the book largely bypasses three important subjects. First is the complex set of interrelat- ed issues of population growth, the environment, conserva- tion, and the development and use of natural resources. There is an urgent need for a solid Biblical analysis of that subject that takes into account fundamental principles of economics, but it requires more extensive analysis than could be done in a chapter or two of a book whose main focus lies elsewhere.[6]

Second is the question of how best to help the poor of other nations (and by "other" I mean generally nations other than the one in which any reader resides, though specifically nations other than the United States). This, too, is a complex and thorny issue that needs much careful Biblical and econom- ic analysis. Answers appear to lie more in development than in charitable gifts (though not to their exclusion), particularly for the Third World, much of which lacks developed economic structures essential to lifting whole societies out of poverty. Precisely how development is to be done and what are the appropriate roles of churches, civil governments, corporations, and individuals—these questions need considerably more exploration than could have been done here.[7]

Third, liberation theology, which attempts to mix

Marxist and Christian concepts but succeeds better in smothering the latter in the former, deserves a far more thorough critique than could be offered here. Unfortunately, few of its critics thus far have challenged it on the important turf of exegeting specific Biblical texts—to many of which it appeals, though it interprets them through Marxist-colored glasses. The job greatly needs doing from a decidedly evangelical perspective.[8]

PART ONE

STEWARDSHIP AND THE SPIRITUAL LIFE

YOU CANNOT SERVE GOD AND MAMMON

*J*esus' encounter with the rich young man (Matthew 19:16-22) has given rise to many interpretations. Some see in it a require- ment that Christians abandon their worldly goods, others a specif- ic command to a specific individual designed to point to his chief spiritual problem. Whatever else we might learn from it, however, we can surely conclude that a man's willingness to part with his possessions and give to the poor at Christ's command is an accu- rate measurement of his spiritual maturity: "If you wish to be complete,[1] go and sell your possessions and give to the poor, and you shall have treasure in heaven; and come, follow Me" (v. 21).

The maturity measured in this command may be defined as self-abandonment, trust in God's provision, care for others, and commitment to following Jesus. Spiritual maturity in attitudes toward and use of possessions as individuals, members of families and churches, and citizens of communities and nations should be the goal toward which Christians always strive. It begins by for- saking the urge to serve self and trusting in God's provision instead, leads to pouring ourselves out for others, and culminates in following Jesus as the highest means of service. Christians are called to reenact in our own lives "the grace of our Lord Jesus Christ, [who] though He was rich, yet for [our] sake He became poor, that [we] through His poverty might become rich" (2 Corinthians 8:9).

Jesus made self-denial the heart of Christian maturity: "If anyone wishes to come after Me, let him deny himself, and take up his cross daily, and follow Me" (Luke 9:23). Here is the same progression of thought that was in Jesus' instructions to the rich young man: deny self, serve others, and follow Him. Serving oth- ers is the point of taking up the cross. As Jesus came not to be served but to serve by giving Himself as a ransom for many (Matthew 20:28), so the Christian's cross is his work of service to those in need.

THE GOAL IS MATURITY

Jesus began His answer to the rich young man in a strange way: "*If you wish to be complete* . . . " The young man had asked not about "completeness," or "maturity," but about eternal life (Matthew 19:16). But gaining eternal life is not God's goal for His people, and doing a good work is not the means to it. On the contrary, while salvation is " . . . by grace . . . through faith . . . not of [ourselves] . . . not as a result of works . . .," God's goal for us is much more: "For we are His workmanship, created in Christ Jesus *for good works*, which God prepared beforehand, that we should walk in them" (Ephesians 2:8-10). If we do not desire to attain to Christian maturity, it is no use our asking Jesus about eternal life—or anything else—for we, like the rich young man, will go away empty and sorrowful.

SELF-ABANDONMENT

"If you wish to be complete," Jesus said, "*go and sell your possessions* . . . " In Jesus' day, as in every age, the great temptation was to trust in possessions instead of in the Provider, and the rich young man did just that. To another person Jesus said, "Beware, and be on your guard against every form of greed; for not even when one has an abundance does his life consist of his possessions" (Luke 12:15). Immediately Jesus launched into the parable of the rich fool (vv. 16-21); warned against anxiety for physical needs (v. 22); urged His followers to seek for His Kingdom with the assurance that all their physical needs would be met (v. 31); and concluded, "Sell your possessions and give to charity; make yourselves purses which do not wear out, an unfailing treasure in heaven, where no thief comes near, nor moth destroys. For where your treasure is, there will your heart be also" (vv. 33, 34).

Jesus insists on knowing of each of us, "Where is your treasure? Is it in barns, hoarded away for some expected tragedy? Is it in tax shelters, bearing little fruit for God's Kingdom or man's needs? Is it tied up in 'securities' that cannot secure the body, let alone the soul? Or is it at work for others' benefit, even at risk to yourself? Are you storing up treasure in Heaven, or on earth?"

In insisting that this man sell his possessions, Jesus established no universal principle requiring all Christians to give away all their wealth. That would contradict His explicit exclamation, upon Zaccheus' repentance and promise to repay fourfold anything he had defrauded and to give half his possessions to the poor, "Today salvation has come to this house, because he, too, is a son of Abraham" (Luke 19:9). To be a "son of Abraham" is to have genuine, saving faith in God (Romans 4). In Zaccheus Jesus saw that faith, expressed in repentance and charity. But the rich young man lacked such faith. He clung to his possessions instead of following Jesus.

Nevertheless, Jesus does set forth a different universal principle: that every believer must count following Jesus worth more than all his possessions, and so be willing to give up everything for Jesus' sake. He calls us to strip away all security but God. Our possessions and families (Matthew 19:29; Luke 14:26), our wisdom and knowledge and even personal holiness (Philippians 3:4-9)—these and any other things on which we depend for our security must be cast aside and replaced by trust in God alone (cf. Psalm 62:1, 2, 7).

SERVING OTHERS

"If you wish to be complete, go and sell your possessions," Jesus said, *"and give to the poor . . ."*[2] Mere self-abandonment is not enough for the Christian. It may be the goal of Hinduism and Buddhism, which strive for negation of all desire and absorption into universal spirit, but Christianity demands something quite different. We abandon ourselves not to become idle, but to become redemptively active, pouring out ourselves and our possessions to serve others.

Unlike idle pietism (and not all pietism is idle),[3] charitable giving demonstrates the reality of Christian faith and life. Just as faith without works is dead (James 2:26), so love without works is dead, for ". . . whoever has the world's goods, and beholds his brother in need and closes his heart against him, how does the love of God abide in him? Little children, let us not love with word or with tongue, but in deed and truth. We shall know by this that we are of the truth, and shall assure our heart before Him . . . " (1 John 3:17-19).

ETERNAL VALUES

"If you wish to be complete, go and sell your possessions and give to the poor," Jesus said, *"and you shall have treasure in heaven..."* There is a promise that comes along with self-abandonment for Jesus' sake. Christ does not ask us to cast ourselves away without hope, but to cast away all that stands between us and the greatest hope of all.

It is simultaneously a blessing and a curse that much Christianity has abandoned the "pie in the sky by-and-by" mentality. That mentality represented at least as much a rejection of the Church's duty to care for the world as a rejection of worldliness itself. But the present about-face often brings with it an inversion of Biblical values, placing temporal above eternal. In contrast, Jesus' attitude is unequivocal:

> Do not lay up for yourselves treasures upon earth, where moth and rust destroy, and where thieves break in and steal. But lay up for yourselves treasures in heaven, where neither moth nor rust destroys, and where thieves do not break in or steal; for where your treasure is, there will your heart be also. The lamp of the body is the eye; if therefore your eye is clear, your whole body will be full of light. But if your eye is bad, your whole body will be full of darkness. If therefore the light that is in you is darkness, how great is the darkness! (Matthew 6:19-23)

Jesus equates clarity of vision with steadfast attachment to things above, not things below. Just so Paul urges, "If then you have been raised up with Christ, keep seeking the things above, where Christ is, seated at the right hand of God. Set your mind on the things above, not on the things that are on earth. For you have died and your life is hidden with Christ in God" (Colossians 3:1-3).

The great risk for Israel on entering the Promised Land was that it would lose its singular attachment to its God. Immediately after impressing the great commandment on Israel, "... you shall love the Lord your God with all your heart and with all your soul and with all your might" (Deuteronomy 6:5) and urging them to keep God's commandments uppermost in mind, Moses warned:

> Then it shall come about when the Lord your God brings you into the land which He swore to your fathers, Abraham, Isaac and Jacob, to give you, great and splendid cities which you did not build, and houses full of good things which you did not fill, and hewn cisterns which you did not dig, vineyards and olive trees which you did not plant, and you shall eat and be satisfied, then watch yourself, lest you forget the Lord who brought you from the land of Egypt, out of the house of slavery. You shall fear only the Lord your

God; and you shall worship [literally "serve"] Him,
and swear by His name. You shall not follow other
gods.... (Deuteronomy 6:10-14a)

Riches are as likely as anything to entice us to violate the
First Commandment, "You shall have no other gods before Me"
(Deuteronomy 5:7). The great danger is that they will gain our
first allegiance instead of God, that we will trust them instead of
God for security, and that, when a choice must be made, we will
cling to them instead of to God. That is why Jesus insisted, ". . . it
is hard for a rich man to enter the kingdom of heaven...it is easier
for a camel to go through the eye of a needle, than for a rich man
to enter the kingdom of God" (Matthew 19:23, 24).

FOLLOWING JESUS

"If you wish to be complete, go and sell your possessions and give
to the poor, and you shall have treasure in heaven," Jesus said,
"and come, follow Me." Here is the height of self-abandonment.
Jesus calls us to follow Him, not ruling our own lives but obeying
Him.

Nothing must substitute for the self-abandonment of being
like Jesus—and even sharing in His work—as the believer's highest goal. Paul made that point when he wrote:

> . . . whatever things were gain to me, those things I
> have counted as loss for the sake of Christ. More than
> that, I count all things to be loss in view of the sur-
> passing value of knowing Christ Jesus my Lord, for
> whom I have suffered the loss of all things, and count
> them but rubbish in order that I may gain Christ, and
> may be found in Him, not having a righteousness of
> my own derived from the Law, but that which is
> through faith in Christ, the righteousness which
> comes from God on the basis of faith, that I may
> know Him, and the power of His resurrection and the
> fellowship of His sufferings, being conformed to His
> death; in order that I may attain to the resurrection
> from the dead. (Philippians 3:7-11)

"In a word," writes Sinclair Ferguson, *"maturity equals
Christlikeness.* No other standard may be allowed to substitute."[4]
Following Jesus means being willing to cast aside anything
He tells us to abandon. It means trusting God alone for all that we

need, pouring ourselves out to serve others, focusing our lives on things eternal rather than temporal. It means absolute, total commitment. And for anyone who longs for salvation, it is not optional.

NO ONE CAN SERVE TWO MASTERS

One of the most damnable heresies in the history of Christianity is the teaching—all too common in every age—that Jesus can be "Savior" without being "Lord." It belittles every command of Christ. It crashes head-on into the insistent words of Jesus:

> If you love Me, you will keep My command-ments....He who has My commandments and keeps them, he it is who loves Me; and he who loves Me shall be loved by My Father, and I will love him, and will disclose Myself to him. (John 14:15, 21)

Anything that usurps Christ's place as absolute Ruler of our lives becomes His rival. It divides our allegiance and so cripples our usefulness in His Kingdom. And, because "the love of money is a root of all sorts of evil," wealth is among Jesus' most common rivals, tempting those who long for it to abandon the faith (1 Timothy 6:10).[5]

That is why, immediately after urging believers to lay up treasures in Heaven, Jesus insists, "No one can serve two masters; for either he will hate the one and love the other, or he will hold to one and despise the other. You cannot serve God and mammon"[6] (Matthew 6:24). Mammon ". . . inevitably becomes the master if a man tries to make himself its master by acquiring it for its own sake."[7]

Jesus does not say, "You must not," or "You ought not," or "It would be unwise for you to serve both God and possessions," but "You *cannot* serve God and mammon." Serving both is as impossible as squaring a circle or making two plus two equal five. The Lord our God is a jealous God (Exodus 20:5), and will not share His glory with another (Isaiah 42:8). He demands absolute rule in our lives, and anything that challenges His rule must go lest it ruin us.

That is the sense of the covenant between God and His people. The Christian stands toward God in the relation of vassal to feudal lord. He is bound by a treaty of suzerainty by which God asserts His absolute right of dominion over him.[8] God has purchased him from slavery to sin, and has set forth His demands on him (Exodus 20:2). He promises blessings on obedience and curses on disobedience (Deuteronomy 8 and 28). So long as the vassal serves his feudal lord, he is protected and provided for. But the moment he allies himself with a rival, he faces the brunt of his lord's anger.

Anything that usurps God's authority is an idol—a false god. And whenever we put possessions—whether material wealth, health, power, even friendships—above God, whenever we serve them instead of serving God, we commit idolatry. When we exercise godly stewardship over such things, they all become tools (like the money in the parable of the talents) for building God's Kingdom and maturing in spiritual life. But when we serve them as ends in themselves, they lead us away from God. That is why Jesus said of anyone who tried to serve two masters, ". . . either he will hate the one and love the other, or he will hold to one and despise the other" (Matthew 6:24).

Nothing is more debilitating to true Christian stewardship than allowing anything to usurp God's authority in our lives. Good stewardship requires obedience, and we cannot obey God when we rebel against Him and serve other gods.

CONQUERING THE IDOL OF MAMMON

Spiritual growth is a prerequisite to proper stewardship. So a major step toward a proper understanding and application of Christian stewardship is conquering the idol of Mammon. How can we do that? This is not the place for detailed answers to that question, but here are three fundamental principles:[9]

DISCIPLINE FOR GODLINESS

We are "by nature children of wrath" (Ephesians 2:3), and sin, not righteousness, comes to us naturally, even though we are Christians (Romans 7:14-24). Therefore we must discipline ourselves for godliness (1 Timothy 4:7b).

The "discipline" of which Paul wrote—*gumnasia*—was no easy matter. It referred to exercise in preparation for competition. It carried the sense not of transitory attention merely, but of consistent, long-term training that made habits of all the activities involved.[10]

Rigorous self-discipline in prayer (Psalm 63:1), in the study of God's Word (Psalm 119:11), in submission to spiritual guidance from mature brothers and sisters in the Body of Christ (Ephesians 4:11-16; 5:21), and in decisive obedience despite contrary feelings (Deuteronomy 30:19) are essential to spiritual growth. "Where your treasure is, there will your heart be also" (Matthew 6:21) is not a proof-text for fund-raising, but a measure of our devotion to God. When we intentionally invest our best time and energy in pursuing God in Scripture and prayer, we show that our treasure is in God. When we put off the pursuit of God until it becomes convenient, we put off spiritual maturity (Luke 9:59-62).

If we pursue God heartily, our minds will be renewed and our values transformed so that we no longer worry about material possessions or needs.

GIVING TO OTHERS

We must also wean ourselves from the love of possessions and train ourselves to trust God. That is the point of Jesus' instruction to the rich young man who had made an idol of his wealth. So long as that idol remained enthroned, he could pay no attention to God's claims on his life. Therefore Jesus insisted that he sell his possessions and give to the poor. Only radical surgery could break his bondage. But as cancers may be incipient or far advanced, so surgery may be major or minor. In the case of Zaccheus the tax-gatherer, health was restored by fourfold restitution to all whom he had defrauded and by giving half his wealth to the poor (Luke 19:1-10).

However mild or radical, the surgery always takes the same form: *giving.* Nothing else so certainly and powerfully breaks the bonds of Mammon. Indeed, many people testify that a sure way to rid themselves of financial worries is to give more than they think they presently can afford.

TAKING UP THE CROSS

Finally, to conquer the idol of Mammon we must take up the cross, mimicking Jesus in service to others.

So long as our minds are fixed on ourselves and our own needs, we will worship Mammon. We will cling to what we have, thinking it necessary for present and future security. We will envy those with more, coveting what is theirs, grasping for more and more and more.

Scripture calls the believer to a wholly different way of life: "Do nothing from selfishness or empty conceit, but with humility of mind let each of you regard one another as more important than himself; do not merely look out for your own personal interests, but also for the interests of others" (Philippians 2:3, 4).

Ultimately, worshiping Mammon means worshiping self. For despite appearances to the contrary, we covet wealth not for its own sake, but for the benefit we think we will gain from it. And that perspective betrays a broader and deeper attitude in our hearts: everything, we think, exists to serve us. In so thinking, we put ourselves in the place of God, for whose pleasure all things were created (Revelation 4:11, *KJV*).

There is but one cure to such selfishness: pouring ourselves out for the sake of others, as Jesus did:

> . . . who, although He existed in the form of God, did not regard equality with God a thing to be grasped, but emptied Himself, taking the form of a bond-servant, and being made in the likeness of men. And being found in appearance as a man, He humbled Himself by becoming obedient to the point of death, even death on a cross. (Philippians 2:6-8)

Only when we are resolved to make this our attitude are we ready to learn and apply the principles of Biblical stewardship.

WORKING AS A SERVANT OF GOD

*T*he Fourth Commandment instructs all people to work: "Six days you shall labor and do all your work" (Exodus 20:9)[1]. Work is an essential economic activity, and Chapters Six through Eight will discuss ways of maximizing its productivity. But first we will examine some spiritual aspects of work.

WORK EXPRESSES THE IMAGE OF GOD

Work expresses who we are, what we are, and what we believe.[2] Just as the created order, God's work, expresses His character (Psalm 19:1-6), so our work makes visible our invisible spiritual nature. It shows our character, just as truly as good works make visible the presence of faith in the heart of one who professes it (James 2:18). In work, we reflect the image of our Maker (Genesis 1:26), for He too is a worker (Genesis 2:2; John 5:17), and at the very time He created us He commanded us to work: "Be fruitful and multiply, and fill the earth, and subdue it; and rule over the fish of the sea and over the birds of the sky, and over every living thing that moves on the earth" (Genesis 1:28).

This means that work—including what we think about it and how we do it—is closely related to our spiritual maturity. God's goal in believers is that we should become "conformed to the image of His Son" (Romans 8:29), who in turn is "the image of the invisible God." It was by Him that "all things were created . . . and in Him all things hold together" (Colossians 1:15-17). The Son of God is, like the Father whose image He displays, a worker (John 5:17), creating, sustaining, and redeeming the world (Colossians 1:15-20). Growth in Christian maturity then means not only increasing righteousness, holiness, and truth (Ephesians 4:23, 24),[3] but also growth as workers fulfilling God's purpose for all mankind to cultivate and keep the earth (Genesis 2:15).

Just as the Son of God into whose image we are to be conformed is Creator, Sustainer, and Redeemer, so there are creative, sustaining, and redemptive aspects to human work. We see the creative and sustaining aspects in Genesis 2:15: cultivation increases and directs the earth's natural productivity to meet man's needs, while guarding sustains it against degradation. Apart from the fall, these would have been the only aspects of work, but man's sin brought death and corruption, and so man was assigned a redemptive work, restoring earth's productivity by the sweat of his brow (Genesis 3:19).

WORK, THE FALL, AND THE CURSE

Work is not part of the curse God cast on man for sin. The curse promised *hardship* in multiplying (Genesis 3:16) and in subduing the earth (vv. 17-19), the latter because the ground itself was cursed so that its natural productivity would be perverted. But that man should work as part of his expression of the Creator's image was ordained prior to the fall (Genesis 1:26-28; 2:15, 18). Work is therefore a privilege, and sloth is condemned not only as rebellion against God's immediate command, but also as a dehumanizing repression of the image of God.[4]

Implicit in the need to work is the idea of scarcity, a fundamental concept of economics.[5] Left to itself, nature does not provide all man's needs or wants. Instead man must work, both to turn raw materials into finished goods, and to conserve the effects of his work so that he can build on them. This means man bears responsibility for the manner in which he uses the world over which God has given him dominion. As Calvin aptly put it:

> . . . the custody of the garden was given in charge to
> Adam, to show that we possess the things which God
> has committed to our hands, on the condition, that
> being content with a frugal and moderate use of them,
> we should take care of what shall remain. Let him
> who possesses a field, so partake of its yearly fruits,
> that he may not suffer the ground to be injured by his
> negligence; but let him endeavour to hand it down to
> posterity as he received it, or even better cultivated.
> Let him so feed on its fruits, that he neither dissipates
> it by luxury, nor permits [it] to be marred or ruined by
> neglect. Moreover, that this *economy*, and this diligence, with respect to those good things which God

has given us to enjoy, may flourish among us; let every one regard himself as the *steward* of God in all things which he possesses. Then he will neither conduct himself dissolutely, nor corrupt by abuse those things which God requires to be preserved.[6]

WORK IS A MEANS OF DOMINION

When God created man and woman, He said, ". . . let them have dominion over . . . all the earth . . ." (Genesis 1:26, KJV). Part of the purpose for which God created man was that man should rule over the earth ". . . in order that by his care and culture he might make it into a transparent mirror of the glory of the Creator."[7] A major purpose of our work is to make it serve our needs for God's glory.[8]

In this respect work's redemptive aspect takes on special importance. Because of the curse, the earth and its plants and animals are in rebellion against man. Before the fall work ". . . was pleasant, and full of delight, entirely exempt from all trouble and weariness."[9] "[F]ood was abundant and cheap, and man did not have to spend much time in search of sustenance and refreshment. Instead, his time was spent in scientific, productive, and aesthetic activity (Gen. 2:15, 19-20). Most of his labor involved investigating and beautifying his environment."[10]

But after the fall, God's curse meant that without man's redemptive activity the ground would become less and less fruitful, leaving even basic physical needs unmet. Work thus becomes a means of restoring the earth—insofar as possible— to its pre-fall productivity. That is, by working we begin to reestablish the dominion over the earth that God originally intended for man but that was broken by the fall and the curse. The increase of that dominion involves the increase of provision for man's needs and, consequently, the increase of man's opportunity to rest. The goal toward which we work is the restoration of the original created order on earth; rest is a symbol of the ultimate achievement of that goal, just as the sabbath is a symbol of ultimate salvation.[11] "Far from being a bitter consequence of the Fall, then, work is a vital aspect of God's overall purpose for man. In fact, 'a man can do nothing better than find satisfaction in his work' (Ecclesiastes 2:24, 3:22)."[12]

WORK, WEALTH, AND POVERTY

In all three of its aspects—creative, sustaining, and redemptive—work produces wealth. That is, it produces goods and services (both physical, like food, clothing, or transportation, and nonphysical, like knowledge or information) valued by human beings. This makes work the chief means of overcoming the poverty that ensued from the curse (Genesis 3:17-19). Work makes earth's natural fertility produce edible fruits, grains, and vegetables instead of briars and thistles. Work reshapes and recombines minerals from their natural states into bricks, concrete, iron, and steel. Work moves things from where they aren't needed to where they are.

Work, in short, is an essential factor in reducing poverty and building wealth.[13] It is "the only means of moving up and out of poverty, and in fact the only means of fulfilling God's purpose for our lives. . . ."[14] Even people who own no land or capital but are free to offer their labor in return for payment can produce wealth, and in general the more wise, diligent, and energetic the labor the more wealth it will produce: "Poor is he who works with a negligent hand, but the hand of the diligent makes rich. He who gathers in summer is a son who acts wisely, but he who sleeps in harvest is a son who acts shamefully" (Proverbs 10:4, 5).

THE NECESSITY OF WORK
Work is not an option for anyone who wishes to prosper, whether materially or spiritually. All must work to gain not only food, clothing, shelter, and the amenities of life, but also spiritual maturity. Those who refuse not only risk physical poverty, but also stunt, stop, or reverse their growth in Christian maturity —that is, in the restoration of the image of God that has been tarnished by sin.

An important part of all Christian endeavor, then, is helping people to work wisely and diligently. Later chapters will focus more closely on the strictly economic aspects of stewardship, keeping in mind that economics is the study of ethical principles and practical methods of allocating scarce resources to achieve optimal production, distribution, and consumption of wealth.[15] They will describe principles and practices that can encourage work and enhance its productivity, and others that can discourage it and diminish its productivity. But first let's consider the other side of the Fourth Commandment: rest.

THREE

RESTING IN THE PROVIDENCE OF GOD

W hen Jesus instructed the rich young man to sell all and give to the poor, He challenged him to trust God instead of riches, to serve God instead of Mammon.[1] He challenged him to learn the fundamental Biblical principle of *resting* in the grace of God expressed in His providence. Had the young man done so, he would have learned that God meets the needs of those who seek Him above all else (Matthew 6:33), and so would have learned the lesson of salvation by grace through faith instead of works.

Jesus called him to strip away all security but God.[2] The Biblical command to rest (Exodus 20:8-10) requires the same thing. By resting, Christians commemorate the completeness of God's creative and redemptive work (Exodus 20:11; Deuteronomy 5:15; cf. 6:10-14a), and acknowledge that all of our work is not for ourselves but for the Lord and His Kingdom (Colossians 3:23, 24; cf. Ephesians 6:5-8; 1 Corinthians 7:22). Thus we confirm that we depend not on ourselves but on God to provide for all of our needs. This includes not only salvation but also food, clothing, shelter—everything necessary to living and serving according to His will. By resting when God tells us to rest, we testify that we serve a Master who takes care of His servants.

COMMAND AND INVITATION

"Remember the sabbath day, to keep it holy. Six days you shall labor and do all your work, but the seventh day is a sabbath of the Lord your God; in it you shall not do any work, you or your son or your daughter, your male or your female servant or your cattle or your sojourner who stays with you" (Exodus 20:8-10). Jesus recast the Fourth Commandment as an invitation when He said, "Come to Me, all who are weary and heavy-laden, and I will give you rest.

Take My yoke upon you, and learn from Me, for I am gentle and humble in heart; and you shall find rest for your souls. For My yoke is easy, and My load is light" (Matthew 11:28-30).

The commandment is no more burdensome than the invitation. Indeed, the invitation makes explicit what the commandment—because of the context in which it was given—implies: that man finds his only real rest in serving God, and that the yoke of God is always easier than the yoke of man. That is why, in introducing the Ten Commandments, God said to Israel, "I am the Lord your God, who brought you out of the land of Egypt, *out of the house of slavery*" (Exodus 20:2; cf. Deuteronomy 5:6). God had redeemed the nation from slavery in Egypt so that it could serve Him, and the guiding principles of its service were embodied in the commandments. The yoke of slavery in Egypt had been hard and heavy; God's yoke would be easy and light (Matthew 11:30). No wonder after Paul argued that justification is by grace through faith (Romans 3:21–5:21), he quickly reminded believers that God still demands works as its fruit (Romans 6)! It must be so, for in salvation those who once were slaves of sin have become "slaves of righteousness"; "having been freed from sin" they have been "enslaved to God" (Romans 6:18, 22).

The sabbath commandment reminded Israel of its deliverance from slavery in Egypt: ". . . the seventh day is a sabbath of the Lord your God; in it you shall not do any work. . . . And you shall remember that you were a slave in the land of Egypt, and the Lord your God brought you out of there by a mighty hand and by an outstretched arm; therefore the Lord your God commanded you to observe the sabbath day" (Deuteronomy 5:14, 15). While its ceremonial aspects are done away in Christ, whose finished work they prefigured (Colossians 2:16, 17), its substance is as important now as it was then.[3] It reminds us of our deliverance from slavery under sin. When we conscientiously rest from our labors—not as a legalistic observance of ceremony but as a grateful acceptance of the rest Jesus offers us—we testify that His deliverance is complete.

Rest for the body commanded in the Fourth Commandment prefigures, then, rest for the soul initiated in a saving relationship with Jesus Christ and perfected in the life to come (Hebrews 4).

WHY RESIST REST?

Why then, if the sabbath commandment teaches such a wonderful lesson, are we so prone to resist its claim on us? Why, when we long—wistfully sometimes—for the rest Jesus promises in His invitation to come to Him, do we find every imaginable way to circumvent the commandment reiterated in that invitation? Why do people so commonly burn the candle at both ends, working seven days a week? Might we doubt the core of commandment and invitation alike—that every benefit comes from God and not from ourselves (James 1:17)? Is it our desire to be self-sufficient, to be independent, to provide for our own needs? Is this what drives us to resent this blessed commandment, "Remember the sabbath day, to keep it holy. . . . in it you shall not do any work"?

By commanding us to rest one day in seven, God vividly reminds us that it is not by our own efforts or our own goodness that we flourish, but by His gracious blessing (Deuteronomy 7:6-8; cf. Psalm 127:1). And to those who take pride in themselves, that reminder is a rebuke. But it is a necessary rebuke, for by it God portrays the gospel in physical life: just as God provides for the physical, so also He provides for the spiritual needs of those who trust Him, though in neither case do they work for them. "Now to the one who works, his wage is not reckoned as a favor, but as what is due. But to the one who does not work, but believes in Him who justifies the ungodly, his faith is reckoned as righteousness . . ." (Romans 4:4, 5). Grace working through faith, not self-generated works, is the means God uses to meet all needs. (Of course, physical provision by grace through faith no more negates the necessity of works in obedience to God than does spiritual provision by grace through faith.)[4]

Following the sabbath commandment, then, helps us to experience God's providence in daily life. It teaches us to work not for ourselves but for the Lord, trusting Him to meet our needs as we obey Him. Then we can truly rest in the assurance that, as A. Wetherell Johnson said, "If I do a good day's work for the Lord, He sees that I do not lack."[5] Then at last Jesus' words in the Sermon on the Mount can be more than a rebuke; they can be a pattern for life:

> . . . do not be anxious for your life, as to what you shall eat, or what you shall drink; nor for your body, as to what you shall put on. Is not life more than food, and the body than clothing? Look at the birds of the air, that they do not sow, neither do they reap, nor gather into barns, and yet your heavenly Father feeds them. Are you not worth much more than they?
>
> And which of you by being anxious can add a single cubit to his life's span? And why are you anxious

about clothing? Observe how the lilies of the field grow; they do not toil nor do they spin, yet I say to you that even Solomon in all his glory did not clothe himself like one of these. But if God so arrays the grass of the field, which is alive today and tomorrow is thrown into the furnace, will He not much more do so for you, O men of little faith?

Do not be anxious then, saying, "What shall we eat?" or "What shall we drink?" or "With what shall we clothe ourselves?" For all these things the Gentiles eagerly seek; for your heavenly Father knows that you need all these things.

But seek first His kingdom and His righteousness; and all these things shall be added to you. (Matthew 6:25-33)

LEARNING BY DOING

It is tempting, though, to say, "But I understand the point of the sabbath commandment. I understand that salvation is by grace through faith, as daily food and drink and clothing are by God's providence. Why should I go through the motions of fulfilling the commandment when I've already learned its lesson?" Tempting, but mistaken. For God "knows our frame; He is mindful that we are but dust" (Psalm 103:14). He knows that because we are earthy people, we do not learn spiritual things but through earthy parables. That is why Jesus' parables took common occurrences as models of eternity.

We may, in other words, learn the intellectual principle of resting in the gracious providence of God by a mere *study* of the sabbath commandment; but we will only take the lesson to heart when we *obey* it. God calls us to be doers of the Word, not hearers only, for those who only hear it "delude themselves"; each of them "is like a man who looks at his natural face in a mirror; for once he has looked at himself and gone away, he has immediately forgotten what kind of person he was. But one who looks intently at the perfect law, the law of liberty, *and abides by it,* not having become a forgetful hearer but an effectual doer, this man shall be blessed in what he does" (James 1:22-25).

In reality, when we mouth the lesson of the sabbath commandment—salvation by grace through faith—but don't live by it, we become like the Israelites who claimed they would hear and do all that the Lord required if only Moses would face Him for them— and then rebelled against God at every turn. Of them God said, "Oh that they had such a *heart* in them, that they would fear Me, and keep all My commandments always, that it may be well with them and with their sons forever!" (Deuteronomy 5:29). For not by hearing only, but by doing are God's people blessed (Deuteronomy 5:32, 33).

CREATURES NEED TO REST

Indeed the lesson goes deeper. Were we, like God, to remember our frame, that we are but dust, we might recognize more readily that we need physical renewal through rest as much as we need spiritual renewal through the rest that is faith. God has woven into the very fabric of the earth and its inhabitants this fundamental reality: all of them get tired and, if not renewed regularly by rest, wear out before their time.

Creatures do not share the Creator's omnipotence,[6] so they must get regular rest. That is why the commandment applied not only to human beings but also to animals. Even the earth itself was to enjoy a sabbath every seventh year (Exodus 23:10,11; Leviticus 25:1-5)—a requirement God took so seriously that He threatened Israel with devastation if it refused to let the land rest (Leviticus 26:14, 21, 27-35, 43). Seventy times seven years later God remembered His covenant with the *land*—not the people but the earth that needed restoration through rest—by sending Judah into a seventy-year exile to make up for seventy unobserved sabbatical years (2 Chronicles 36:20, 21; cf. Jeremiah 27:5-7).[7]

Perhaps this is why Solomon wrote, "Unless the Lord builds the house, they labor in vain who build it; unless the Lord guards the city, the watchman keeps awake in vain. It is vain for you to rise up early, to retire late, to eat the bread of painful labors; for He gives to His beloved even in his sleep" (Psalm 127:1, 2). God knows that His creatures need restoration by rest, and so He not only commands but even invites us to get it.

BENEFITS OF SABBATH KEEPING

There are two chief benefits of sabbath keeping beyond those that we have already mentioned (seeing a regular demonstration of God's gracious providence and getting the regular physical rest we need). They appear in the extension of the sabbath commandment in the form of the sabbatical and jubilee year laws.[8]

LIMITS ON DEBT

The first is that the sabbatical and jubilee year laws put automatic limits on the amount and term of debt people living under the Covenant could incur. The *amount* of permissible debt was limited to what someone could secure by collateral, the collateral being either some physical possession or the value of his own indentured labor (Leviticus 25:13-17, 23-55; cf. Exodus 22:25-27). The maximum *term* of permissible debt was the number of years remaining until the next year of jubilee, a maximum of fifty years (Leviticus 25)—and even then no payments were to be exacted during sabbatical years (every seventh year; Deuteronomy 15:1-3). These limits were designed to protect believers from financially ruining themselves and, even more important, their families and descendants. God expected His people to leave inheritances for their children and grandchildren (Proverbs 13:22a; cf. Proverbs 22:28; 23:10, 11, and regulations about inheritance in Deuteronomy 19:14; 27:17).[9] Making oneself and one's descendants destitute through nonessential debt, and thus leaving one's wealth to a creditor instead of one's descendants, was sin (Proverbs 13:22b). This was at least partly because, by borrowing, debtors enslave themselves (and potentially their heirs) to lenders, symbolizing their rejection of God's liberating work for them (Proverbs 22:7), much as those who trade the gospel of salvation by grace through faith for the counterfeit of salvation by works choose slavery to sin instead of liberation in Christ (Galatians 4:21—5:5).[10]

The limits on the amount and duration of debt also, by implication, limited the amount and duration of the alienation of productive property (as collateral) from a family. A family living in accord with the sabbatical and jubilee year regulations on debt would not face long-term loss of the means of production. Thus these laws were as much a protection of the family as of the individual, and of family property as of individual property. Indeed, they make it clear that individuals hold property as trustees for families and heirs.[11]

ASSURANCE OF REST

The second benefit of the sabbatical and jubilee year laws grew directly from the first. Since debts were limited in amount and extent, debtors were assured of at least periodic rest from the toil of paying off their debts. God had commanded all His people to rest every sabbatical and jubilee year. But someone paying off a debt would almost surely not be able to survive without regular employment (either by himself or by someone else). The release of debts every seven years—which was a suspension of collection rather than a complete remission[12]—and the termination of every debt in the year of jubilee[13] meant that debtors could share in the rest and restoration involved in the sabbath commandment.

Interestingly, the prohibition of debt collection during the sabbatical years did not apply to debts owed by foreigners (Deuteronomy 15:3). Why not? Because salvation, which is prefigured by the rest and restoration embodied in these laws, is available only under the Covenant. These laws applied, therefore, only to those who lived under the Covenant—children of Abraham by blood or conversion. Compliance with God's Law would make Israel a lender to and therefore a ruler over, rather than a borrower from and therefore a slave of, many nations (Deuteronomy 15:6). The exclusion of foreigners from the benefits of the sabbatical and jubilee year laws testified to them that they were still alienated from God and thus slaves of sin. Their slavery to sin was depicted physically in their unbroken bondage to debts, for contracting debts is self-chosen slavery (Proverbs 22:7).[14]

At the same time that God gave the command to rest, then, He also provided assurance that no one among His people need be excluded from that rest by excessive debt. They were not, like foreigners, alienated from the Covenant, but members of it. To have required their continuing to make payments on debts during those years would have required their continuing to work, which would have implied that they were not among the redeemed.

God calls Christians to live obediently and to trust Him to provide for all their needs. The sabbath commandment and its nonceremonial applications provide practical models for resting in the providence of God. They picture the eternal spiritual rest of believers, but they also have clear temporal benefits. They instruct people to set aside time for the physical rest they, their servants, their livestock, and even their land need, and they protect personal and family property by limiting the amount and duration of debt.

In calling His people to rest, God calls them to depend on Him rather than on their own labors for the essentials of life. Thus the sabbath commandment attacks the selfishness that can motivate economic activity, and suggests another motive altogether: faithful service to God as stewards in His household.

PART TWO

STEWARDSHIP AND JUSTICE

A CHRISTIAN VIEW
OF ECONOMIC JUSTICE [1]

*T*he Lord ". . . is a God of justice . . ." (Isaiah 30:18c). ". . . I, the Lord, love justice, I hate robbery in the burnt offering," He says (Isaiah 61:8).

As God is just, so man must be: "O house of David, thus says the Lord: 'Administer justice every morning; and deliver the person who has been robbed from the power of his oppressor, that My wrath may not go forth like fire and burn with none to extinguish it, because of the evil of their deeds'"(Jeremiah 21:12). "How blessed are those who keep justice," wrote the psalmist, "who practice righteousness at all times!" (Psalm 106:3). Through Jeremiah God said

> Do justice and righteousness, and deliver the one who has been robbed from the power of his oppressor. Also do not mistreat or do violence to the stranger, the orphan, or the widow; and do not shed innocent blood in this place. (Jeremiah 22:3)

WHAT JUSTICE IS

For all its importance, justice is a virtue often misunderstood. The word is an ideological football cast to and fro by foes accusing each other of injustice. Few are eager to define it clearly—particularly not in light of Scripture.

TWO IMAGES OF JUSTICE

In the Bible the two chief images of justice are conformity with a right standard and rendering to each his due.

CONFORMITY WITH A RIGHT STANDARD

Justice and truth are integrally interrelated, for the sense of justice is the practice of truth in human relationships. "You shall do no wrong in judgment," God warned the Israelites in Moses' day, "in *measurement of weight, or capacity. You shall have just balances, just weights, a just ephah, and a just hin*: I am the Lord your God, who brought you out from the land of Egypt" (Leviticus 19:35, 36). "And I will make justice the measuring line," God declared through Isaiah, "and righteousness the level" (Isaiah 28:17). "Can I justify wicked scales and a bag of deceptive weights?" God asked incredulously through Micah (Micah 6:11).

Such passages are of particular interest to us because they all deal with *economic* relationships. Standards of measurement— whether of dimension or of weight—were used in commerce, and God demanded that they be "just" or "true." They must not vary. If someone claimed to sell an ephah of flour, he should sell exactly that and no less. If another claimed to pay with an ounce of silver, it should be precisely that and no less.[2]

But the standards of measurement God mentioned in connection with justice do not indicate that justice stops at truthfulness in economic transactions or even at economic relationships as a whole. They indicate that all behavior should be governed by the same unbending standards. This is the chief sense in which justice and equality are related: the same standards apply equally to all people and relationships.

TO EACH HIS DUE

God Himself illustrates most perfectly the second chief image of justice in Scripture, rendering to each his due: "Far be it from God to do wickedness, and from the Almighty to do wrong. For *He pays a man according to his work* . . . and the Almighty *will not pervert justice*" (Job 34:10b-12).

"Render to all what is due them," Paul tells us (Romans 13:7). St. Thomas Aquinas explains that ". . . justice is a habit whereby a man renders to each one his due by a constant and perpetual will."[3] John Calvin says that justice "embraces all the duties of *equity* in order that to each one be rendered what is his own," and refers to Romans 13:7.[4]

Twentieth-century Christian philosopher Russell Kirk writes:

> Now our traditional idea of Justice comes to us from two sources: the Judaic and Christian faith in a just God whom we fear and love, and whose commandments are expressed in unmistakable language; and the teachings of classical philosophy, in particular the

principles expressed in Plato's *Republic* and incorporated into Roman jurisprudence by Cicero and his successors. The concept of Justice upon earth which both these traditions inculcate is, in substance, this: the idea of Justice is implanted in our minds by a Power that is more than human; and our mundane Justice is our attempt to copy a perfect Justice that abides in a realm beyond time and space; and the general rule by which we endeavor to determine just conduct and just reward may be expressed as "To each man, the things that are his own."[5]

Biblical Law and Natural Law as Standards of Justice

The Christian and classical traditions agree that justice is rendering to each his due according to a right standard. They disagree about what the standard is—though the two standards overlap significantly. Classical tradition appeals mainly to natural law, its concepts strongly influenced by Plato, Aristotle, and such great Roman philosophers as Cicero. Christian tradition appeals ultimately to the Decalogue, though it has often appealed to natural law as well.

The Christian understanding of natural law rests largely on Paul's statement in Romans 2:14, 15, that the "work of the Law" is written on every heart. Calvin, for instance, says "that the law of God which we call the moral law is nothing else than a testimony of natural law and of that conscience which God has engraved upon the minds of men."[6] Thus Christian thought widely recognizes that the fundamental requirements of God's Law are recognized by all men everywhere.[7]

Most Christian philosophers appeal freely to secular thinkers for elucidation of the idea of justice, though they judge them by Scripture. Even Luther and Calvin, despite their Reformation commitment to *sola scriptura*, drew heavily on natural law tradition. And Aquinas, though known in Protestant circles as a representative of natural law philosophy, drew ideas about justice more from Scripture than from classical tradition.[8]

This methodology is common to later Christian thinkers, Roman Catholic and Protestant alike, including the American Founding Fathers.[9] The ability of natural men to recognize—though certainly not to conform to—righteousness is assumed in Moses' promise to Israel that the statutes and judgments commanded by God would be their "wisdom and . . . understanding in the sight of the peoples who will hear all these statutes and say, 'Surely this great nation is a wise and understanding people'" (Deuteronomy 4:5, 6).

According to Christian thought, then, the two standards of justice—Biblical Law and natural law—are really one, though Biblical Law is more clearly revealed. Where there is a conflict between natural law *tradition*, which is distinct from natural law itself, and Biblical Law, the latter must correct the former.

TWO DOMAINS OF JUSTICE

There are also two chief domains of justice, the personal and the social.

"Personal or private justice," writes Kirk, "is attained by that balance and harmony in character which shines out from those persons whom we call 'just men'—men who cannot be swayed from the path of rectitude by private interest, and who are masters of their own passions, and who deal impartially and honestly with everyone they meet."[10] Personal justice, in other words, has to do with controlling oneself—in thought and act alike—in conformity with the standards of rightness. It has to do with an individual and his relationships with God, with himself, and with others.

True social justice—a term sadly corrupted in our day—is closely related to personal justice. It ". . . is similarly marked by harmony and balance," writes Kirk; "it is the communal equivalent of that right proportion and government of reason, will, and appetite which the just man displays in his private character. Socrates says to Glaucon, 'And is not the creation of justice the institution of a natural order and government of one faculty by another in the parts of the soul? And is not the creation of injustice the production of a state of things at variance with the natural order?'"[11] Plato's idea of the natural order differed from the Biblical idea, but the principle that social justice aims for conformity with the natural order is itself Biblical. We aim for conformity with the order God has providentially created by giving individuals differing aptitudes, abilities, and stations in life.

Just as no member of the Body of Christ can complain of injustice solely because his position or function differs from another's (1 Corinthians 12), so no member of society can complain of injustice solely because his function differs from another's. To prove injustice one must prove that his position, function, wealth, and so on are contrary to what are *due* him—not merely that they differ from another's.

Just as personal justice is individual conformity with the standards of rightness, so social justice is societal conformity with the standards of rightness. Understanding this should prevent our falling into the mistaken idea that social justice has something to do with a particular distribution of goods, privileges, or powers in society. Real social justice, on the contrary, attends only to the question whether goods, privileges, and powers are distributed in conformity with the standards of rightness. Whatever factual distribution results from conformity with those standards is just regardless how far it strays from conditional equality—the real idea behind many uses of the term *social justice* today.

SOCIAL JUSTICE *vs.* EQUALITARIANISM

It should be clear now that justice has to do with more than compensation for behavior, whether good or ill. It has to do also with such things as position, function, privilege, and power in society. As personal justice—maintenance of conformity with right standards in one's thought and behavior—requires the happy congruity of one's reason, will, and appetites or emotions, the several components of the person, so social justice requires the happy congruity of the various components of society, namely, individuals and groups, voluntary and involuntary. Everyone must play his appropriate role given his character in relation to others around him, according to the standard of rightness.

Because social justice pays attention to the fittedness of persons for various roles and circumstances in society, it must not be equated with equalitarianism.[12] The Bible recognizes differences among people that necessitate differences in their stations in life: "Under three things the earth quakes, and under four, it cannot bear up: under a slave when he becomes king, and a fool when he is satisfied with food, under an unloved woman when she gets a husband, and a maidservant when she supplants her mistress" (Proverbs 30:21-23).

Classical philosophy recognized the same thing:

> The happy man, Socrates maintains, is the just man; and the happy society is the just society. It is the society in which every man minds his own business, and receives always the rewards which are his due. The division of labor is a part of this social justice; for true justice requires "the carpenter and the shoemaker and

the rest of the citizens to do each his own business, and not another's." Injustice in society comes when men try to undertake roles for which they are not fitted, and claim rewards to which they are not entitled, and deny other men what really belongs to them.[13]

The varying gifts God has given people fit them for varying roles in society. Social justice prevails to the extent that people fill the roles for which God fits them; social injustice prevails to the extent that people are forced into roles for which God has not equipped them. Because God equips people unequally, social justice requires that their roles—and consequently their wealth and many other circumstances—be unequal as well,[14] despite the fact that justice requires equality before law.

This is a lesson the Pilgrims learned soon after they arrived in New England. Initially they endeavored to live communally, i.e., to share equally in all the possessions of the commonwealth. But quickly this "Common Course and Condition" proved impossible. Governor William Bradford later wrote that it bred "much confusion and discontent" among the people. It removed incentives for productive work by forcing everyone to work for others' benefit rather than for himself and his own family, "without any recompense." The equal sharing of benefits among those whose contributions to production were highly unequal "was thought injustice." Older, wiser men thought it an indignity to be treated just like the young and inexperienced. "Upon the point all being to have alike, and all to do alike, they thought themselves in the like condition, and one as good as another; and so, if it did not cut off those relations that God hath set amongst men, yet it did at least much diminish and take off the mutual respects that should be preserved amongst them."[15]

Economist William A. Orton writes:

> The goal of commutative justice is equality. Not egalitarianism, which seeks to flatten out, usually by force, the natural diversities of endowment, heredity, aptitude, and luck; not even equality of opportunity, though that is an inseparable part of the general aim; but *moral equality*. It protects a man's right "to live a human life, to perfect his moral nature, to be treated as a free, intelligent, responsible human being." Its practical rule is the familiar "do as you would be done by," which, when Christianity started applying it

without exception to all sorts and conditions of men,
turned out to be a radically progressive principle. This
is the rule of *reciprocity*, without which neither
democracy nor economic freedom can be
maintained.[16]

The Bible recognizes the justice of societal differences of
position, privilege, and power, as well as of material wealth and
personal relationships. It does not, as do some idealists, pretend
that there are no significant differences among men. Indeed, it
sees only one significant equality among them: that they all bear
the image of their Creator and are therefore morally accountable
and due respect for their lives, liberties, and properties consistent
with their behavior toward themselves and others. In all other significant ways men differ, and differ gloriously.

The Body of Christ exhibits this sense of social justice: "For
through the grace given to me," Paul writes, "I say to every man
among you not to think more highly of himself than he ought to
think; but to think so as to have sound judgment, as God has
allotted to each a measure of faith. For just as we have many
members in one body and all the members do not have the same
function, so we, who are many, are one body in Christ, and individually members one of another. And since we have gifts that
differ according to the grace given to us, let each exercise them
accordingly . . ." (Romans 12:3-6).

TWO FORMS OF JUSTICE
Roughly parallel to the two domains of justice—personal and
social—are its two forms, commutative and distributive.

Commutative justice has to do with the commutation of
value from one person to another. It governs exchanges among
individuals. "'Commutative' justice, in the words of old Jeremy
Taylor three centuries ago, is 'that justice which supposes
exchange of things profitable for things profitable.' It is that righteous relationship by which one man gives his goods or services
to another man and receives an equivalent benefit, to the better-
ment of both."[17]

It is to commutative justice most directly that Biblical laws
against false weights and measures apply. Parties in economic
exchanges owe it to each other, as a matter of justice, to be truthful about the quantity and quality of goods and services, or the
quantity and quality of money, that they offer in exchanges. So
"clipping" of coins—shearing off the edges to reduce the amount

of precious metal given in purchase and retain some for melting down and reusing—and other manners of debasing currency were always condemned by the Christian church, just as monetary inflation, false advertising, and false labeling ought to be.[18]

As personal justice relates to social justice, so commutative justice relates to distributive. In each pair, the former refers primarily to individuals, the latter to societies.

The very term *distributive justice* occasions misunderstanding. It leads people at first to imagine some person or institution that "distributes" goods and services, or privileges and powers and positions, to other members of society. But in fact the "distributive" nature of justice is a function of all the interdependent workings of all the individuals in society as each exercises commutative justice. It is a function of system, not of person or group. "Now 'distributive' justice, again in Jeremy Taylor's words, 'is commanded in this rule,"Render to all their dues."' Distributive justice, in short, is that arrangement in society by which each man obtains what his nature and his labor entitle him to, without oppression or evasion. Commutative justice is righteous dealing between particular individuals; distributive justice is the general system of rewarding each man according to his deserts. Both concepts of justice have been badly misunderstood in our time, but distributive justice has fared the worse."[19]

Distributive justice does not demand some ideal distribution of goods and services, privileges, powers, and positions in society. Neglect or contempt of this fundamental understanding of social justice has led to the proliferation of claims to "rights" that are in truth mere privileges, and to the mistaken notion that the equal rights in which all men share are rights to equal things. Rather, society is, as the great Christian statesman Edmund Burke put it, like a partnership: "In this partnership *all men have equal rights; but not to equal things*. He that has but five shillings in the partnership has as good a right to it as he that has five hundred pounds has to his larger proportion; but he has not a right to an equal dividend in the product of the joint stock. . . ."[20]

Each man's contribution to society ought, in justice, to determine his share in its benefits. The "distributor" in "distributive justice" is actually each man himself, acting as producer and trader of his goods and services. Any other distributing usurps this proper distributive authority. Those who pretend to know—better than all members of society acting in concert and limited only by the Biblical prohibitions against fraud, theft, and violence—who ought to have or to do what—such people forget that they are not God and so cannot know all the ins and outs of a great population.[21] Better to leave distributive justice to the choices of free individuals than to entrust it to the proud.

TWO SPECIAL GOALS OF JUSTICE

Aside from the commutative and distributive functions of personal and social justice, there are two other important functions of justice, remedial and retributive, prescribed in Scripture and practiced—well or poorly—throughout the history of civilization.

Remedial justice is the standard by which reparation is made for malicious injury to life, liberty, or property—those things to which a person has rights. It is, in other words, the standard for reparation of violations of right. It demands that when life, liberty, or property is taken from someone unjustly—that is, without that person's consent unless he is being punished for a crime—what has been taken must be returned by the one who took it.

The Bible requires the exercise of remedial justice by God's people and by every state: "Thus says the Lord, 'Do justice and righteousness, and deliver the one who has been robbed from the power of his oppressor'" (Jeremiah 22:3). It contains explicit instructions regarding the kind and amount of restitution to be required in cases of theft (e.g., Exodus 22:1-5, 7-9) or negligent destruction of property (e.g., Exodus 22:6), and even considers property so protected by justice that one is morally required to do what he can to find the owner of lost property (Exodus 23:4-9).[22]

At the same time that the offended party is to receive back what was taken from him, if possible, the offender is to be punished in some manner consistent with the injustice he has committed. This is retributive justice. Scripture tells us that God has ordained civil government to enforce justice (Romans 13:1-7), including temporal vengeance, which is retributive justice (Romans 13:4). So David writes, "The righteous will rejoice when he sees the vengeance; he will wash his feet in the blood of the wicked. And men will say, 'Surely there is a reward for the righteous; surely there is a God who judges on earth!'" (Psalm 58:10, 11). Again, throughout the Mosaic Code there are explicit instructions about the kind of punishment, or retributive justice, to be exercised on criminals of various sorts.

JUSTICE AND IMPARTIALITY

Another important aspect of justice is impartiality. It is the principle of applying all the standards of morality—including those related to economics—to all people alike, without exceptions for rank, privilege, power, or wealth. God Himself demonstrates this principle, for "there is no partiality with God" (Romans 2:11). Whoever ". . . does wrong will receive the consequences of the wrong which he has done, and that without partiality" (Colossians 3:25). "God takes His stand in His own congregation," writes David; "He judges in the midst of the rulers. How long will you judge unjustly, and show partiality to the wicked? Vindicate the weak and fatherless; do justice to the afflicted and destitute. Rescue the weak and needy; deliver them out of the hand of the wicked" (Psalm 82:1-4).

Of particular significance for *economic* justice are commands against partiality to rich and poor alike: "You shall not show partiality in judgment; you shall hear the small and the great alike. You shall not fear man, for the judgment is God's" (Deuteronomy 1:17). "You shall do no injustice in judgment; you shall not be partial to the poor nor defer to the great, but you are to judge your neighbor fairly" (Leviticus 19:15). God is not "on the side of the poor," despite protests to the contrary.[23] Any law, therefore, that gives an advantage in the economic sphere to anyone, *rich or poor*, violates Biblical justice. Laws requiring government agencies to give minority or handicapped businesses an advantage in bidding on contracts, for instance, are unjust, just as would be laws giving majority or nonhandicapped businesses the same advantage. The aim of such laws is conditional equality, but the Bible never presents conditional equality as an appropriate goal of justice.[24] Instead, the Bible demands impartiality, which—because people differ in interests, gifts, capacities, and stations in life—must invariably result in conditional inequality.

JUSTICE AND PROPORTIONALITY

Closely related to impartiality is proportionality. Rendering to each his due means rendering what is in proper proportion to his acts. Again God Himself demonstrates this principle, for He "will render to every man according to his deeds" (Romans 2:6). What a man sows he reaps (Galatians 6:10). This is the sense of Burke's statement that while all have equal rights, they do not have rights to equal things: a man's due is in proportion to his investment, positive or negative. Aristotle expressed the same idea by saying that justice means rendering equal things to equals and unequal things to unequals in proportion to their relevant inequalities[25]—and relevant inequalities in economics have nothing to do with race, sex, or handicap, but with one's contribution to the economic enterprise in question.

THE STANDARDS OF JUSTICE
IN ECONOMIC RELATIONSHIPS

We have said that justice is rendering impartially to each his due in conformity with the standard of rightness, whether in personal or in social relations, whether in voluntary exchange or in forced restitution and retribution for crimes. But what is that standard? Jesus summarized it in the Golden Rule: ". . . however you want people to treat you, so treat them, for this is the Law and the Prophets" (Matthew 7:12). He stated this rule as a *summary*—not a replacement—of the Law and the Prophets.

The standard of rightness that defines justice, then, is the Ten Commandments, with the many applications and explanations of them that make up the moral and civil elements of Old Testament Law.[26] Focusing as we are on economic justice, we will discuss here only a few of the laws dealing most directly with economic relationships.[27]

WORK, PROPERTY, AND ECONOMIC LIBERTY

The Fourth Commandment requires men to work six days out of every seven and rest one. What God requires of men cannot justly be forbidden or prevented by others (Acts 5:29). Men have not only the *duty* but also the *right* to work and to rest. As a reward for their work comes a right to property, protected by the Eighth Commandment, which forbids stealing. According to Jesus the laborer is "worthy of his wages" (Luke 10:7); there is an inherent connection between work and its fruit.

With the right to property comes the right to use it freely short of violating the rights of others by damaging their lives, liberties, or properties. Peter affirmed this when he chastened Ananias for lying about the price of land sold to donate to the church in Jerusalem and reminded him, "While [the land] remained unsold, did it not remain your own? And after it was sold, was it not under your control? Why is it that you have conceived this deed in your heart?" (Acts 5:3, 4). Jesus, too, affirmed this principle when in the parable of the laborers in the vineyard He represented the owner of the vineyard (who symbolized God and thus cannot be accused of injustice in the matter) as replying to complaints about his having paid laborers the same amount for different hours of work, "Friend, I am doing you no wrong; did you not agree with me for a denarius? . . . Is it not lawful for me to do what I wish with what is my own?" (Matthew 20:13, 15).[28]

Justice in economic relationships requires that people be permitted to exchange and use what they own—including their own time and energy and intellect as well as material objects —freely so long as in so doing they do not violate others' rights. Such things as minimum wage laws, legally mandated racial quotas in employment, legal restrictions on import and export, laws requiring "equal pay for equal work," and all other regulations of economic activity other than those necessary to prohibit, prevent, and punish fraud, theft, and violence are therefore unjust.[29]

LIBERTY, EQUALITY, AND FRATERNITY?

The drive toward economic equality in the modern world owes its origin not to a Christian understanding of justice but to a decidedly anti-Christian understanding, one that gained power especially before and during the French Revolution and then influenced Karl Marx. Its proponents have been men of Enlightenment mind, like Condorcet, eminent among the philosophers who ushered in the French Revolution and who proclaimed that "Not only equality of right, but equality of fact, is the goal of the socialist art."[30]

The Bible clearly approves of both economic liberty (Matthew 20:13, 15; Acts 5:4) and economic inequality (Proverbs 22:2; 2 Thessalonians 3:10). The outcome of any successful drive toward equality of condition in any society is not equality but tyranny. "The delusion that justice consists in absolute equality," writes Kirk, "ends in an absolute equality beneath the weight of a man or a party to whom justice is no more than a word."[31] Why? Because all men have different gifts, talents, interests, and abilities. Left free, they will exercise those in different ways and will produce different fruits. The only way to arrive at equal fruits is to equalize behavior; and that requires robbing men of liberty, making them slaves. Thus the French Revolutionary cry, "Liberty, Equality, Fraternity," was a double self-contradiction. For liberty produces inequality, and equality can be enforced only by tyranny—the denial of fraternity.[32]

Far from demanding economic equality of condition, justice—precisely because it demands impartiality and proportionality—demands economic inequality. To cite Kirk again:

> The great classical philosophers of politics argued that justice amounts to this: "to each his own." Every

man, ideally, ought to obtain the things which best suit his own nature; he ought to do the work for which he is fitted, and to receive the rewards of that work. Men's talents and desires vary conspicuously from individual to individual; therefore a society is unjust which treats all men as if they were uniform beings, or which allots to one sort of nature the rights and duties which properly belong to other sorts of human beings.[33]

Because the idea is so common today that justice requires equality of economic condition—or some close approximation to it—the next chapter will examine specific Biblical passages that some people allege require economic equalitarianism.

DOES JUSTICE DEMAND EQUALITY?

Various persons and groups throughout the history of Christianity have claimed that a Christian understanding of justice requires economic equality of condition. Rarely have these people comprised a significant proportion of the whole Body of Christ, but they have almost always shown intense dedication to their ideals. Their fervency shines through in the claim of the Taborites, the radical Bohemian party of the Hussite wars of the early fifteenth century: "In these days there shall be no king, ruler, or subject on the earth, and all imposts and taxes shall cease; no one shall force another to do anything, for all shall be equal brethren and sisters. As in the town of Tabor there is no mine or thine, but all is held in common, so shall everything be common to all, and no one own anything for himself alone. Whoever does so commits a deadly sin."[1]

Particularly important among communistic[2] and semi-communistic groups in church history—those preaching and practicing obligatory community of goods—were Thomas Münzer and his followers in the early Reformation, along with many (particularly the Moravian) Anabaptists.[3] In America, small Christian communistic movements have grown up frequently, most of them short-lived.[4]

Although in most instances Christian communistic groups have begun simply by teaching that Biblical justice requires voluntary equality of economic condition, they have almost invariably reached the conclusion that equality had to be established and maintained by force.[5] In both logic and practice, this has led to the renunciation of private property, not only voluntarily by individuals but also in principle. Some, treating the Seventh Commandment as they did the Eighth, rejected the exclusivity of marriage, practicing a community of wives.[6]

Today there is a resurgence of equalitarianism among some Christians, including some evangelicals and Roman Catholics.[7] They appeal to four principal precedents in Scripture to sustain their position: the sabbatical year, the jubilee year, the community of goods in Jerusalem, and the Pauline collections. Let's examine each of these.

THE SABBATICAL YEAR

The Biblical regulations for the sabbatical year were designed to give relief to the poor from repaying debts, since no one was supposed to work during it, and the likelihood of their acquiring enough both to support themselves and to make payments on debts without work would be extremely small:

> At the end of every seven years you shall grant a remission [Hebrew *shemittah*] of debts. And this is the manner of remission [Hebrew *shemittah*]: every creditor shall release [Hebrew *shamat*] what he has loaned to his neighbor; he shall not exact it of his neighbor and his brother, because the Lord's remission [Hebrew *shemittah*] has been proclaimed. From a foreigner you may exact it, but your hand shall release [Hebrew *shamat*] whatever of yours is with your brother. (Deuteronomy 15:1-3)

Of these regulations Ronald Sider writes, ". . . it is crucial to note that the Scripture prescribes justice[8] rather than mere charity. The sabbatical release of debts was an institutionalized mechanism for preventing an ever-growing gap between rich and poor."[9] But a careful exegesis of the passage shows such ideas to be untenable.

The most crucial point is the understanding of the word here translated "remission," the Hebrew *shemittah*, "a letting drop of exactions, a (temporary) remitting."[10] In its margin the *New American Standard* offers the alternative translation "release," which is in fact closer to the literal sense of the Hebrew.[11] The noun appears only in Deuteronomy 15:1, 2 (first and third clauses), 9, and 31:10, in every instance in reference to the *shemittah* connected with the sabbatical year. Because in each instance the context does not clearly determine between the two alternate understandings—a permanent or a temporary release—we must look at the usage of the verb *shamat*, "let drop, fall,"[12] from which the noun is formed.

The earliest Old Testament use of *shamat* is in Exodus 23, again in the context of the sabbatical year. In this instance, however, it describes what the Israelites were to do not with debts but with land: "And you shall sow your land for six years and gather in its yield, but on the seventh year you shall *let it rest [shamat]* and lie fallow, so that the needy of your people may eat; and whatever they leave the beast of the field may eat. You are to do the same with your vineyard and your olive grove" (Exodus 23:10, 11). Were the Hebrews to abandon a particular plot of ground forever after the sabbatical year? Clearly not. They were to "release" it for the duration of a year, neither plowing, nor planting, nor systematically harvesting it, but allowing it to produce freely. They were to harvest from it each day only what they needed for that day, and to allow needy people and wild beasts to do likewise. That this was a temporary release is even clearer in light of the parallel verse that immediately follows it: "Six days you are to do your work, but on the seventh day you shall cease from labor in order that your ox and your donkey may rest, and the son of your female slave, as well as your stranger, may refresh themselves" (v. 12). If we are to argue that the release of the land was permanent, not temporary, then we must—to be consistent in the immediate context—argue also that the rest on the seventh day was to be permanent, not temporary. The most anyone could ever work in a lifetime, then, would be six days. Both the Biblical context and common sense show that conclusion to be ludicrous.

The next appearance of the verb in the Old Testament is in Deuteronomy 15:2, 3: "And this is the manner of remission [*shemittah*, the noun, "release"]: every creditor shall release [*shamat*, the verb, "let drop"] what he has loaned to his neighbor; he shall not exact it of his neighbor and his brother, because the Lord's remission [*shemittah*] has been proclaimed. From a foreigner you may exact it, but your hand shall release [*shamat*] whatever of yours is with your brother." Nothing in the context indicates that the verb should be understood differently from how we understood it in Exodus 23. Indeed, the last clause strongly implies the opposite. What the hand should "release" is "whatever of *yours* is with your brother." It remains the legal property of the lender, though it is possessed, for the time being, by the brother.

The verb appears elsewhere in the Old Testament only five times: in 2 Samuel 6:6 (parallel to 1 Chronicles 13:9), indicating that oxen "let fall" the Ark of the Covenant; 2 Kings 9:33, where Jehu instructed officials to "throw down" Jezebel from a window;

Psalm 141:6, describing wicked judges who are "thrown down"; and Jeremiah 17:4, where the prophet warns that the people of Judah will, by refusing to forsake their sins, "let go" their inheritance in the land so that they will serve their enemies in a foreign land. In all but the last use, the sense is strongly physical, not metaphorical, and conveys simply the idea of physical dropping or throwing down, implying nothing about whether what was released could or would be picked up again. But in the last instance the verb has its metaphorical sense again, and the rest of Jeremiah's prophecies clearly show that the "letting go" of the inheritance would be only temporary (cf. Jeremiah 29:10). Indeed, it was to be connected with the sabbatical year law, for it was to last seventy years—precisely long enough to restore to the land the sabbatical years the Israelites had before refused to give it (2 Chronicles 36:21; cf. Leviticus 26:34, where God warned that failure to keep the sabbatical year law would bring exile, during which the land would keep its sabbaths).

Thus in every instance in which *shamat* and *shemittah* are used regarding the sabbatical year, they must be understood in the sense of a temporary, not permanent, release. The passage in Deuteronomy enlarges upon that in Exodus, and must not be interpreted contrary to it.[13] The passage in Exodus unquestionably envisions a temporary, not a permanent, release.[14] The passage in Deuteronomy must, therefore, be understood the same way; as we have seen, that interpretation is also consistent with the contextual hint involved in the words "whatever of *yours* is with your brother."

It is also consistent with another contextual hint. The Israelites were explicitly permitted to continue to exact loan payments from foreigners (Deuteronomy 15:3), though they were forbidden to do so from brethren. But if the release were, as Sider understands it, a matter of abstract justice, then we would be forced by this exception to conclude either that the Hebrews did not owe foreigners justice, or that justice means something different for believers from what it means for unbelievers. Either conclusion is, of course, untenable in light of Scriptures that insist that we do justice to widows, orphans, *and foreigners* (Exodus 22:21; 23:9; Leviticus 19:33f; Deuteronomy 24:17f).

The release, then, must be viewed not as a matter of abstract justice, but as necessitated on some other basis. What was that? It was that God had commanded the Israelites not to work their land during the sabbatical year, but to let it rest. The land being the chief means of production, a command not to work the land was, by implication, a command to cease from productive labor (consistent with the weekly sabbath). And that, as we saw in Chapter Three, was an important aspect of the sabbatical year regulation. But requiring borrowers to continue payments on loans during that year would also mean, by implication, requiring them to work during that year. It would mean preventing their obeying God's command to rest and enjoying the restoration involved in it.

It was, then, a matter of justice that the Hebrews' debts should be "released" during the sabbatical year. But it was not a matter of economic equality, but of equal responsibility to and enjoyment of the Law of God, for the sabbatical year release of debts meant that debtors, along with lenders, could enjoy the sabbatical rest and obey the command not to work the land. If debtors could be required to continue to make payments on their debts during the sabbatical year, they could not enjoy that God-required rest that others could. "If no harvest was gathered in, and even such produce as had grown without sowing was to be left to the poor and the beasts of the fields, the landowner could have no income from which to pay his debts."[15] But foreigners living among them were not prohibited from working the land during the sabbatical year. (Indeed most probably were nonagriculturalists, since the land was divided among the Israelites.) Their activities, therefore, were not restricted during the sabbatical year. They could earn enough both to survive and to make payments on their debts.

Meredith G. Kline argues that because the jubilee year law and the sabbatical year law "belonged to one symbolical unit," and because debts were canceled (a term that doesn't actually fit the jubilee regulation, as we shall see shortly) in the jubilee year, the sabbatical regulation must also call for "a permanent cancellation of debts. . . ."[16] But this argument fails for two reasons: (1) It fails to consider carefully the mechanism by which debts came to an end in the year of jubilee (a matter that we will consider in detail below). Such consideration would show that the debts were not canceled but paid off, and necessarily so because the production of land used as collateral to secure them belonged to the lender during the term of the debt, and the amount of a loan was determined by the projected value of the land's production. (2) Kline's argument is actually backward, for the jubilee law is an extension of the sabbatical year law, not vice versa, just as the sabbatical year law is an extension of the Fourth Commandment's requirement of a weekly sabbath, not vice versa. The jubilee law must then be interpreted in light of the sabbatical year law, which in turn must be interpreted in light of the weekly sabbath law.

The sabbatical law simply required that God's people not demand payment of debts *during* the sabbatical year *from their brethren*. This allowed their brethren to enjoy God's legislated rest with them. Otherwise an observance designed to depict past and future deliverance and rest could, for some, become the occasion of their entering bondage by default on debts.[17] But payment was to resume in the following year, to ensure that justice—rendering to each his due—was done. Only because Sider assumes that justice demands equality of condition—or at least a limitation on the gap between rich and poor[18]—instead of impartiality and the rendering of what is due, can he write that the permanent cancellation of debts would be "justice rather than mere charity."[19] It would, in fact, be neither justice nor charity, for the lender would not be paid his due (required by justice), the debtor would be prevented from doing his duty (also required by justice), and the cancellation would be forced rather than voluntary and so not charitable.

THE YEAR OF JUBILEE

An extension of the sabbatical year requirement was the year of jubilee, which occurred every fiftieth year, or the year following every seventh sabbatical year (Leviticus 25). This also made special provisions for the poor, bringing a regular end to debts and to indentured servanthood, thus restoring personal and economic liberty, but not—as we shall see—equality.

When God brought Israel into the Promised Land, He divided among the tribes the land that He gave them, providing each family with a plot over which it became steward and that it should hand down to its descendants. Differences in personal diligence and intelligence, differences in the productive capacities of the land, sometimes oppression or natural tragedies, however, made it inevitable that economic inequalities would develop among the people. These were not necessarily unjust.[20] But to preserve family unity and family possession of land,[21] as well as to restrain any one person from squandering all the family's wealth by contracting debts he could not pay, God gave Israel the jubilee regulations.

According to these regulations, land in ancient Israel was not to be sold permanently, because it belonged to God (Leviticus

25:23). It could, however, be presented as collateral for an emergency loan to provide for a family's immediate needs. The loans secured by this collateral were to be made for a period not exceeding the number of years remaining until jubilee (presumably shorter terms could be made). The amount of the loan would then be determined by the number and value of the harvests to be expected in the term of debt (Leviticus 25:13-16), "for it is a number of crops he is selling to you" (v. 16). Total income from the land (worked, during the term of the loan, by the lender) would constitute repayment. When jubilee came, therefore, complete repayment would have been made and the collateral, or pledge, was to be returned to its original owner. If, however, the debtor were able to earn enough to pay off the remainder of the loan, he could do so at any time and regain possession of his land.

Careful examination of the jubilee year's regulations should help us to avoid the errors of modern proponents of Christian socialism who believe that it required redistribution of wealth in society. When Waldron Scott writes of the jubilee, "Every fifty years, all land was to go back to the original owners *without compensation*, for the land . . . was actually the Lord's,"[22] he clearly neglects the process by which the original price was determined. No compensation was needed upon return of the land since none was due: the harvests during the term of the loan repaid the creditor, and when the loan was repaid, the collateral had to be returned to the (at that point *former*) debtor. Thus while the jubilee regulation put a maximum term on debts—significantly, on debts *secured by collateral*—it did not require cancellation of any unpaid debts.

Sider makes the same interpretative error in writing of the jubilee, and then compounds it by insisting that the jubilee not only required cancellation of unpaid debts but also required equality among God's people:

> Leviticus 25 is one of the most radical texts in all of
> Scripture. At least it seems that way for people born
> in countries committed to either laissez-faire eco-
> nomics or communism. Every fifty years, God said,
> all land was to return to the original owners—with-
> out compensation! Physical handicaps, death of a
> breadwinner or lack of natural ability may lead some
> people to become poorer than others.[23] But God does
> not want such disadvantages to lead to greater and

greater divergence of wealth and poverty. God therefore gave his people a law which would equalize land
ownership every fifty years (Lev 25:10-24).[24]

A more thorough case of reading into a text what one hopes
to find can hardly exist. Leviticus 25 would indeed seem radical to
laissez-faire capitalism, but not for the reason Sider thinks it
would. It would seem radical because it put a strict requirement
on borrowers by requiring collateral to secure all loans, and
because it put a maximum limit on the number of years for
which a loan could be extended. But it would not—as Sider
implies by emphasizing that land was to be returned "without
compensation!"—mean that any unpaid debts were canceled. On
the contrary, it required making sure loans were repaid by putting
productive collateral in the hands of lenders. (Apologists of the
Left are fond of saying this law required keeping capital in the
hands of the poor—a variation on Marxist dogma. On the contrary, it took capital out of the hands of poor borrowers until their
loans were paid, so that it could not be squandered and the loans
left unsecured.)

It would be radical for communists, too, because rather than
requiring redistribution and equalization of wealth it required protecting the property of both lender and borrower. It protected the
lender's property by ensuring repayment of the debt; it protected
the borrower's property by ensuring return of collateral after
repayment. Nothing in it stood in the way of some people's
becoming poorer than others.

Sider adds, "It was to be the poor person's *right* to receive
back his inheritance at the time of jubilee. Returning the land
was not a charitable courtesy that the wealthy might extend if
they pleased."[25] It was indeed the borrower's right, not because
God intended to "equalize land ownership every fifty years," but
because the land was collateral for a loan paid in full. Indeed
"returning the land was not a charitable courtesy"; it was instead
a matter of justice as we have defined it. It was a matter of rendering to each his due (in this case the return of security for a loan paid
in full), not of the equalitarian "justice" Sider thinks he finds here.

The jubilee regulations said nothing of newly-created
wealth, only of land used as collateral in loans. If one farmer produced far more per acre of land than did another, or if he gained
riches through industry or trade, nothing in Scripture demanded
equal distribution of that wealth to others. It was not because the

land belonged to God that it had to be returned to its original owner at the year of jubilee. Rather, it was because the land belonged to God that it could not be permanently sold, and it returned to its original owner at jubilee because the loan secured by it was paid off.

The actual provisions of the jubilee year were in accord with the Biblical principle of justice as we have understood it. The law of jubilee was designed not to promote economic equality, but to prevent one family member's destroying an entire family's means of productivity, not only in his own generation but also in generations to come, by contracting huge debts and selling, permanently, the family's means of production.

Further, the jubilee regulation set an upper limit on the size of loans. They could not exceed the projected value of the harvests during the period of lease plus, in cases in which a person sold himself into indentured service (that is, made his forced labor collateral for an even larger loan), the value of the indentured servant's labor for that period of time.[26] No one, therefore, could squander his family's and heirs' means of living—at least not permanently. The return of the land to the original family of ownership represented not a redistribution of wealth but the return of collateral upon repayment of a loan.[27]

THE COMMUNITY OF
GOODS IN THE JERUSALEM CHURCH

A third Biblical precedent for economic equalitarianism used by many communistic writers is the sharing of property among the early Christians in Jerusalem. The two key texts are as follows:

> And all those who had believed were together, and had all things in common; and they began selling their property and possessions, and were sharing them with all, as anyone might have need. (Acts 2:44, 45)

> For there was not a needy person among them, for all who were owners of land or houses would sell them and bring the proceeds of the sales, and lay them at the apostles' feet; and they would be distributed to each, as any had need. (Acts 4:34, 35)

The degree to which different writers press these texts varies. One document, *An Evangelical Commitment to Simple Lifestyle*,[28] takes the passages as indicative of the great love the

Christians had for each other, but stops far short of inferring communism. Instead, it acknowledges that "selling and giving were voluntary, and some private property was retained," but adds that the property "was made subservient to the needs of the community. . . . That is, they were free from the selfish assertion of proprietary rights."[29] While this restraint is commendable compared with the extremes we will see, it certainly creates at least one false impression: that all assertion of private property rights is selfish.

If we agree with that assessment, then we face some difficult questions in light of Biblical Law. Why, for instance, does the Eighth Commandment, "You shall not steal" (Exodus 20:15), explicitly protect private property? Why does Scripture require restitution, including multiple restitution, in cases of theft, even if paying the restitution requires selling oneself into slavery (Exodus 22:1ff)? Why does God's Law specifically permit the use of force—even lethal force—to protect private property in case of a break-in at night (Exodus 22:2, 3)? And why does God's Law require showing respect for others' property by returning lost animals and helping overburdened animals even if they belong to enemies (Exodus 23:4f)?

In light of such requirements, it seems hardly reasonable to conclude that God condemns all assertions of private property rights as selfish.[30] To do so necessarily implies that God's Law fostered selfishness—something quite the opposite of its actual effect, if we are to believe Jesus when He tells us that it is summed up in love for God and neighbor (Matthew 22:39f; 7:12; cf. Romans 13:10).

The key to understanding the practice of the Jerusalem church is to remember that giving occurred "as any had need"—a condition that must have been fairly restrictive, since Paul teaches us to be content so long as we have food and covering (1 Timothy 6:8).[31] The love of Christ should make any Christian willing to give of his own property to meet the actual *needs* of fellow Christians; but it need not make him feel guilty of selfishness for retaining possessions entrusted to his stewardship by God if he is not convinced of another's need.

Waldron Scott, in *Bring Forth Justice*, goes a bit farther, first saying that the practice was a matter of justice,[32] and then adding, "Even early Christians seemed to know instinctively that to preach effectively to the Gentiles required within their own commonwealth an effort, for example, at economic and racial *equality*. . ."[33] Nothing in the context, however, implies economic equality among the believers. The passages tell us that believers sold property from time to time as needs arose, and distributed the proceeds to the needy. They do not tell us that the end result was economic equality of sellers, distributors, and recipients. Only a predisposition toward equalitarianism can have forced such an interpretation.

Arthur G. Gish, in *Living in Christian Community*, apparently recognizes that the sharing was voluntary: "They shared everything not because they had to (Peter made this clear to Ananias [cf. Acts 5:4]), but because they wanted to. And in Jerusalem apparently all did."[34] Yet he also cites approvingly from Eberhard Arnold, "Communal life with its white-hot love began [in the Jerusalem church]. In its heat property was melted away to the very foundations. The icy substructures of age-old glaciers melt before God's Sun. The only way to *abolish private property* and personal assets is through the radiant power of the life-creating Spirit.[35] All ownership feeds on stifling self-interest. When deadly selfishness is killed by love, and only then, ownership comes to an end. Yet it was so in the early church: under the influence of the Spirit of community, no one thought his goods were his own. Private property was an impossibility; here the Spirit of love and unity ruled."[36] Here again we find belief in private property equated with selfishness, implying that God promoted selfishness in His laws protecting private property. No wonder Gish precedes his admission that the sharing was voluntary with the assertion, "Because of their love and unity, the boundaries of private property dissolved."[37]

Gustavo Gutierrez, a major theorist of liberation theology,[38] holds that the Jerusalem church's example was of a "common ownership of goods,"[39] bolstering the idea by citing Hebrews 13:16: "Never forget to show kindness and to share what you have with others, for such are the sacrifices which God approves."[40] However, the passages in question do not propound common ownership of goods, but use of goods (including sale and giving) by their owners for the good of those in need. To give the sense Gutierrez wants, Hebrews 13:16 would have to say something like, "Never forget to receive kindness and to take for yourself a share in whatever others have. . . ."

Jose Miranda, in *Communism in the Bible*, surely takes as radical a position on the Jerusalem church as can be:

> Luke's normative intention stands out. There is no question of a special lifestyle that could be considered

peculiar to some Christians in contrast with the general mass of Christians. His insistence on the universality of *communism* from a literary point of view is even a little affected—*pantes hoi pisteusantes* (2:44), all the believers, all who had believed in Jesus Christ, all Christians; *oude heis* (4:32), not a single one said anything was his; *hosoi ktetores* (4:34), whoever possessed fields or houses, whoever had anything. If they wanted to be Christians the condition was *communism.*[41]

For Miranda, the Jerusalem church's example is normative and Luke goes to literary extremes to impress on us that to be a Christian one must be a communist. But Miranda ignores two important aspects of the passages.

First, the giving was always voluntary. Thus when Ananias and Sapphira, perhaps motivated by a mistaken notion that giving was mandatory or by prideful desire to be thought more generous than they really were, sold a piece of land and laid *part* of the price at Peter's feet, but alleged that they gave *all* of it, Peter responded, "Ananias, why has Satan filled your heart to lie to the Holy Spirit, and to keep back some of the price of the land? While it remained unsold, did it not remain your own? And after it was sold, was it [i.e., the money received in payment for the land] not under your control? Why is it that you have conceived this deed in your heart? You have not lied to men, but to God" (Acts 5:3, 4). Then the Holy Spirit struck Ananias dead; when Sapphira came later and repeated her husband's lie, He struck her dead, too.

Peter's rebuke is telling against the communist interpretation of the early church's practice: the land belonged to Ananias and he was under no obligation to sell it. The money received when it was sold also belonged to him, and he was under no obligation to give it to the church. Not abolition of but respect for property rights (and the inevitable inequalities that accompany them) was the principle of the Jerusalem church. To that principle was added that of loving concern for fellow believers by which property owners were motivated to give to meet their needs. But that loving concern and the resultant giving were voluntary, not mandatory. Thus Sider, who elsewhere finds every reason to lean toward communistic interpretations, explains the *koinonia* (community, or fellowship, or partnership) of goods among the Jerusalem Christians:

> The earliest church did not insist on absolute economic equality. Nor did they abolish private property. Peter reminded Ananias that he had been under no obligation either to sell his property or to donate the proceeds to the church (Acts 5:4). Sharing was voluntary, not compulsory. But love for brothers and sisters was so overwhelming that many freely abandoned legitimate claims to private possessions.[42] . . . That does not mean that everyone donated everything. Later in Acts we see that John Mark's mother, Mary, still owned her own house (12:12). Others also undoubtedly retained some private property.[43]

Second, the selling and giving occurred over a period of time, not all at once, as would have been required had the whole idea of private property been rejected. When we are told that owners of property "would sell" it and bring the proceeds to the apostles' feet, the verb is in the imperfect tense, denoting an action beginning and repeated over and over.[44] The idea is not that anyone sold everything he had all at once and turned over all the proceeds all at once, but that people would sell bits and pieces of their property from time to time, turning over the proceeds as need arose.[45]

Far from the early church's practice supporting communism, complete with economic equalitarianism and abolition of private property, it exemplifies both respect for private property and voluntarism in charitable giving. Furthermore, giving was done to meet *needs*, not to equalize economic conditions.

THE "EQUALITY"
OF THE PAULINE COLLECTIONS

A fourth Biblical precedent claimed by the Left to support equalitarianism is the collection of gifts from churches in Macedonia, Greece, and Asia Minor by Paul to meet the needs of hungry Christians in Jerusalem (1 Corinthians 16; 2 Corinthians 8, 9). The key passage for the equalitarians is 2 Corinthians 8:13-15:

> For this is not for the ease of others and for your affliction, but by way of equality—at this present time your abundance being a supply for their want, that their abundance also may become a supply for your want, that there may be equality; as it is written, "He who gathered much did not have too much, and he who gathered little had no lack."

Though in commenting on passages about the Jerusalem church in Acts (2, 4, 5) Sider acknowledges that "the earliest church did not insist on absolute economic equality,"[46] he does an about-face here: "This may be startling and disturbing to rich Christians in the Northern Hemisphere. But the Biblical text clearly shows that Paul enunciates the principle of economic equality among the people of God to guide the Corinthians in their giving."[47] This, he claims, ". . . was simply an application of the basic principle of the jubilee."[48]

First, we may note that the passage has nothing to do with the jubilee. The jubilee affected not all property but only what had been used as collateral to secure loans (including indentured labor). Only if Sider could show that the property Paul hoped the Corinthians would give to those in Jerusalem was collateral securing loans the Corinthians had made, and only if he could show that those loans had been paid off, would this exemplify the genuine jubilee principle. Sider has forced his idea of the jubilee onto the text in 2 Corinthians, perhaps because his idea of both texts is that they promote economic equality—something we have already seen was not the case with the jubilee.

Second, Sider's interpretation is disastrous for charitable motives for giving. For then Paul's argument runs thus: You are to give to solve the Jerusalem brethren's material poverty, so that if someday you are in the same straits they will be able to give to solve your material poverty. In other words, Sider's understanding makes Paul's picture of charitable giving selfish, while Biblical charity means giving with no expectation of receiving anything in return (Luke 6:27-35).

The key to understanding the equality Paul intends is to be found in the preceding verses:

> But just as you abound in everything, in faith and utterance and knowledge and in all earnestness and in the love we inspired in you, see that you abound in this *gracious* work also. I am not speaking this as a command, but as proving through the earnestness of others the sincerity of your *love* also. For you know the *grace* of our Lord Jesus Christ, that though He was rich, yet for your sake He became poor, that you through His poverty might become rich. And I give my opinion in this matter, for this is to your advantage, who were the first to begin a year ago not only to do this, but also to desire to do it. But now finish

doing it also; that just as there was the readiness to desire it, so there may be also the completion of it by your ability. For if the readiness is present, it is acceptable according to what a man has, not according to what he does not have. (vv. 7-12, emphasis added)

The equality envisioned is not of economic condition but, as John Calvin pointed out, of proportionate giving—giving in proportion to what one has, not in proportion to what one does not have—and of needs being met.[49]

Yet there is a further sense to this equality that should subsist between the believers in the two cities. As Calvin recognized, the equality of giving was indeed to be proportionate to what each had—and in this instance, the Christians in Corinth had something different from what those in Jerusalem had. They should indeed meet each other's needs, and do so equally, but not in the same respect, for the needs were not the same. As R. C. H. Lenski carefully argues, the Jerusalem Christians had, out of their spiritual abundance, once filled up—or equalized—the Corinthians' spiritual lack, sending missionaries to shine the light of the gospel into their darkness. Now Paul tells the Corinthians that they will fill up—or equalize—the physical need in Jerusalem by their physical gift. And by the same act, they will fill up—or equalize—their own *spiritual lack*, a lack of performance of their stated willingness to give. "The equalization is accomplished the moment the Corinthian readiness and willingness become finished action by relieving the Jerusalem deficiency and raising it to abundance, for by this action that grace and that spiritual enrichment will be the Corinthians' as God and Christ purpose. The *isotes* [equality] will be effected."[50]

This view is thoroughly consistent with what Paul later writes to the Corinthians about giving:

Now this I say, he who sows sparingly shall also reap sparingly; and he who sows bountifully shall also reap bountifully. Let each one do as he has purposed in his heart; not grudgingly or under compulsion; for God loves a cheerful giver. And God is able to make all grace abound to you, that always having all sufficiency in everything, you may have an abundance for every good deed; as it is written, "He scattered abroad, he gave to the poor, his righteousness abides forever." Now He who supplies the seed to the sower and bread for food, will supply and multiply your seed for sowing and increase the harvest of your righteousness; you will be enriched in everything for all liberality, which through us is producing thanksgiving to God. (2 Corinthians 9:6-11)

The very act of giving to the poor would become a means of spiritual growth to the Corinthians, and that "harvest of righteousness" would in turn enrich them so that they would be able to give liberally again in the future. The equalization was to be made by the Corinthians' giving materially to those who had already given to them spiritually—the very point Paul made more explicitly elsewhere in describing the purpose and motive of his collections for the poor in Jerusalem: ". . . but now, I am going to Jerusalem serving the saints. For Macedonia and Achaia have been pleased to make a contribution for the poor among the saints in Jerusalem. Yes, they were pleased to do so, and they are indebted to them. For if the Gentiles have shared in their spiritual things, they are indebted to minister to them also in material things" (Romans 15:25-27).

Finally, the whole motive for the Jerusalem collections was not—as Sider and other Christian Leftists claim—justice but gracious love, as is clear throughout Paul's discussion in 2 Corinthians 8 and 9. He tells us contributions for the poor in Jerusalem are a "gracious work" (8:7), compares them with "the grace of our Lord Jesus Christ" (8:9), calls them a "generous gift" (8:20) and "the proof of your love" (8:24). He twice calls the donation a "bountiful gift" (9:5), reminds us that it is to be done by each "as he has purposed in his heart; not grudgingly or under compulsion" (9:7),[51] and insists that the generosity springs not from a sense of duty but from "the surpassing grace of God in you" (9:14).

The equality Paul envisioned was not economic equalitarianism, forced or voluntary. It was a filling up of the needs of all parts of the Body of Christ, whether spiritual or material.

WE MUST DEFEND BIBLICAL JUSTICE FROM EQUALITARIANISM

Justice is one of the most fundamental principles on which human society depends. A right understanding of it is essential to the preservation of a just society. The wise and unfairly maligned moral philosopher Adam Smith,[52] writing in *The Theory of*

Moral Sentiments, warned that society "may subsist . . . without any mutual love or affection. . . ." But it "cannot subsist among those who are at all times ready to hurt and injure one another. . . . Beneficence, therefore, is less essential to the existence of society than justice. Society may subsist, though not in the most favorable state, without beneficence; but the prevalence of injustice must utterly destroy it." This, he argued, is why justice may be enforced and injustice punished by civil government, while love may only be urged and its lack bemoaned. Love he compared to an ornament that embellishes society. "Justice, on the contrary, is the main pillar that upholds the whole edifice. If it is removed, the great, the immense fabric of human society . . . must in a moment crumble into atoms. In order to enforce the observation of justice, therefore, nature has implanted in the human breast that consciousness of ill desert, those terrors of merited punishment, which attend upon its violation, as the great safeguards of the association of mankind, to protect the weak, to curb the violent, and to chastise the guilty."[53]

Justice is rendering to each his due in accord with the standard of God's Law. It demands impartial application of all laws to all people. It respects natural, divinely ordained spiritual and physical differences among men and, respecting these, also respects their inevitable effects: diversity of intellectual, social, economic, and spiritual attainments. It recognizes rights to life, liberty, and property, and protects them by prohibiting and punishing their violation. It demands proportionality in reward and punishment. It demands not equality of economic condition, but equal application of God's Law to all men everywhere.

Justice is the rule of order in the soul and order in the commonwealth. For the preservation of a civilization in which men respect each other's rights, we must understand justice properly and pursue it in our personal and social lives with vigor. And we must defend it against those who make it a pretext for establishing a communistic society instead of the free and just society God intends for man.

PART THREE

STEWARDSHIP AND ECONOMIC PRINCIPLES

WORKING HARDER

Work is an essential factor in reducing poverty and producing wealth, but it is not the sole factor. Insofar as it is isolated from other necessary factors, it falls short of its potential productivity. Work must make diligent and wise use of natural resources[1] in order to bear much fruit. This chapter will discuss the diligence that increases the productivity of work; the next will consider wisdom.

HARD WORK COMES FIRST

"The hand of the diligent will rule," wrote Solomon, "but the slack hand will be put to forced labor" (Proverbs 12:24). Diligence—hard work—must precede the application of wisdom. Why? Because any able-bodied person can work hard, but only those who have the leisure necessary to study can work smart. The first priority for anyone who hopes to climb out of poverty is the willingness to work hard; afterward, as a fruit of that labor, he can begin to learn how to work smarter, and as he learns more his added wisdom will multiply the effectiveness of his effort. Soon he will find that he can produce the same amount with less effort, or more with the same effort; and before long his wisdom will enable him to produce more with less effort. But effort must come first.

The economic history of the West illustrates this lesson on a large scale. In rising slowly from the almost universal poverty that preceded the fourteenth and fifteenth centuries, the Western world first employed labor-intensive means of bettering its condition.[2] In the seventeenth and eighteenth centuries, as the fruits of all that labor began to accrue, people found more leisure in which to think up and experiment with ways to make labor more fruitful.[3] Slowly at first, and then increasingly rapidly, invention joined invention, organizational innovation joined organizational innovation, until the same human effort that once barely fed a single man could feed a whole family—and later fifteen families—instead.[4]

The economic history of various waves of immigrants to the United States illustrates the same point on a smaller scale. Tens of thousands of people who arrived in the United States penniless took on backbreaking employment and saved everything they could, until at last the second—or perhaps third—generation was sufficiently provided for to enable it to focus its energies on education instead of scraping for a living. Almost overnight the general economic condition of the given immigrant group changed dramatically as one generation was enabled to work smarter because an earlier generation had worked harder.[5] "The first principle [of overcoming poverty] is that in order to move up, the poor must not only work, they must work harder than the classes above them."[6]

And the same lesson appears on a yet smaller scale—at the level of the individual. Every man who works his way through college by scampering feverishly around in a supermarket warehouse at night, picking up boxes and loading them onto pallets until he thinks he's ready to collapse—and then staying at it for another four hours; every woman who flips hamburgers in a hot, greasy fast-food kitchen to earn tuition for the classes she attends during the daytime; every individual who patiently works to support his family while he earns a four-year degree in seven years—every such person, when he graduates and gets a job for which he has been educated, working at a higher wage than he had during his schooling, illustrates this same lesson. Hard work is the *sine qua non* for overcoming poverty.

THE BIBLE COMMANDS HARD WORK

No wonder Solomon called diligence ". . . the precious possession of a man" (Proverbs 12:27)! Without it individuals, families, ethnic groups, and whole civilizations are bound to perpetual poverty. "He who tills his land will have plenty of food, but he who follows empty pursuits will have poverty in plenty" (Proverbs 28:19).[7] If anything marks the "excellent wife" of Proverbs 31:10-31, it is diligent labor. Because she works so hard, "She is not afraid of the snow for her household, for all her household are clothed with scarlet" (v. 21). Her work helps her husband to rise to prominence in the community so that he dispenses justice with the other elders of the land (v. 23).[8] Her labor is a sign that she "fears the Lord" (v. 30), and she enjoys "the product of her hands" (v. 31).

This emphasis on hard work is not peculiar to the Old Testament. The Apostle Paul takes it up too:

> . . . we urge you, brethren, to excel still more, and to make it your ambition to lead a quiet life and attend to your own business and work with your hands, just as we commanded you; so that you may behave properly toward outsiders and not be in any need. (1 Thessalonians 4:10-12)

> Now we command you, brethren, in the name of our Lord Jesus Christ, that you keep aloof from every brother who leads an unruly life and not according to the tradition which you received from us. For you yourselves know how you ought to follow our example, because we did not act in an undisciplined manner among you, nor did we eat anyone's bread without paying for it, but with labor and hardship we kept working night and day so that we might not be a burden to any of you; not because we do not have the right to this, but in order to offer ourselves as a model for you, that you might follow our example. For even when we were with you, we used to give you this order: if anyone will not work, neither let him eat. For we hear that some among you are leading an undisciplined life, doing no work at all, but acting like busybodies. Now such persons we command and exhort in the Lord Jesus Christ to work in quiet fashion and eat their own bread. But as for you, brethren, do not grow weary in doing good. And if anyone does not obey our instruction in this letter, take special note of that man and do not associate with him, so that he may be put to shame. And yet do not regard him as an enemy, but admonish him as a brother. (2 Thessalonians 3:6-15)

Refusing to work was considered a moral matter so serious as to warrant official discipline by the congregation, and even breaking of fellowship with those who did not readily respond to the church's admonition.

Elsewhere Paul explains the chief motive that should underlie all the believer's work:

Slaves, in all things obey those who are your masters on earth, not with external service, as those who merely please men, but with sincerity of heart, fearing the Lord. Whatever you do, *do your work heartily, as for the Lord rather than for men;* knowing that from the Lord you will receive the reward of the inheritance. It is the Lord Christ whom you serve. (Colossians 3:22-24)

While work has its rewards (Colossians 3:24), and so the expectation of reward is one legitimate motive for it, the highest motive should be to express, by diligent service, gratitude to the Lord for deliverance from slavery (Exodus 20:2). We serve a faithful Lord who fulfills His promise to provide for us if we obey Him. Hence, though we must work hard, we need not drive ourselves to collapse, but can enjoy rest (Matthew 11:28-30). Because our chief reward is not in this world but in the next (Colossians 3:1ff), we can stop short of grasping for every bit of wealth we can get, "For wealth certainly makes itself wings, like an eagle that flies toward the heavens" (Proverbs 23:5), and so we can take seriously Solomon's admonition, "Do not weary yourself to gain wealth . . ." (Proverbs 23:4).

THE SELF-DEFEATING NATURE OF LAZINESS
Yet confidence must not become an excuse for lazy complacency. God appoints means to ends. One of the means He has appointed to prosperity is hard work. So Solomon warns:

Go to the ant, O sluggard, observe her ways and be wise, which, having no chief, officer or ruler, prepares her food in the summer, and gathers her provision in the harvest. How long will you lie down, O sluggard? When will you arise from your sleep? "A little sleep, a little slumber, a little folding of the hands to rest"—and your poverty will come in like a vagabond, and your need like an armed man. (Proverbs 6:6-11)

Warnings against sloth echo like a refrain throughout Proverbs: "The soul of the sluggard craves and gets nothing, but the soul of the diligent is made fat" (13:4); "In all labor there is profit, but mere talk leads only to poverty" (14:23); "Laziness casts into a deep sleep, and an idle man will suffer hunger" (19:15); "Do not love sleep, lest you become poor; open your eyes, and you will be satisfied with food" (20:13).

SLOTH AVOIDS RISK

Laziness has more than one detriment to it. Not only is it simple unwillingness to work, but also it is an impediment to one of the most important economic activities: risk-taking. "The sluggard says, 'There is a lion in the road! A lion is in the open square!' As the door turns on its hinges, so does the sluggard on his bed" (Proverbs 26:13, 14; cf. 22:13). The mentality of sloth is the mentality of cheap security. It refuses to go out on a limb in the hopes of finding fruit. Thus it won't take the risks that are absolutely essential to economic growth: risks involved in testing new technologies or investing capital in untried ventures. And such risk-taking has contributed to the discoveries that have multiplied the effectiveness of labor.[9]

JEALOUSY, ENVY, AND RESSENTIMENT

Laziness also contributes directly to the growth of covetousness: "He who tills his land will have plenty of bread, but he who pursues vain things lacks sense. The wicked desires the booty of evil men, but the root of the righteous yields fruit" (Proverbs 12:11, 12; cf. 13:4). Because wealth, the fruit of hard work, exalts a man (Proverbs 22:29), lazy people, whose sloth keeps them poor, become jealous of the wealthy. Before long their jealousy is transformed into envy, a burning hatred for those whose wealth the envious covet, a hatred that can boil over into destructive acts and even hatred for God Himself as the envious shift blame for their ill fortune to Him (Romans 1:29; cf. Galatians 5:19). "Envy is the feeling that someone else's having something is to blame for the fact that you do not have it. The principal motive is thus not so much to *take*, but to *destroy*. The envier acts against the object of his envy, not to benefit himself, but to cut the other person down to his own level—or below."[10]

The Philistines who ruined Abraham's wells did so because they envied him (Genesis 26:12-15). Their act benefited them not at all; but it injured a hard-working man of God who had been blessed with abundant fruit for his labors. Haman's envy of Mordecai—even though Mordecai was poor and Haman was a personal aide to the king—led him to connive for Mordecai's death (Esther 5:11-13).

Jealousy and envy ultimately produce *ressentiment*, a vengeful hope for and delight in calamity's coming upon those one envies.

> *Ressentiment* has its origin in the tendency to make
> comparisons between the attributes of another and
> one's own attributes: wealth, possessions, appearance,
> intelligence, personality, friends, children. Any per-
> ceived difference is enough to set the pathology in
> motion. *Ressentiment* "whispers continually: 'I can
> forgive everything, but not that you *are*—that you are
> *what* you are—that I am not what you are—indeed
> that I am not *you*.'" . . . *Ressentiment* values its own
> welfare less than it does the debasement or harm of
> its object.[11]

Ultimately the covetousness, jealousy, envy, and *ressentiment* that grow from laziness are economically as well as spiritually paralyzing. They prevent the one who harbors them from
addressing his own problems for himself. He sees the cause of all
his distress in others, and focuses his emotional and even physical
energy on hating them, striking out against them verbally and
physically. Should the state try to alleviate his poverty by outright
gifts, he resents the state as much as he does the wealthier individuals around him since clearly the state, too, has more than he
does. The crimes that frequently arise from this complex of sin
often bring the punitive power of the state into play against him,
increasing his troubles and so giving him yet another reason to
hate. And if he should be so rational as to realize, at last, that he
has brought his troubles on himself, the chances are good that his
hatred will turn inward and lead to consciously self-destructive
acts, including, ultimately, suicide.

THE WISDOM OF FOOLS

Might the lazy man be helped by spiritual counsel? Perhaps—and
that is the only effective means of helping him. But laziness and
its fruit—covetousness, jealousy, envy, and *ressentiment*—often
prevent his receiving any such counsel: "The sluggard is wiser in
his own eyes than seven men who can give a discreet answer"
(Proverbs 26:16).

The pride of the lazy stands in the way of his learning more
efficient techniques of working, because learning is itself hard
work. Often learning means trying something again and again
without success; the lazy man simply isn't willing to expend that
effort without the guarantee of immediate reward. And so he continues to use his unproductive methods year after year, limiting
his productivity to a small fraction of what it could be.

Willingness to learn can make the difference between continuing in poverty (or losing wealth) and climbing into prosperity: "Poverty and shame will come to him who neglects discipline, but he who regards reproof will be honored" (Proverbs 13:18).

Ironically, the sluggard's way is self-defeating (and this is as true of whole societies as it is of individuals). He hates work, but his very laziness condemns him to more and harder work than he would have to endure if only he would take the risks and gain the skills necessary to increase his productivity. God's moral order in this, as in many other kinds of sin, is simple: those who transgress suffer in ways fitted to their transgressions (Psalm 109:14-20).[12]

Clearly only spiritual transformation will deliver the lazy from the economic and spiritual bondage they suffer. Such a transformation can only come when they are made new creatures in Christ, when old things have passed away (2 Corinthians 5:17) and they are enabled, by the power of the indwelling Spirit of God, to conquer sin and walk in righteousness (Romans 8:1-4). This points to the tremendous importance of evangelism and discipleship in the church's efforts to help the poor out of poverty.[13]

WORKING SMARTER

S weat cannot replace thought. For any society, family, or individual to prosper beyond bare subsistence, hard work must be supplemented by devices—tools and relationships—that multiply its effectiveness. Developing those tools and relationships requires *wisdom*, the "perceptual and rational powers [needed] to live in this world efficiently and effectively, carrying out practical enterprises with skill and satisfaction."[1]

Wisdom is not, of course, solely an economic virtue. It is first and foremost spiritual, beginning with the fear of the Lord and characterized by obedience to His Law (Psalm 111:10). It is incomparably more valuable than any material benefit (Proverbs 3:13-18; cf. 16:16; 8:10, 11; Psalm 19:7-11); its great advantage is that it leads to eternal life, while riches are world-bound (Ecclesiastes 7:11, 12).

Yet there are economic benefits to wisdom. One who "fears the Lord" receives God's instruction "in the way he should choose," so that "His soul will abide in prosperity, and his descendants will inherit the land" (Psalm 25:12, 13). Says wisdom:

> I love those who love me; and those who diligently seek me will find me. Riches and honor are with me, enduring wealth and righteousness. My fruit is better than gold, even pure gold, and my yield than choicest silver. I walk in the way of righteousness, in the midst of the paths of justice, to endow those who love me with wealth, that I may fill their treasuries. (Proverbs 8:17-21)

The wise are fitted for economic productivity, honor, and positions of influence over the surrounding culture (Proverbs

24:3-5; 22:29). In contrast, folly leads to collapse, even for kings (Ecclesiastes 4:13, 14). While riches, honor, and power are fitting for the wise, they are unnatural for the foolish (Proverbs 26:1; 14:24; 19:10; 30:21-23). Those who neglect wisdom are warned that she will neglect them, laughing when their naivete leads to destruction (Proverbs 1:24-33). Given all wisdom's benefits, and the dangers inherent in neglecting her, it is no wonder that Solomon wrote:

> Acquire wisdom! Acquire understanding! Do not for-
> get, nor turn away from the words of my mouth. Do
> not forsake her, and she will guard you; love her, and
> she will watch over you. The beginning of wisdom is:
> Acquire wisdom; and with all your acquiring, get
> understanding. (Proverbs 4:5-7)

Gaining wisdom makes the difference between working harder and working smarter, one of the most important differences in economics.[2] It is the difference between brain and brawn. Applying wisdom to economic problems—problems of how best to allocate scarce resources for the production, distribution, and consumption of goods and services that people value—sets millions of people free from the tasks of bare subsistence so that they can produce, trade, and enjoy goods and services unheard of even by their own parents, let alone by peoples of earlier centuries.

The vast majority of the West's population was involved in growing or raising food through all the centuries until the Industrial Revolution. But steady accumulation of wisdom made possible increasing division of labor[3] and mechanization of farming. As a result, the percentage of a population that had to devote itself to agriculture to feed everyone began to fall steadily. By 1930, only about 25 percent of the American population lived on farms, and only 10 percent was employed in agriculture. By 1982, only 2.4 percent of Americans lived on farms, and only 1.6 percent were employed in agriculture.[4] Yet those 3,773,000 people raised enough food to feed over 234 million Americans and still have huge surpluses to ship overseas and fill government warehouses. The average American farm worker today raises enough food to feed himself and over sixty-one others. Yet he needn't work nearly so hard as agricultural workers five hundred, one hundred, or even fifty years ago did to feed just one or two people in addition to themselves. Why? Accumulated wisdom in machines, tools, and fertilizers.

The rest of this chapter will look at seven particular aspects of wisdom as applied to economics: planning, division of labor, absolute and comparative advantage, competition and cooperation, profit and loss, saving and investment, and submission to God. The better we understand and apply these principles, the better we will be able to make the most efficient allocations of scarce resources to the production, distribution, and consumption of wealth for the broadest possible benefit.[5]

PLANNING

About a year ago a young couple told me that they were building a house across the road, and I looked forward to welcoming them to the area. But a few weeks ago, with the foundation and frame of the house finished, a "For Sale" sign appeared. The couple has run out of money and can't complete the job. Now they must try to get enough from the sale to pay taxes and mortgage, lest they lose everything. Even then they'll have lost all the time and effort, and much of the money, that they've already put into the property. Their intentions were excellent, but they failed to foresee the extent of the sacrifices they would have to make to complete their house.

In warning people to count the cost of following or rejecting Him, Jesus assumed that all sensible people recognize the wisdom of planning ahead (Luke 14:26-33). "The plans of the diligent lead surely to advantage," wrote Solomon, "but everyone who is hasty comes surely to poverty" (Proverbs 21:5; cf. 27:12). Clearly, planning is essential to economic prosperity.[6]

GOALS AND STEPS

An obvious sort of planning is setting goals and determining the intermediate steps necessary to achieve them. Someone who wants to manufacture and sell computers will see that he must invest a certain amount of capital (money, time, effort) up front to get the project off the ground. He will need to find suppliers of all the components, from steel or plastic chassis to memory chips and disk drives; hire managers for the various aspects of his business—procurement, plant, design, assembly, shipping, and marketing, to name a few—and skilled laborers to design and assemble the machines; buy or rent land and a building on which to operate his business, and all the equipment for production. Each of these intermediate steps—and there are many others—will cost time and money.

If he doesn't foresee how much each step will cost, how long it will take, how many people (and with what skills) must be involved, and what are the risks of failure at any point along the way, he probably will never reach his goal. And even if he does plan properly for all these things, he will fail if he has misjudged the market: Is some other company already making an equivalent computer at a price he can't meet? Do enough consumers want the product to support production at the cost level he predicts—and are they willing to pay? What if someone has just made a new breakthrough in computer technology—one he doesn't even know about—that will enable a competitor to produce faster computers with bigger memories and more capabilities, and at half the cost he expects for his own? Why, if that happens, he'll have to adapt almost overnight, or fail. Careful planning is a way of minimizing—but never eliminating—risks of disaster in the future.

BUDGETING

Budgeting, another type of planning, is an essential part of the fundamental economic task of allocating scarce resources to the production of goods and services. It involves the allocation of scarce resources—income—to their alternate uses.

We might wish we could dine out every night at expensive restaurants, or buy a new set of Bible commentaries, or give $500 to support a missionary this month, but we must weigh each of those desires against other desires and needs. If we dine out every night, will we still be able to pay rent or mortgage or electricity or car insurance? If not, and if we must pay for some or all of those, then we must moderate our dining out—perhaps to twice a month, and at less expensive restaurants. If we give $500 to support the missionary, will we be able to pay next month's hospital bill when the new baby is born? Maybe we need to give $100 instead, recognizing that our prior responsibility is to pay for services received.[7]

Businesses, just like individuals and families, must also budget. They must decide how much of their income can be allocated to payroll for additional workers or raises for present workers, to capital improvement (to buy new computers or ships, build whole new factories, or upgrade assembly line equipment), to acquiring raw materials, to research and development for future products, to advertising and distribution, and so on. The business that fails to plan ahead for equipment breakdowns or obsolescence, or that allocates too little for wage increases, will suffer when a printing press breaks down or a competitor attracts its workers by offering them more pay or better benefits or working conditions. By the same token, if it pays its workers too highly, or buys more new equipment than it can use efficiently, or advertises heavily in an area where people don't need its products, it will also suffer in the long run. The wisely run business will keep an eye on the condition of its facilities, tools, and raw materials (Proverbs 27:23-27). "A prudent man sees evil and hides himself, the naive proceed and pay the penalty" (Proverbs 27:12).

DIVISION OF LABOR

Suppose you're a tailor and want twenty pins to hold a seam together until you've sewn it up. What do you do? You could try making the pins yourself, from scratch. Here's a partial recipe:

(1) Make a shovel.

(2) Find, dig, and transport some iron ore.

(3) Build a small blast furnace. (You might need somebody to teach you how.)

(4) Find, dig, and transport some coal to heat the furnace.

(5) Put the iron ore into the furnace and, through a complicated process that might take you years to learn, turn it into steel.

(6) Form the hot steel into long, thin wires, straighten them, cut them into proper lengths, cool them, and sharpen their points.

(7) Put heads on the pins, using more steel or some plastic beads you make from oil you pump from the ground, transport, refine, and process into plastic.

With luck you might have your twenty pins in three to five years, if you survive all the dangers of mining and refining ore and drilling and refining oil. (This assumes that you learn how to do each of the steps from somebody who already knows how; if you have to teach yourself by trial and error, figure on centuries.) Of course it might take you longer if you have to grow your own food while you're at it. And in any case, by the time you've got your pins, your customer will have gone elsewhere for his garment, and your fabric will probably have rotted. (Oh, by the way: where'd you get the steel for the shovel you made to dig the ore and coal to make steel for the pins?)

Let's face it, it's a whole lot easier to buy pins from somebody else. And it's a whole lot easier for pin-makers to let somebody else dig the iron ore and coal, make the steel, pump the petroleum, and make the plastic. While other folks are doing those things, you can be sewing garments that you sell to earn the money you spend on the pins—and needles and threads and fabrics, and food for yourself and your family too.

ADVANTAGES OF SHARING THE WORK

For many centuries, most people personally produced everything, or almost everything, that they consumed or used for other production. Buying and selling—trade—made up only a tiny proportion of most families' economic activity. Needless to say, they didn't produce much, which explains why the vast majority of the world lived in dreadful poverty until about two hundred years ago, when increasing application of the principle of the division of labor in the factory system—along with other principles people began to understand at about the same time—resulted in booming productivity growth that has lifted a large part of the world's population out of poverty and shows no signs of stopping. (Unless, of course, people turn their backs on the accumulated economic wisdom that has led to the growth.)

Division of labor is the arrangement in which individual people do little jobs that contribute to finished products. It is inherent to the spiritual functions of the Body of Christ as well as to economies: "For just as we have many members in one body and all the members do not have the same function, so we, who are many, are one body in Christ, and individually members one of another" (Romans 12:4-5; cf. 1 Corinthians 12). How many pastors bemoan the common attitude, "If the pastor doesn't do it, it won't get done"? That isn't the way God intended things in the church; He intended the various members of the Body to perform different functions, each making his own contribution to the growth of the Kingdom. If everyone does his work, the Body grows; if everyone lets the pastor do everything, it withers. And no one can say that just because his work isn't particularly visible, it isn't important to the growth of the Body; ". . . God has placed the members, each one of them, in the body, just as He desired. And if they were all one member, where would the body be?" (1 Corinthians 12:18, 19).

In a justly famous paragraph of his giant *Inquiry into the Nature and Causes of the Wealth of Nations*, moral philosopher Adam Smith (1723-1790), whose ideas on economics were among the most powerful in shaping the economies of the West, explained the effect of the division of labor on the pin-making trade. Those not familiar with the trade, he wrote, would be hard pressed to produce one pin per day, and certainly could not produce twenty. But the application of the division of labor in factories of his time greatly multiplied that productivity.

> One man draws out the wire, another straights it, a third cuts it, a fourth points it, a fifth grinds it at the top for receiving the head; to make the head requires two or three distinct operations; to put it on, is a peculiar business, to whiten the pins is another; it is even a trade by itself to put them into the paper; and the important business of making a pin is, in this manner, divided into about eighteen distinct operations, which, in some manufactories, are all performed by distinct hands, though in others the same man will sometimes perform two or three of them.

As a result of this division of labor, he wrote, he had observed ten men, even in small factories with poor equipment, producing "about twelve pounds of pins in a day," or about forty-eight thousand. Thus the division of labor multiplied the product of each man by at least 240, and perhaps by 4,800.[8] Clearly, division of labor contributes significantly to economic prosperity.

DIVISION OF LABOR
AND WORKER ALIENATION

Some people have criticized the division of labor and the factory system for "alienating" workers from their products. According to this theory, factories with high degrees of division of labor so remove, or alienate, individual workers from the end product that they can have no significant psychological satisfaction from their work. These critics also say that any individual's contribution to the finished product is so slight that it becomes difficult to determine its value. That, they say, results in difficulties in determining appropriate wages.[9] Are there answers to these criticisms?

To the claim that division of labor alienates workers from products, there are several answers:

First, the relationships people need are not so much with products as with *people*. Bringing people together to cooperate in production fosters such relationships. Notice the stress Paul lays on the unity of the Body of Christ, despite the different tasks performed by its many members (1 Corinthians 12:14-22). The division of labor is really precisely that: a division of *labor*, not of laborers. It is a *uniting* of laborers in a common enterprise.

Second, while the relationship between worker and end product is closer when there is less division of labor, the total amount of end product is also significantly smaller. The worker may feel a closer bond to what he has produced, but he will have produced far less. Is it better to feel satisfaction in doing most of a little thing, or in doing a little of a big thing? Different people will answer differently. But it seems impossible to argue that either the population as a whole or the individuals in it would be better off with fewer finished products—that is, poorer instead of richer.

Third, this criticism appears to arise from the desire to be praised—whether by ourselves or by others—for what we do. But that motive doesn't comport well with the Bible's emphasis on humility or with its assurance that what really counts is what God thinks of us, not what others think. That is Paul's point when he writes, "And the eye cannot say to the hand, 'I have no need of you'; or again the head to the feet, 'I have no need of you.' On the contrary, it is much truer that the members of the body which seem to be weaker are necessary; and those members of the body, which we deem less honorable, on these we bestow more abundant honor, and our unseemly members come to have more abundant seemliness, whereas our seemly members have no need of it. But God has so composed the body, giving more abundant honor to that member which lacked, that there should be no division in the body, but that the members should have the same care for one another" (1 Corinthians 12:21-25). The workers who fit body to chassis on a car are more closely connected in time and space with the end product than those who make the pistons, but can anyone seriously argue that their contribution is more important?

Does alienating worker from end product necessitate difficulties in determining appropriate wages? This criticism assumes that the price of a worker's labor ought to be related directly to the percentage his contribution comprises of the total price of the end product. But when people are free to offer products and services at whatever prices they're willing to accept, and others are free to offer whatever prices they're willing to pay, prices are determined by the relationship of supply and demand. The only alternative to this free market arrangement is a market controlled by civil government, in which people's God-given liberties are drastically reduced—by force if necessary.[10]

In a free market, wages are established by free agreements

between buyers (employers) and sellers (employees) of labor. Buyers compete for laborers and so bid prices (wages) up, while sellers compete for employment and so bid prices (wages) down.[11] As the supply of able and willing workers increases relative to employers' demand for their work, the price for their work necessarily falls (unless artificially controlled by civil government);[12] as supply decreases relative demand, the price for work will rise.[13] This is not to prejudge whether this pricing mechanism is morally good (although we will argue later that it is); it is only to say that the criticism we're dealing with rests on a false conception of reality.[14]

ABSOLUTE AND COMPARATIVE ADVANTAGE

Let's suppose now that you work in a pin-making factory. You have exceptionally large, strong hands with thick, stubby fingers; a fellow worker has thin, delicate hands with long fingers. Your hands are ideal for lifting heavy crates of finished pins, but you'd have a terrible time putting heads on the pins. Your friend, however, can fit heads on pins easily, but can barely lift the crates. Which of you ought to do which task? The answer's obvious.

This principle of *absolute advantage* tells us that it's to everyone's benefit for people to specialize in the things they can do more efficiently than others—that is, the things in which they have an advantage over others. This does not mean that everyone ought to do what he does better than anything else he can do. If by sewing shirts Jim can produce more product value per hour than by any other activity, yet Tom can sew shirts even faster, perhaps Jim ought to do what he does second best—but at which Tom can't come close to competing—and then trade some of his products for some of Tom's. This way more units of both products are made, meaning that the members of the producing society are wealthier than they otherwise would be.

This holds true for aggregates of people—cities, provinces or states, and nations—as well as for individuals. The cities, states, and nations of the world will all be better off if they will specialize in the forms of production at which they have an advantage over others and trade for the goods and services they don't produce. This is why, for instance, we don't grow bananas in North Dakota (though it would be possible in expensive greenhouses) but buy them from the Dominican Republic and other countries, while those countries don't produce wheat (which they could do, but not so well as they grow bananas) but buy it instead from North Dakota.

COMPARATIVE ADVANTAGE

But what if you can do *everything* more cheaply than your friend? Does it no longer matter which of you does what? No, for beyond the principle of absolute advantage is that of *comparative advantage*. Unless your absolute advantage is to the same degree with regard to every item of production (a pretty unlikely case), the two of you together will still produce more total goods if you will focus on the things in which your absolute advantage is greater and he will focus on the things in which his absolute disadvantage is less.

Assume for a moment that you can produce ten pounds of bananas per hour of effort, while your friend can only produce eight. You can produce four blankets per hour, while he can produce only 1.6. (We're also assuming, for the sake of simplicity, that labor is the only cost of production, and that your and his products are of equal quality.) If each of you invests twenty-four hours per week producing bananas and sixteen producing blankets, you will produce 240 pounds of bananas and forty-eight blankets, and he will produce eighty pounds of bananas and 25.6 blankets, for a combined total of 320 pounds of bananas and 73.6 blankets.

Clearly you have an *absolute advantage* in the production of both products. But your absolute advantage in producing blankets is greater than in producing bananas, and his absolute disadvantage is less in producing bananas than in producing blankets. You have a *comparative advantage* in producing that in which you have the greater *absolute advantage,* and he—though he doesn't have an absolute advantage in anything—actually has a *comparative advantage* in producing that in which he has the lesser absolute disadvantage.

If you're both smart, he'll produce all the bananas and you'll produce all the blankets. Then each of you will trade his surplus for the other's; as a result there will be more of each product to share. Thus, if you spend forty hours per week producing blankets and he spends forty hours per week producing bananas, the two of you together will end up with 160 blankets and four hundred pounds of bananas. This represents 117 percent greater total blanket production and 25 percent greater total banana production.[15]

This principle holds true for groups—including nations—as well as for individuals. "Even in the extreme case where one country produces *everything* more cheaply (with fewer resources) than another, there is still a basis for trade between them. If the things it produces are cheaper to *varying* degrees, there will be more total output between the two countries together if the more efficient country concentrates on those things where its production costs are lowest relative to the other, and trades with the less efficient country, which produces those things where the cost differential is least."[16] Only if the degree of one country's absolute advantage over another is the same in every item of production would it be economically more efficient for it to produce all its own products rather than to concentrate on some and trade for the others.

There was an interesting application of the principle of comparative advantage in the early missionary work of the Christian church. The apostles recognized the fruitfulness God had given to Paul in preaching to the Gentiles and to Peter in preaching to the Jews, so they encouraged each to focus on those with whom he was more effective (Galatians 2:7-9). Thus there was a division of labor between them along the lines of their comparative advantages. As a result the gospel spread more rapidly than it otherwise would have.

TURNING THE TABLES

A country's (or individual's) present comparative advantage need not persist through time. Changing economic conditions (availability of raw materials and labor, consumers' preferences, competency of labor, obsolescence of equipment, etc.) can lead to drastic changes in comparative advantage. While the United States once enjoyed overwhelming comparative advantage over Japan in automobile manufacturing, for instance, that advantage has almost disappeared. For the Japanese, changing the picture meant sacrifice. It meant opting for future prosperity over present prosperity; for a certain period Japanese people chose to pay the costs of pursuing an industry in which they were at an absolute disadvantage so that they could develop a comparative advantage in it.

Gaining and maintaining comparative advantage, in other words, almost always requires some sacrifices—investment of time, capital, and energy into one kind of production instead of another. For individuals and countries suffering deteriorating economies because of loss of comparative advantage, or worsening absolute disadvantage, the only nonviolent solution is to make the present sacrifices necessary to gain new skills and productive capital for the future.[17] Using violence—political force—to overcome absolute and comparative disadvantages

impoverishes everyone by directing economic effort into less efficient channels than would be chosen freely.[18] Freely choosing present
sacrifices for the sake of future productivity enriches everyone in
the long run by making all economic effort more efficient. It is
one thing to express concern over nations' deteriorating absolute
and comparative advantages; it is another thing altogether to
translate that concern into proper economic solutions.[19]

COMPARATIVE ADVANTAGE, FREE TRADE, AND NATIONAL SECURITY

If individuals, companies, and states chose consistently with the
principles of absolute and comparative advantage, aggregate production in the world would be maximized, and standards of living
everywhere would rise—though they would not necessarily be
equal.[20] This means that it is in principle better economically to
allow free trade than to set up legal barriers to trade (e.g., tariffs or
import quotas). Consistent with such principles, ". . . frontiers
would be without significance. Trade would flow over them
unhindered."[21]

Barriers to trade, then, can properly be defended only on the
non-economic ground of national security. (This is not to say that
barriers cannot *successfully* be defended on economic grounds.
People are often fooled by economically fallacious arguments.)[22]
No economic argument for free trade, for instance, can properly
counter the argument against selling nuclear weapons to an
enemy nation. Similarly, one might argue for prohibiting all trade
with an enemy nation on the supposition that its economy would
suffer more than the domestic economy and, presumably, weakening its economy compared to the domestic economy would
lessen its martial threat.[23] Free trade between enemy nations,
then, is normally to the martial advantage of the economically
weaker nation. To counter this with the economic argument that
both nations will prosper more with free trade is to ignore the fact
that national security and economic advantage are quite different,
though closely related, kinds of considerations.

COMPETITION AND COOPERATION

Speaking of absolute and comparative advantage naturally leads
to the idea of competition, for only through competition do we
discover where absolute and comparative advantages lie, and only
by discovering such absolute and comparative advantages can we
maximize the productive potential of an economy, whether local,
national, or worldwide.

WHAT IS COMPETITION?

It is important to understand precisely what constitutes economic "competition," for failure to distinguish it properly can lead to advocating inefficient, counterproductive policies. In economics, competition

> . . . is not mere rivalry, but the *conditions* under which the rivalry is carried on. . . . A competitive market is one in which:
>
> 1. There are *large numbers* of buyers and sellers acting independently, no one of whom has sufficient output or demand to affect the market price.
>
> 2. There is sufficient *knowledge* on the part of buyers and sellers to prevent transactions from being made on terms different from those available elsewhere in the market.
>
> 3. The conditions of *entry* and *exit* are such that new firms may be established in an industry on terms very similar to those of existing firms in the industry, and existing firms may leave one industry for another without serious losses from the transition. . .
>
> Where all three conditions for a competitive market exist, certain results may be expected:
>
> 1. There will be one price for everybody throughout the market.
>
> 2. There will be no chronic shortages or surpluses.
>
> 3. There will be one rate of profit throughout the market, and it will be the lowest rate that is sufficient to attract the capital and management necessary to conduct the business.[24]

Put simply, competition results in production sufficient to meet consumers' demands at the lowest possible prices. Businesses in competitive industries tend to have small percentages of profit (though if their markets are very large the profits may be very large in absolute, not proportionate, terms) because as soon as profit percentages rise new competitors will enter the market, adding to supply relative to demand and so forcing prices (and consequently profit percentages) down.

IS COMPETITION IMMORAL?

Many Christians are wary of the idea of competition because they view it as inherently rooted in self-centeredness and individualism. They see competition as necessarily opposed to cooperation. Arthur G. Gish, for example, writes:

> A basic Western assumption since the Renaissance is that the individual is a separate unit. Only secondarily do we have relationships with others, and these are seen as restrictive of our personal freedom. Life is seen as a jungle in which everyone must fight for survival. We work not with others but against them, everyone struggling against nature and competing with others to climb the ladder of success.[25]

COMPETITION ENHANCES COOPERATION

This criticism involves three misunderstandings of the role of competition in economies. First, so long as it does not resort to political force (laws restricting competitors' activities through tariffs, legally enforced monopolies, quotas, etc.), economic competition enhances cooperation for the very reason that it helps participants to identify absolute and comparative advantages. Knowing those, they can focus on endeavors in which they have comparative advantages and so increase overall productivity. Since this means making more goods and services available to consumers, it also means reducing the prices of those goods and services (an operation of the law of supply and demand) and thus making them available to consumers with lower incomes.[26]

COMPETITION IN SERVICE

Second, the nature of the competition itself differs from that in, say, a boxing match. In boxing, competitors try to pound each other into submission; their focus is on each other, not on those observing them. But in economic competition, competitors focus on the observers—consumers—rather than on each other (except to the extent that they try to learn from each other's example how best to serve consumers). Their object is not to pound each other into submission, but to provide more and better goods and services to consumers at lower prices. In other words, economic competition is competition in *service*.

COMPETITION *VS*. COERCION

Third, economic competition is the only peaceful means of determining the allocation of scarce resources. It ". . . is a necessary consequence of scarcity; it is an unavoidable dimension of human existence in this life. Competition exists whenever the scarcity of something people prize or value results in more people wanting it than can have it."[27] The sole alternative to free competition—socialism—is allocation by agents with legal power to enforce their decisions regardless of the consent of those affected by them, and this power ultimately amounts to the threat or actual use of violence.[28]

The key is to distinguish economic competition from coercion by the state. Where economic competition is free of state coercion, its result is cooperation; increased availability of goods and services, and reduced prices. But where state coercion enters the picture, the result is lack of cooperation, decreased availability of goods and services, and increased prices.[29] "The competition of the marketplace is not an end in itself," writes Nash; "it is a means to the end of providing better goods and services at the lowest possible price. The competition of the marketplace ends up encouraging social cooperation. It benefits the masses and increases the productive capacity of the society. We live as fallen creatures in an imperfect world where scarcity abounds. The alternative to nonviolent competition for these scarce resources is the use of force, violence, and theft."[30]

Competition can, of course, be abused. But then, so can all of God's gifts. The Bible can be twisted to justify neo-Nazism or Communism. Sexuality can be exploited outside of marriage. We can so overindulge our appetites as to make our bellies our gods (Philippians 3:19). Susceptibility to abuse doesn't make any of these things inherently evil. The evil, in fact, lies in human hearts, not in the things themselves. The solution to abuse is not to abolish them, but to change human hearts through the gospel and Biblical discipleship.

PROFIT AND LOSS

In discussing competition we saw that rising profit percentages invite new firms into particular markets, increasing product supply and decreasing prices. Watching and responding to trends in profits is how competitive markets keep profit percentages and consumer prices low while ensuring sufficient product availability to meet demand. But it is not the only use of profits.

PROFITS REWARD SERVICE

Profit is the excess of income from sales of products or services over costs of production, marketing, and distribution; loss is the excess of costs over income. Profit and loss may be seen as proportionate or as absolute. Proportionate profit or loss is measured in percentage of gross revenues; absolute profit or loss is measured in actual money value. Profits therefore reward producers for meeting consumers' demands well; losses punish them for failing to meet consumers' demands well. Profits sustained over long periods enable owners to invest in additional productive enterprises by which to serve consumers' needs. Long-term losses drive companies out of business.

The fundamental function of profits (and losses) is to show whether, and to what extent, our endeavors meet others' perceived needs. The more efficiently we meet people's demands, the higher will be our profit percentage, until other producers enter the market and drive down the price, forcing profit to stay at the lowest percentage necessary to attract the capital and management needed to conduct the business.[31] The more demands we meet, the larger will be our absolute profits, even if percentage profits are low.

PANDERING TO EVIL DESIRES?

This understanding of the function of profits has been criticized on the grounds that perceived needs may differ from real needs, resulting in profit-seekers' pandering to consumers' evil desires.[32] This is a legitimate concern; yet it isn't always easy to determine whether something is an evil desire or a real need.

From a Biblical standpoint, for instance, no one has a real need for pornography, but everyone needs food. Yet there are items for which reality or unreality of need cannot be determined universally. Furthermore, Scripture nowhere says that people's desires must be limited solely to their most basic needs. They are to be *content* with food, clothing, and shelter alone (1 Timothy 6:8). But that doesn't mean they cannot desire and, if granted them, enjoy things beyond these (Philippians 4:12).

The economy's task is to meet perceived needs, real or not, within the constraints of God's moral Law. Ensuring that perceived needs conform to real needs, and that desires are godly rather than evil, is the discipling task of the church. Outside of matters clearly proscribed by Biblical Law and over which God grants the state legal jurisdiction (such as those addressed in the Fifth through Ninth Commandments), Scripture teaches us to allow each other freedom of individual conscience (Romans 14). As David Chilton puts it, "The Bible does not want the government to stand idly by while Murder, Inc. negotiates a 'market price' for its service. The *market* is to be free from government regulation, but criminal activity in the market must be abolished."[33]

PROFITS, EFFICIENCY, AND DOMINION

Chapter Two noted that a prime aim of work is furthering man's dominion over the earth, making it serve man's needs to the glory of God. Economic efficiency—maximizing production and minimizing costs to meet people's needs and (godly) desires—is a sign of increasing dominion. Profits, in turn, are the clearest indicator of economic efficiency. Profits therefore are an important means of determining whether, and to what extent, our economic actions contribute to fulfilling the dominion mandate God gave man in Genesis 1.

Profits are earned only by investing wealth—money, land, machines, personal energy, time, etc.—to serve others. This means they are earned only at the risk of loss if investments turn out not to serve others so well as was hoped. In effect, profits are a reward for offering wealth to others ". . . without a predetermined return."[34] They are a (nonguaranteed) reward for self-denial expressed by taking risks for the benefit of others.

We might fear loss so much as not to take the risks involved in investment. Doing so may secure our wealth short-term, but it ensures that we will lose it in the long run. This principle is clearly illustrated in the parable of the talents (Matthew 25:14-30). God expects His servants to take risks for the sake of serving others; when we do so wisely, we meet needs and earn profits. But when we avoid risks, God ultimately removes wealth from us and gives it to those who are willing to take the risks of servanthood and have proved themselves wise investors. To them He gives dominion—increasing responsibilities and the increasing authority needed to fulfill them (Matthew 25:21, 23, 28, 29).

SAVING AND INVESTMENT

"There is precious treasure and oil in the dwelling of the wise," wrote Solomon, "but a foolish man swallows it up" (Proverbs 21:20). Why is it wise to save and foolish to consume everything we earn? Partly because we might one day meet an emergency when we need to live on what we have saved in the past (see Genesis 41 and 47). But that isn't the only reason. Economic productivity is largely limited by the amount we invest in raw materials, tools, buildings, and other factors of production. We cannot invest more than we save.[35] We must save before we can invest, and we must invest in order to produce things for others and earn a profit.

Those who save and invest must forego present pleasures for the sake of future gains. Future orientation is an important part of Christian maturity (Proverbs 21:17). The righteous man, in fact, cares not only about his own future but also about his descendants', conscientiously building an inheritance for them (Proverbs 13:22). Immediate consumption, in contrast, is present-oriented. Because it lies at the root of the failure to save and invest, it is one of the chief factors prohibiting many people and societies from climbing out of poverty.[36] This is why a present-oriented person or society, by putting little emphasis on saving, is bound to suffer economically.

SUBMISSION TO GOD

All of our efforts to produce and save wealth, whatever their immediate rewards, will come to naught in the long run if we do not humbly submit to the rule of God in our lives. This holds true for individuals and societies alike. God will not be mocked. Whatever we sow, we will inevitably reap, sooner or later (Galatians 6:7-10).

We might think that anyone could apply God's principles of economic wisdom and prosper, while rejecting God Himself and other aspects of His moral Law. And indeed, short-term prosperity may come this way. But the same verse that teaches us that the righteous leave an inheritance to coming generations also promises that ". . . the wealth of the sinner is stored up for the righteous" (Proverbs 13:22).[37] God is not an absentee landlord. He sovereignly rules His world. Regardless of our economic efforts, if we refuse to submit to God He will someday take our wealth from us and give it to the righteous. To those who turn from Him to revel in riches and worship Fortune and Destiny, God says:

> . . . I will destine you for the sword, and all of you shall bow down to the slaughter. Because I called, but you did not answer; I spoke, but you did not hear. And you did evil in My sight, and chose that in which I did not delight. . . . Behold, My servants shall eat, but you shall be hungry. Behold, My servants shall

drink, but you shall be thirsty. Behold, My servants shall rejoice, but you shall be put to shame. Behold, My servants shall shout joyfully with a glad heart, but you shall cry out with a heavy heart, and you shall wail with a broken spirit. (Isaiah 65:11-14)

In prophesying this, Isaiah was simply echoing the warning God had given Israel through Moses: that its rebellion would bring God's curse (Leviticus 26:14-33; Deuteronomy 4:23-28; 8:19, 20; 28:15-38; Psalm 92:5-8).[38]

Time and again throughout the Scriptures God promises blessings in response to obedience. Yes, the blessings sometimes are spiritual. But often enough they are material. Economic prosperity is not a matter merely of pushing the right buttons. It is primarily a matter of God's blessing (Deuteronomy 4:40; 5:29, 33; 6:3; 7:11-16; 11:13-17; 28:1-14). "The reward of humility and the fear of the Lord are riches, honor and life" (Proverbs 22:4; cf. Psalm 128:1-4). Only if God confirms the work of our hands will it produce long-term prosperity (Psalm 90:17), and that He will do only in response to humble obedience: "Humble yourselves in the presence of the Lord, and He will exalt you" (James 4:10; cf. 4:6; 1 Peter 5:6, 7). But ". . . the Lord of hosts will have a day of reckoning against everyone who is proud and lofty, and against everyone who is lifted up, that he may be abased" (Isaiah 2:12).

All true wisdom—including the understanding of economic principles—comes by the fear of the Lord and submission to His Law (Psalm 111). Such spiritual maturity comes only as people are brought into increasing conformity to the will of Christ revealed in His commandments (Matthew 28:19, 20). As it was at the close of Chapter Six, so again it is clear that evangelism and discipleship are essential steps toward bettering people's economic condition.

STEWARDSHIP, VALUE, AND PRICE

*R*emember when we assumed for a moment that you were a tailor in need of twenty pins, and then explored how you might have made those pins yourself from scratch? We figured it would probably take you three to five years to make the twenty pins you needed. Obviously you thought better of the project and decided to buy them from somebody else. But what would have happened if someone had decided to make the pins that way for himself and—as we surmised—his customer had gone elsewhere for his garment? If, in fact, another tailor had come and cornered the market? Our hapless do-it-yourselfer would have been out of the tailoring business, of course.

Now what does he do with the pins? Unless he has a personal use for them, he tries to sell them to recoup the costs of making them, right? So, he's labored full-time for five years. At an average annual wage of $18,000, that's $90,000 for labor. He's put about $2 million in capital into the project. (Nobody builds a blast furnace, digs iron and coal mines, builds train cars to transport the iron and coal, and drills for oil to make plastic for pinheads at no cost, after all!) So he figures his total cost of production was $2.09 million.

Now he walks into the new tailor's shop and offers the twenty pins for $2.09 million. But the new tailor offers a nickel. Our do-it-yourselfer's going to have to deal a little! He comes down 50 percent, to $1.045 million. No sale? Okay, he asks $90,000, just enough to cover labor, writing off the capital as dead loss. What a deal—$2.09 million worth of pins for just $90,000!

But the new tailor won't budge. Now our hero gets a little offended. "What's the matter, buster? I worked hard to make these pins! Don't you think five years of my hard labor is worth a

lousy 90,000 bucks? I know what you're trying to do! You're trying to take advantage of me! This is worker exploitation!"

Alas, nothing will bring the tailor up to $18,000, or even a
dollar, or even a dime. You see, he can walk next door and buy
pins at 29 cents per hundred, and those—made by specialists in
pin-making—will be straight, sharp, perfectly regular in size and
shape, and *stainless*!

Where did our friend go wrong—aside from deciding to
make the pins himself in the first place, and never turning back
once he'd gotten started? What was wrong with his whole
approach to bargaining?

He acted under a mistaken sense of *economic value*, and
since economic value determines *price*, he mistook the price he
could expect for his products.

ECONOMIC AND NON-ECONOMIC VALUE

All of us know instantly that twenty crudely made pins aren't
worth $2.09 million, or even one dollar.[1] How do we know it?
Because we have what seems like an almost instinctive sense of
economic value. Unfortunately, when confronted with less
extreme examples of mistaken economic valuing, we sometimes
have difficulty perceiving the mistakes. A closer look at what
determines economic value will help us see those fallacies more
easily, and so help us understand how best to be wise stewards in
God's service.

A first step is to distinguish economic value from non-economic value. Failure to do so has led many people—especially
Christians who rightly recognize the reality of certain absolute
spiritual and moral values—to mistaken economic notions.

God, of course, has the highest value of anything in existence.
Indeed, He alone should be our ultimate value—not a means
toward an end, but the great end of all our efforts. As St. Augustine
put it, just as one who marries for money is contemptible, so also is
one who serves God for money or for anything else. Whoever loves
God only to gain a reward holds the reward more precious than
God. "What then, is there no reward belonging to God? None
except Himself. The reward belonging to God, is God Himself. This
[the godly man] loveth, this he esteemeth; if any other thing he
shall have loved, the love will not be chaste."[2] Whoever seeks and
serves God only for Himself, and not for any other reward, will
always find Him, for God has promised to reveal Himself to those
who seek Him with their whole hearts (Jeremiah 29:13).

But God is not properly an *economic* value, for three reasons. First, the infinite God is not *scarce*. There is plenty of Him to go around. One person's knowing and enjoying God doesn't diminish His availability to anyone else. And, as we shall see shortly, scarcity is a key factor in economic value. Second, we cannot give anything in exchange for knowing God. Salvation is free to all who ask Him for it: "Ho! Every one who thirsts, come to the waters; and you who have no money come, buy and eat. Come, buy wine and milk without money and without cost" (Isaiah 55:1; cf. Romans 6:23).[3] Third, and paradoxically, while we cannot buy God, He still requires that we forsake all, including our own lives, to be His disciples (John 12:25)—not to benefit God, but because otherwise we cannot welcome God's gift of Himself to us.

Some other things have, under normal circumstances and for similar reasons, no *economic* value. Air, on which we all depend for physical life, normally has no economic value. Why? Not because it is of no use, but because it is so common that one person's use doesn't diminish its availability to another. Air in general is enormously useful to us, but the particular air we breathe is of no economic value because if someone took one gallon of it away from us, that gallon would instantly—and without cost to us—be replaced by another from the surrounding atmosphere. Air is not scarce and so, like God, it has no economic value.

THE ROOTS OF ECONOMIC VALUE

Air has no economic value *under normal conditions*. Anyone who's ever done any scuba diving knows that air bottled under pressure and made available for underwater breathing through a regulator is scarce, which is why dive shops can charge for filling tanks. Indeed, even clean outside air can be scarce enough to gain economic value, which is why people put costly catalytic converters on cars and smoke scrubbers on smokestacks to diminish pollution.

SCARCITY

All of these things illustrate the difference between economic and non-economic value. Regardless how useful it is—even how essential it might be to life itself—*something has economic value only if it is sufficiently scarce that there isn't enough of it ready at hand to supply everybody's demands at no cost—that is, without someone's producing more.* This is the economic concept of *scarcity*. And note that it doesn't necessarily mean that there isn't enough to meet everybody's demands, but that there isn't enough to meet everybody's demands without someone's bearing the cost of producing more.[4]

THE EXPLANATORY POWER OF SCARCITY

The concept of scarcity explains a great deal in economics. It is involved in the very definition of economics as "the study of the allocation of scarce resources which have alternative uses."[5] It explains why our friend's twenty pins weren't worth more than a nickel to the new tailor, despite what it had cost him to produce them: pins aren't sufficiently scarce to support a higher price. It also explains why a given item can have a higher value in one place than in another: Sand on the seashore isn't scarce enough (in short, enough quantity relative to demand) for anyone to worry about someone's carting off a cubic yard or two (though if everyone started doing it things could change). But where I live, sand is sufficiently scarce that friends willingly paid $10 for three cubic yards to fill my children's sandbox. A good or service gains economic value when moved from where it is less scarce to where it is more scarce—a fact that explains the motives that underlie the idea of *trade*, from its origin to its tremendous modern expansion.

Scarcity even explains why, when two people freely exchange goods with each other, each with appropriate knowledge of the nature of the goods, both *gain*. They wouldn't make the exchange unless each considered that he had more than he needed of what he traded, and in fact that the excess of possession over need was greater for that item than for the item he received—and preferably that the item he would receive would be one in which he presently had an excess of need over possession.[6] That is, neither would trade if he didn't consider the item the other fellow had more scarce *for himself* than the item he had, and hence more economically valuable *for himself*. Trading, when done freely without deceit, is not a zero-sum game in which one person must lose in order for another to gain, but a positive-sum game in which both parties gain.[7] Another way of saying this is that in trading, two people can *profit*[8] simultaneously, and the size of their profits will depend on the degree of scarcity they are able to alleviate for each other. Thus the idea that profits can be unfairly high in free, nonfraudulent exchanges rests on a failure to understand this fundamental economic concept of scarcity.[9]

SCARCITY AND SUBJECTIVE VALUE

The foregoing discussion leads to another important insight about economics. Economic value is not *objective* but *subjective*. This is not to say that there are no objective, universal values—moral standards that apply to all people everywhere. But economic value addresses not the absolutes of moral standards, but the value of different goods and services to different people with different needs in different circumstances. A cup of water, for someone sitting beside a pure mountain stream, has no economic value because it is not scarce (it can be replaced at no cost); but for someone walking across the desert it may have enormous economic value. The difference is in their circumstances, and the value of the water comes not from its inherent properties but from the subjective needs of the persons involved. Economic value, then, is not *intrinsic* but *extrinsic*, attributed to a thing by people, not inherent to it. It is not *objective*, the same for everyone everywhere, but *subjective*, determined by people in particular situations. And *people determine economic value by the scarcity of a good or service relative to the strength of their desire for it.*

This principle is illustrated by two strikingly contrasting historical situations in the Bible. In 1 Kings 10 we read of the enormous wealth of Israel under the early reign of King Solomon. The nation was so wealthy that "... all King Solomon's drinking vessels were of gold, and all the vessels of the house of the forest of Lebanon were of pure gold. None was of silver; it was not considered valuable in the days of Solomon" (v. 21). Why wasn't silver considered valuable? Because there was so much of it readily available that it wasn't scarce. It was "as common as stones in Jerusalem" (v. 27).

About a century later, in Samaria, conditions were far different. With Samaria suffering famine under military siege, "a donkey's head was sold for eighty shekels of silver" (roughly 138.5 ounces, or $969.50 at $7 per ounce—many times an average year's wages) and "a fourth of a kab of dove's dung [about one pint] for five shekels of silver" (roughly 8.65 ounces, or $60.55 at $7 per ounce) (2 Kings 6:25). Food was so scarce (there's the key economic term) that people were willing to part with almost anything to get even the crudest, smallest meals. (Interestingly, while silver was so common in Jerusalem under Solomon that it had no economic value, there probably was far less silver in Samaria during the famine relative to the number of people. Yet this didn't make silver more valuable, because it was not *scarce*; supply exceeded demand because people couldn't eat silver, and eating was the supreme unmet need. Hence silver had little economic value rela-

tive to food, not because it was absolutely abundant but because
it was abundant relative to demand.)

But with the destruction of the besieging army by the Lord,
the siege ended the next day. Suddenly "a measure of fine flour"
(about eleven quarts) "was sold for a shekel" (1.73 ounces of silver,
or $12.11 at $7 per ounce) and "two measures of barley for a
shekel" (2 Kings 7:16; cf. v. 1). Food prices, though still high, plum-
meted in a single day. Why? Because the goods were less scarce.

Scarcity, then, is *the determinant of economic value*. But
what precisely is scarcity? Is something scarce merely because it
is one-of-a-kind? No. Imagine that there were an object called a
kill-stone. There is only one such stone in the whole world, and
whoever buys it dies within twenty-four hours (he doesn't die if
somebody gives it to him). Would such a stone be economically
scarce? Not at all. There would be no demand for it whatever.
Despite its extreme rarity, supply would forever exceed demand.
Scarcity is not a measure of absolute rarity but of relative rarity, of
the relation of the supply of a good to the demand for it by people
who would like to have it.

SUPPLY, DEMAND, AND MARGINAL UTILITY

This brings us to the commonly recognized phrase "supply and
demand." But recognition isn't synonymous with understanding.
Precisely what are "supply" and "demand"?

SUPPLY

Supply, in economics, is not the total amount of a good in existence, but the total amount that sellers can and will offer at a
given price.[10] Our do-it-yourself pin-maker, though he had only
twenty pins, actually had a surplus; he couldn't sell that many *at
the price he initially wanted*. If he had come down to the price
the tailor was willing to pay, supply would have equaled demand,
the pins would have been sold, and the market would have been
cleared—that is, the surplus would have been replaced by *equilibrium*, the condition in which the quantity of goods offered at a
particular price met the quantity of goods demanded at the same
price, and hence all the goods were sold.[11]

DEMAND

Our definition of "supply" depends on the meaning of "demand."
What, then, is "demand"? Is it the desire people have for goods?
No. All of us desire many things that, because we cannot afford
them, we cannot have. We only create a demand when we couple

with desire the *willingness* and the *ability* to pay. Further, since most of us don't desire to have all of any given good in the world, our demands are limited by the *amount* that we are willing and able to pay for. And our willingness and ability to pay is, of course, limited by the price of the good.[12]

We are able to buy more golden delicious apples at 69 cents per pound than Granny Smiths at 99 cents per pound. Even so, we might buy the Granny Smiths because we prefer their crisp, tart quality to the softer, sweeter quality of the golden delicious. If we do, we exert a demand for one pound of Granny Smiths at 99 cents, but no demand for golden delicious at 69 cents. But if the Granny Smiths' price rises to $1.19, and the price of golden delicious drops to 59 cents, we might change our minds. Now perhaps we'll buy the golden delicious. But will we still spend 99 cents—what we'd have spent on a pound of Granny Smiths? We have the money, but we might not spend it, because we might fear that we can't use up 1.67 pounds of golden delicious in the same time we could use up one pound of Granny Smiths, and the remainder might spoil. So we might limit ourselves to a pound of golden delicious. Now the money magnitude of our demand has dropped, though the weight of goods required to supply it has remained the same. What made the difference? The subjectively perceived quality of the demanded product dropped too.

MARGINAL UTILITY

Notice that in all that figuring—which we'd probably do in split seconds in the produce department, almost without realizing it—we let 2/3 pound of golden delicious apples get away. We could have had them at the same price per pound we paid for the pound we did buy, but we chose not to. Why? Because we perceived a need for a pound at that price, but not for the next 2/3 of a pound. This is a practical demonstration of the economic principle of *marginal utility*: "the rate of change of a consumer's total utility as his consumption of a given good changes."[13]

We buy things because we believe they will satisfy some want or need—whether a self-serving want, like the want to eat, or an other-serving want, like the want to have a typewriter to donate to a missionary. The greater the satisfaction they can render, the higher the economic value we place on them, and hence the more we are willing to pay. But for all economic goods, the degree of satisfaction we receive from *each additional unit* diminishes as the number of units already possessed increases. (This is also known as the "law of diminishing returns," or "Gossen's Law of Diminishing Utility.")[14] Since economic value varies in direct proportion to degree of satisfaction expected from the valued item, economic value must diminish as quantity possessed increases, because for each additional unit we perceive less need than for the prior unit. Solomon expressed the principle of marginal utility this way: "A sated man loathes honey, but to a famished man any bitter thing is sweet" (Proverbs 27:7).

Marginal utility describes the value we attribute to *one more unit* of a given good: it is a measurement of the magnitude of satisfaction we expect from possessing one more apple, or one more car, or one more oil painting than we presently possess. It is, in fact, the term we use to describe the economic value we attribute not to just any unit of a good, but to *the last unit that we are willing to buy at a particular price*, for it is that last unit—the unit *at the margin* of our buying behavior—that will satisfy the lowest degree of want for us, a degree that we would consider not worth satisfying if the unit were a tiny bit more expensive. It is that unit that we *value the least.*

It is because we all habitually think and act in terms of marginal utility that we refuse to pay famine prices for food when our community is not experiencing a famine. When you walk into a grocery store, you don't think, "What if I were on the verge of starvation? What would I be willing to pay for that bunch of bananas then? [The answer of course is "Everything!"] If I'd be willing to pay it then, I'd better pay it now!" Instead, you think to yourself, "I think I'd like a few bananas. Here's a good-looking bunch. No, too big. Last week I bought a bunch that big and two of them rotted before I ate them. I'll break two off and buy these five." And then you look at the price, and it's gone up 20 cents per pound since last week, so you say to yourself, "Ooops! Not at that price! I'd rather have peaches at that price!" And you walk over to the peach bin. And all the while you never consider what you might be willing to pay if you were on the verge of starvation, because in fact you're not.

You would expect much greater satisfaction of want from a bunch of bananas if you were starving than you do otherwise. Therefore you value the bananas less when you're not starving. And you expect much greater satisfaction from the five bananas you estimate you can eat in a week than from the two more you figure will spoil; so you value the five more highly and are willing to buy them, but not the other two, even at the same price per pound. And when you compare the prices of bananas and peaches, you suddenly say to yourself, "Gee, at that price I'd get more satisfaction from the peaches than from the bananas," so you buy them instead. At each juncture you've made a judgment of *marginal utility*—the degree of satisfaction you expect from one more unit of a given product. That degree of satisfaction has determined the amount you're willing to pay for the product. Thus, *"The value of a good is determined by the magnitude of its marginal utility."*[15]

MARGINAL UTILITY, VALUE, AND PRICE

The concept of marginal utility is so fundamental to all understanding of economics that the late Eugen von Böhm-Bawerk, whose massive study of value and price[16] remains the most comprehensive in the history of economics,[17] calls it "the crux of our theory of value" and "the key that opens the door to an understanding of the broadest fundamentals underlying the behavior of economizing men with respect to goods."[18]

> Everywhere we see men making valuations of goods on the basis of their marginal utility and ruling their *actions* in accordance with the results of those estimations. And in view of that the doctrine of marginal utility may be regarded as the crux, not only of the theory of value, but of every explanation of man's economic behavior, and hence indeed of the entire field of economic theory.[19]

Marginal utility is the measurement of value we put on the last unit of a good that we are willing to buy at a particular price—that is, the lowest economic value we attach to a given good. This, in turn, means that we will not pay more for any one unit than we would for the least valued one. We won't walk into the produce section and say, "Boy, I'd love a nice juicy grape right now! I'd pay a dime for just one grape!" and then pick up a bunch of grapes and conclude, "Well, with 175 grapes on this bunch, it's worth $17.50 to me." No, we realize that after the delight of the first grape, we'd get less satisfaction from the second, still less from the third, fourth, fifth, and so on, down to the 175th, which might in fact not delight us but sicken us. So we pay no more for the first than we're willing to pay for the last, not because we don't value the first more but because, there being plenty of grapes in the store, we know we needn't pay more for the first than for the last.

No wonder Solomon wrote, "Have you found honey? Eat only what you need, lest you have it in excess and vomit it" (Proverbs 26:16), and "A sated man loathes honey, but to a famished man any bitter thing is sweet" (Proverbs 27:7)! He understood the principle of marginal utility.

All of this means that our judgment of marginal utility—the degree of satisfaction we expect from the last unit of a given good that we'd buy at a given price—actually determines the price we're willing to pay for any of that good. That is why the store manager would have to reduce the price of grapes to near zero to persuade us to buy his whole stock of 400 pounds; we wouldn't foresee any use for any but the first few pounds. (Unless we hoped to resell them, an idea we'd best examine carefully before concluding that we, as nonspecialists, can sell the grapes better than the grocery store manager can. Remember our pin-maker's debacle!)

The market price of any good, then, is necessarily determined by the marginal utility it is judged to have by consumers—what consumers are willing to pay for the unit of the good that they value the least.[20]

IMPLICATIONS OF MARGINAL UTILITY THEORY OF VALUE AND PRICE

This understanding of the determination of market prices has some important implications. First, it means that, in a competitive market, prices automatically tend toward the lowest level that will meet the necessary costs of production (including distribution to points where the good encounters buyers). These prices, in turn, will make the goods available to the largest possible proportion of buyers granted the cost of production—that is, they will tend to make the goods available to less and less wealthy people. Allowing a market price for goods, therefore, is of particular benefit to those with low incomes.

Second, "under conditions that are otherwise identical, equal quantities of goods have quite unequal value for the rich and for the poor, that value being greater for the poor and smaller for the rich."[21] This is because the quantities that the poor can afford are directed toward satisfying more important wants than those the rich can afford; the poor man satisfies his hunger with an apple, the rich man his taste. Thus, being able to buy at prices established by marginal utility—the lowest prices that can support the costs of production—not only benefits the poor but also benefits them more than it does the rich.

Third, according to this understanding of value and price, there is no such thing as a "just price" or a "fair wage" among people acting freely in the marketplace, other than that at which buyer and seller freely agree, without deception.[22] Understanding marginal utility warns us ahead of time what legislated increases and decreases in price will cause. Increases (minimum prices) will cause surpluses—not necessarily more total units of the good available than under the market price, but more than can be sold at the higher price—because they will push prices above those that the former marginal consumers, who judged the good at the lowest marginal utility that still brought about an exchange, are willing to pay. (Hence our huge stockpiles of dairy products.) Legislated decreases (maximum prices) will cause shortages—not necessarily fewer total units of the good available than under the market price, but fewer than are demanded at the lower price—because they will push prices below those that the former marginal sellers, those who judged the marginal utility at the lowest money price that still brought about an exchange, were willing to accept. (Hence the shortage of rental housing in cities with rent control.)[23]

This last point explains why some well-meant proposals for helping the poor are counterproductive when carried out.[24] Ronald Sider, for instance, in his *Rich Christians in an Age of Hunger*, bemoans the low price Central American countries get for bananas, implying that it ought to be raised, perhaps by export taxes levied by the countries of origin, perhaps by exporting companies' voluntarily contracting to pay higher prices to growers.[25] He forgets (or doesn't understand) that consumers, acting on the principle of marginal utility, will respond to higher prices by decreasing consumption, creating a surplus. That surplus will have to be alleviated either by lowering the price (quickly, since bananas spoil quickly) or by decreasing production (also quickly). The former would mean a return to a market price; the latter would mean unemployment for plantation workers. Recognizing this fundamental economic reality doesn't mean we're any less compassionate toward the poor than Sider; it only means that we realize that in this case the proposed cure would be worse than the disease.

ALTERNATE THEORIES OF VALUE AND PRICE

There have been other theories about how economic value and price are determined. Since the profound theoretical analysis of value and price by Böhm-Bawerk at the turn of the century, few economists continue to endorse any of them, but they underlie certain political ideologies and many popular misconceptions held by people who don't even realize they've based their thinking on mistaken notions of value and price. The most prominent are the theories that value and price are (or ought to be) determined by: (1) cost of production; (2) labor in production; (3) a central planning authority.

COST OF PRODUCTION AND PRICE

At first thought it would seem natural that the cost of production would determine the price of a good. But looking at concrete examples quickly warns us to think again. Without doubt it cost our do-it-yourself pin-maker $2.09 million to make his twenty crude pins, but that didn't mean he could sell them at that price. The selling price was determined by the marginal utility of the pins to their potential buyer(s). Marginal utility is the true determinant of price, not cost of production.

In fact, causation runs in the opposite direction. Because consumers are willing to pay a certain price for goods, producers are willing to spend something just under that price to produce them, the difference being profit (usually reinvested to meet other consumer demands, not pocketed). Thus selling price, determined by marginal utility, causes production cost, not vice versa. (If production cost runs above selling price, producers take a loss instead of earning a profit.)

LABOR THEORY OF VALUE

Karl Marx and other Socialist thinkers attribute the value of goods not to their marginal utility for potential buyers but to the value of the labor involved in making them.[26] It is easy to see how this is, in fact, simply a variation on the cost of production theory of value, for once one reduces all costs of production to labor, as Marx did,[27] the two theories are identical in principle. This means, of course, that the labor theory of value is subject to precisely the same criticism that destroys the cost of production theory.

But the labor theory is also subject to another criticism:

> . . . it disregards differences in the quality of labour.
> For Marx all human labour is economically homoge-
> neous, because it is always the "productive expendi-
> ture of human brain, muscles, nerves, hands, etc."
> "Skilled labour is only intensified, or rather multi-

plied simple labour, so that a small quantity of skilled labour equals a larger quantity of simple labour. Experience shows that this resolution of skilled into simple constantly happens. A commodity may be the product of highly skilled labour, but its value equates it to the product of simple labour and represents only a certain quantity of simple labour."[28]

Marx's argument is circular; he assumes precisely what he needs to prove. Ludwig von Mises' analysis is fatal to it. He points out that different skills produce different qualities of goods, and it is consumers' judgment of the qualities of the goods that determines the price at which the goods will sell. That price, in turn, determines the value of the labor that produced the goods, not vice versa. Any other means of valuing the labor must be wholly arbitrary.[29]

Marx thought the value of labor determined the value of products; but we only know the value of labor by what its products will bring in the market, which means that value is imputed in the reverse order from what Marx thought. By Marx's labor theory of value, the just price of the twenty crude pins would indeed have been $2.09 million (including the stored labor represented by the $2 million in capital). But we can bet our last dollar (the one with the highest marginal utility and hence the most valuable to us, of course!) that Marx, had he been the new tailor in town, wouldn't have paid that price!

The Command Theory of Value

One particular ideology—socialism—holds that values, and hence prices, ought to be dictated by central governing authorities.[30] The great advantage of this arrangement, say proponents, is that it ensures that everyone will receive a "fair price" or a "just wage" for his goods or services. Under a command economy,[31] bureaucrats (or civil servants, as they prefer to be called) determine "fair prices" and "just wages" and require everyone to pay them.

We have already seen one problem with this arrangement. Legislated minimum prices must, unless they are below the natural market price and therefore devoid of effect, produce surpluses; legislated maximum prices must, unless they are above the natural market price and therefore devoid of effect, produce shortages. Thus, if they have any effect at all, it must be pernicious.[32]

A second problem with command prices is simply that it is impossible for any small group of people to master all the facts necessary to establish prices that will be as optimal to consumers as those set by the market acting freely under the principle of marginal utility.[33] The price-setting agency cannot know the degrees to which various goods would satisfy various people's various degrees of various wants and needs. Nor can it possibly know how much consumers are willing and able to sacrifice to see their wants met, or how much producers are willing and able to sacrifice to meet consumers' needs.

In a free market, economic calculation takes place in the form of billions of tiny, interrelated decisions and actions. These decisions go on constantly, every minute of every day, constantly revising the total economic information in the marketplace. All that information is passed around the market by means of the prices naturally produced by voluntary exchanges between buyers and sellers based on their subjective perceptions of the marginal utilities of products and money. A price-setting committee cannot keep all of these bits of information tabulated and updated, and in fact by controlling prices artificially it actually destroys the one mechanism that makes it possible to process the information.[34] Command pricing mechanisms are therefore self-defeating, disrupting the whole working of the economy by making "rational economic activity impossible."[35]

CONCLUSION

In the parable of the laborers in the vineyard (Matthew 20:1-16), Jesus told of a landowner who hired laborers at the typical day's wages to harvest his grapes. As the day wore on, it seems to have become clear that he would need more laborers to get the job done (leaving grapes on vines even a day or two too long can result in costly reduction of quality), so he hired more laborers.[36] This happened repeatedly through the day. At the end of the day, he paid those who had worked only an hour the same amount as those who had worked the whole day. The latter complained that they were paid unfairly, but the landowner replied to one, "Friend, I am doing you no wrong; did you not agree with me for a denarius? Take what is yours and go your way, but I wish to give to this last man the same as to you. Is it not lawful for me to do what I wish with what is my own? Or is your eye envious because I am generous?" (Matthew 20:13-15).

While the central spiritual point of this parable is that man cannot rightly complain against the sovereign grace of God in salvation, it demonstrates that point by presupposing three fundamental economic lessons:[37]

(1) That a wage (or price) reached freely between two parties without deceit is just; it does nobody any harm.[38]

(2) That the marginal utility theory of value may well lead us to pay different prices for the same products or services, or the same prices for different products or services, based on our perceived needs and the capacity of the products or services to satisfy those needs, and that there is no injustice in the differences. The landowner perceived his need to get his crop in before it began to deteriorate, and so valued the labor of the last workers more highly, on an hourly basis, than he had valued the labor of the first. Hence he was willing to pay a higher price for it, and that higher price was no injustice to those who had contracted for a lower price before.

(3) That the underlying motive of complaints about differences in payment, offered by those who have entered free, non-fraudulent exchanges, is not concern for justice, but plain envy.[39]

The inescapable conclusion of a competent analysis of the factors determining economic value and price is that permitting markets to function freely (without coercion, either governmental or private, by fraud, theft, or violence) results in prices and availabilities of goods and services that are most beneficial to the most people in society, particularly to those most in need and least able to pay for the satisfaction of their needs and to defend themselves against fraud, theft, and violence: the poor.

STEWARDSHIP, MONEY, AND INFLATION

*N*ormally we think of stewardship mainly as charitable giving of money. Giving is indeed part of it, but not all. Indeed, it isn't even the majority of it. Stewardship is what we do with everything God entrusts to us. If we assume the tithe as the Biblical standard of giving,[1] giving would normally be understood as only about 10 percent of stewardship.

The degree to which we use whatever God entrusts to us to further the growth of God's Kingdom determines the degree to which we are good or bad stewards. And we mean by the growth of God's Kingdom not solely numbers of souls saved and discipled, but equally the expansion and intensification of man's dominion over the earth—his rule and development of it such that it serves man and glorifies God (Genesis 1:28).[2] This means that stewardship and economics are intimately related. If, as we have seen, economics is the study of the allocation of scarce resources to the production, distribution, and consumption of goods and services, then stewardship is the very practice economics studies.

In this chapter, then, we will focus on the connection not between giving and money,[3] but between all the rest of our stewardship—our economic activity—and money.[4] As we will see, our understanding and use of money, as individuals and whole societies, have a profound effect on the quality of our stewardship. A faulty monetary system can cause people to misjudge the value of their money and, hence, their ability to afford goods and services. Their misjudgments can lead to unwise purchases which, in turn, can cause producers to flood the market with goods the demand for which will suddenly disappear, forcing the producers to suffer major losses and their employees to lose their jobs. In short, a faulty monetary system can cause us to waste resources—resources over which God has made us stewards and for the use of which He will hold us accountable.

WHAT IS MONEY?

Economists define money as any object that can function as, and is used in a given society as, three things: (1) a medium of exchange; (2) a unit of account; (3) a store of value.

A MEDIUM OF EXCHANGE

As a medium of exchange, money eases trade by eliminating the need for barter. In barter, exchanges occur only when two people encounter each other, each having a good or service that the other desires, and each willing to part with it in exchange for the other's good or service. In barter, two pigs might be exchanged for a horse, or a wagon load of rough lumber for a hundred pounds of flour. The frequency of exchanges is severely limited by the frequency of meetings between traders each having precisely the goods or services that the other wants. Since, as we saw in Chapters Seven and Eight, marginal utility (economic value) increases through trade (as each party receives something worth more *to him* than what he gives), slow trade necessarily means slow economic growth, which itself means slower growth in the number and quality of goods and services available to all members of the community.

As a medium of exchange, money speeds trade—and so speeds the satisfaction of people's needs and wants—by allowing trade to occur without direct matching of barterers. With money, the man with flour can sell it to someone with money, knowing that he can later use the money to buy lumber from someone else who doesn't need flour but might later use the same money to buy a new rim for his wagon wheel.

A UNIT OF ACCOUNT

As a unit of account, money permits communication of precise valuations from one person to another and throughout the whole of a market (the buying and selling society, which includes everyone). Listing assets in terms of pigs, horses, boards, and acres of land is inherently imprecise: pigs, horses, and boards come in different sizes and qualities, acres of land in different fertilities and shapes. Money, on the other hand, has fairly precise market value readily known to both parties in an exchange.[5]

A STORE OF VALUE

As a store of value, money permits people to "save something for a rainy day" without fear that it will deteriorate rapidly. A banana grower can't store ten tons of bananas for six months to be exchanged for new banana tree seedlings at planting time; by then they'll rot and he'll have to pay someone to clean out the warehouse. But he can sell the bananas for money that won't rot, put some of the money into savings where it can earn interest, and use it six months later to buy seedlings.

MONEY IS NO MYSTERY

Clearly money plays an important part in the healthy functioning of any economy. Without money trade would be restricted to barter, greatly slowing the rate of growth in production and distribution of goods and services people need. Without it accounting would be much less precise. And without it, storing wealth for use at times of greater need would be considerably more difficult—particularly for perishable goods. Its use saves time, labor, and other resources in any society, allowing that society to redirect those resources from inefficient barter to more efficient productive activities. In that way, a society's use of money greatly enhances its productive potential.

Granted these clear uses of money, it is difficult to see why some Christians evidence such confusion over it. Jacques Ellul, for instance, in his book *Money & Power*, looks at money as something utterly mysterious:

> It is a strange sort of convention which leads people to attribute, both by judgment and by will, value to something [money] which in itself has no value of use or of exchange.

> This is completely unexplainable and irrational. Nothing, whether in human nature or in the nature of things, whether in technology or in reason, adequately explains the original act of creating and accepting money. Nothing explains the blind confidence that we continue, in spite of all crises, to place in money. This is an absurdity which neither economists nor sociologists are able to clarify. The collective attitude of all humankind, this consensus, this submission, are incomprehensible if they are not traced back to the spiritual power of money. If money is not a spiri-

tual power which invades us, enslaving our hearts
and minds, then our behavior is simply absurd. If people everywhere place such importance on the symbol
of money, it is because they have already been
seduced and internally possessed by the spirit of
money.[6]

Ellul's declaration that money "has no value of use or of
exchange" is simply false. Nor is it true that "neither economists
nor sociologists are able to clarify" why people value and use
money. While there are minor variations in explanations, the fundamental facts have been clear for centuries.[7] To attribute people's
acceptance and use of money to irrational, demonic forces, as
Ellul does, is to ignore the simple and valuable roles that money
plays in economic activity. Perhaps Ellul had in mind primarily
the greed with which some people hoard money; but then hoard-
ing anything else is subject to the same criticism (see the parable
of the rich man who built more barns to store his crops, Luke
12:16-21). Also, as Whittlesey points out, "The convenience and
other benefits conferred by the possession of ready cash are entirely different from the more or less pathological considerations that
motivate the miser."[8]

ESSENTIAL CHARACTERISTICS OF MONEY

In order for anything to perform as a medium of exchange, a unit
of account, and a store of value, it must have five essential characteristics: divisibility, portability, durability, recognizability, and
scarcity ("high value in relation to volume and weight").[9]

Without divisibility, money couldn't function as a unit of
account. It could not represent minute variations in value depending on the identity, quantity, and quality of the good or service
being exchanged. Without portability, money couldn't function as a
medium of exchange; it would be as easy, if not easier, to barter.
Without durability, money couldn't function as a store of value, for
rapid deterioration would soon make it valueless. Without recognizability, it couldn't function as a medium of exchange, since a
seller might not acknowledge its value in a transaction. And without scarcity it couldn't function either as a medium of exchange or
as a store of value, since value is, as we saw in the last chapter,
determined by scarcity (the law of supply and demand).

Anything that has these five properties can, at least in theory, function as money. Historically, many different things have
been used: beads, gold and silver bullion or coins, grain, lumber,

pearls, sea shells, even cigarettes. Items that have these properties to higher degrees will serve better as money than items that have them to lower degrees, at least up to a point. (Some things, like platinum, are too scarce to serve *widely* as money; there isn't enough available for many people to use them. This doesn't mean they won't be used at all—platinum is used as money—but that they won't be widely used and so will have less impact on the overall economy than things that are less scarce and so can be more widely used.)

MOST MARKETABLE COMMODITY

Another way of looking at money is as the most marketable commodity in a given population.[10] That is, money is an item that everyone, or nearly everyone, desires and accepts for one or more of its three uses (exchange, unit of account, store of value). Therefore everyone is willing to exchange other things for it, knowing that he can in turn exchange it for yet other things since everyone else is also willing to exchange for it.

Note that this doesn't mean that anyone wants money more than anything else. It merely means that more people want money than want any other particular thing, but that they want it not for itself but for the access it gives them to other things. Money is not an end in itself, but a means to many ends. In fact, we could say that it is when we make money an end in itself rather than a means to other ends that it becomes *Mammon*, the object of idolatry.[11] When we allow money to become *Mammon* in our lives, there is every reason to believe that it can assume tremendous spiritual power over us, including enticing us to reject God Himself. This is as true of anything that takes God's place in our lives as it is of money.

If one or more of the five essential characteristics disappears, or is greatly weakened, in a given commodity, the commodity's efficiency in performing the important tasks of money diminishes as well. That is, whatever reduces the divisibility, portability, durability, recognizability, or scarcity of a commodity makes it a less effective medium of exchange, unit of account, and store of value. It therefore reduces money's *value* in the marketplace. Unfortunately, it is easy for that to happen, and when it does the effects on the overall economy can be devastating, greatly hindering our ability to perform the tasks of stewardship. The most common way it happens is by a reduction in the *scarcity* of money, and so we'll look at that problem closely.

UNDERMINING THE VALUE OF MONEY

Suppose for a moment that you're nearing the end of a day at work. It's Friday, and your boss walks up to you and says, "We just doubled your salary. Here's the first check at the new level. I wanted to hand it to you myself." Stunned, you shake his hand gratefully, look at the $1,000 check, and think, "At last I can get my wife that microwave I promised her. What a lot of time she'll save! And we can afford the tuition to send Liz to Ivystone Prep now, too; she'll get a much better education there than at Redwood Country Day School." Walking to your car you think, "Boy, wouldn't Cheryl be excited if I showed up tonight with the microwave! I'll pick one up on the way and surprise her."

So you go to the department store, buy the best microwave available, and present it to her at home. "But, honey," she says, "we can't afford that—not now anyway. I wish you'd talked with me about it first."

"Can't afford it?" you say. "Take a look at this!" You hand her the check, and her drawn look changes to a bright smile. "It's a permanent raise," you add. "Now we can send Liz to Ivystone Prep—and it's not too late to register her, either. Classes don't start till next Wednesday. We can register Monday. Of course we'll lose the $50 deposit at Redwood, but that's a small price to pay for the better education she'll get at Ivystone."

Right away the two of you sit down and write out a check to your church, not just doubling your old tithe, but giving a double tithe on this new salary as an expression of gratitude to God. Monday morning Cheryl takes Liz to Ivystone, pays the $350 nonrefundable registration fee, and signs the tuition agreement for the coming year. Then she goes shopping for the first time since Friday. To her surprise, she finds all the prices in the supermarket precisely double what they were last week. Refusing to pay such ridiculous prices, she goes down the street—same story. Everywhere she checks—supermarkets, clothing stores, gas stations, everyplace—has doubled its prices. She heads home in horror, picks up the mail, and finds bills with telephone and utility rates precisely double what they once were.

She runs inside and calls you, sobbing. "Henry! Henry, I don't know what to do! We can't afford groceries for the week!"

"What do you mean? We just got that double-sized paycheck."

"Yes, yes, but I just tried to go shopping, and all the prices are exactly double what they were last week. Your doubled pay won't make any difference now. And we've already spent the $350 each on the microwave and Liz's registration, and given the $200 to the church. The hundred dollars left would normally be more than enough for groceries for a week. But now it's just barely half what we need. And we're tied into tuition payments at Ivystone now, and can't even get the registration fee back if we put Liz back in Redwood. Henry, what are we going to do?"

Meanwhile, millions of other people all over the country are going through similar traumatic experiences. All have their incomes doubled, and all go to the stores on Monday to find all the prices doubled. And most, like our hapless couple, make what seemed to be wise purchases over the weekend, only to find themselves coming up short once the prices change.

Oh yes, one other thing: Next April 15 you and all the others find yourselves in higher income tax brackets, though your actual purchasing power, after your raises, has fallen.[12]

THE PERNICIOUS EFFECTS OF INFLATION

Although this story is exaggerated and a little simpler than what typically happens in the real world, it is in principle precisely what happens when *inflation*—an increase in the money supply—occurs, at whatever rate. In this illustration the rate of inflation is greatly increased over what we're accustomed to. We've imagined an instant doubling of the money supply, i.e., instant 100 percent inflation. In common experience the money supply tends to grow more slowly, but it can grow much more rapidly, and has.[13] But the effects of lower inflation rates, though spread over a longer period of time and thus less readily noticeable because they occur in small increments instead of large chunks, are precisely the same.[14]

DIMINISHED PURCHASING POWER

Let's analyze our story and see precisely what happened. The first thing we *notice* is that people everywhere got sudden raises amounting to doubling of income. What isn't apparent on the surface, though true of necessity, is that those raises were made possible by an equally sudden doubling of the money supply. That is what had the pernicious effect. Had all wages doubled in *purchasing value* without any change in money supply, things would have been great. That would simply have meant that prices would have been cut in half, hurting no one since every sector of the economy would have benefited equally from it.[15] But because the doubled wages were made possible by the greater money supply, their purchasing power—that is, the value of goods and services that each dollar could command in the market—was simply cut in half. That is what we learn from the fact that prices doubled. The doubled prices are simply a way of saying that the value of money was cut in half.

DISTORTED CONSUMER DEMAND

But the slashed purchasing power wasn't immediately apparent to income earners. Initially they thought each dollar could purchase as much as before, and for two days they were right. So during those two days they made economic decisions based on the illusion that their temporarily doubled purchasing power was permanent. In other words, *they thought they could afford* things that in fact, in view of the unforeseen impending doubling of prices, they could not.

In the terms we used in Chapter Eight, this means that people made judgments of *marginal utility* under false assumptions. Before Friday they had delayed buying microwaves because they had considered the degree of satisfaction (utility) they would get from them as less than what they could get from other uses of the money needed to buy them. But from Friday afternoon through Sunday night, they mistakenly thought the purchasing power of their incomes had doubled *permanently*. Now they thought they could get microwaves without having to forego some other things they had previously chosen instead. So they bought microwaves, and when all prices doubled Monday morning they found themselves in the same situation they'd have been in had they bought the microwaves without the raises in pay: short of cash for more essential goods and services. :

DESTRUCTION OF SAVINGS

Actually they weren't in *precisely* the same situation. If they had had savings before the inflation, the purchasing power of those savings was cut in half on Monday morning. That means they were actually *worse off* than they would have been had they simply bought the microwaves without the increases in income. On the other hand, if they had had debts before the inflation, the purchasing power of the debts—that is, the market value of the dollars necessary to pay them off—also was cut in half. This means debtors were better off after the inflation than before it, being able to pay off their debts with dollars worth only half what the dollars they originally borrowed were worth.[16] And this in turn means that anyone who was owed money by anyone else was worse off after the inflation than before it, since the purchasing power of the dollars in which he would be paid back would be only half that of those he had loaned out.[17] In inflation, savers and lenders, the very people the Bible considers most responsible (Proverbs 13:22a; Deuteronomy 15:6), lose, while debtors, whom the Bible normally considers irresponsible if their debts are not contracted in emergency (Proverbs 22:7; Romans 13:8a), gain.[18]

MISALLOCATION OF RESOURCES

Another, and in the long run probably more devastating, unnoticed effect of the inflation (increase in money supply) that made the doubled incomes possible is a result of the temporarily distorted consumer demand. The rash of microwave buying over the weekend creates the illusion that microwaves will continue to sell much better than before. When this happens over a longer period of time (as it normally does under inflation), producers divert some capital and labor from other activities into producing more microwaves, hoping to enjoy some of the profits from the newly expanded demand. Perhaps some companies start making microwaves that never made them before, and some wholly new companies may even be formed for that purpose. Soon there are more machines, factories, and workers making microwaves than before, and there are more microwaves on the market than before. But in time it becomes clear that the increased demand for microwaves was only a temporary aberration created by the sudden growth in money supply. If the money supply doesn't continue to increase just as rapidly—or perhaps even more rapidly[19]—the demand will drop off, probably to a level below what it was before the inflation since consumers who overstretched themselves under the illusion of prosperity will be forced to curtail non-essential purchases for some time to come. When the demand drops off, workers will be laid off, factories left idle, and some companies will go out of business.[20]

What has happened is that the sudden influx of new money into the economy has created a temporary change in the *pattern* of demands in the marketplace.[21] Not only have consumers demanded more goods, but also they have demanded *different* goods, and in different relative quantities. This is because their illusion of prosperity changed their judgments of marginal utility. Their changed patterns of demand, in turn, caused producers to change the patterns of production, i.e., to change their *allocations of resources* (raw materials, capital, and labor). Until the illusion fades and consumption (guided by judgments of marginal utility) readjusts to reality, resources will be *misallocated*—directed to supplying wants that would not be so strongly expressed by willingness to buy were it not for the illusions caused by inflation.[22]

IRRATIONALITY: DISRUPTION OF THE MARKET'S INFORMATION PROCESSING SYSTEM

In short, inflation causes irrational judgments of marginal utility, which translate into irrational consumer demands, to which producers respond with irrational production made possible by irrational allocation of resources (raw materials, labor, and capital). And as soon as rationality returns to the demand side of the consumption/production equation, with contraction of consumer spending, producers will have to reallocate resources again, causing unemployment and waste of raw materials and capital in the transition.[23]

DO WE NEED MORE OF THE HAIR OF THE DOG THAT BIT US?

A common response to this scenario is that unemployment and other difficulties resulting from inflation won't occur if money supply continues to grow. They will occur only when inflation halts. This argument holds that it is not inflation but "tight money policies" that cause unemployment. Logically, this is equivalent to blaming a bullet, rather than the man who pulls a trigger, for killing someone. For "tight money policies" would never cause unemployment if labor, capital, and raw materials were not first misallocated into avenues of production that would not have appeared profitable had inflation not distorted consumer demand.

When money supplies are stable—and thus, since economic value is determined by the relationship of supply to demand, money value is stable—consumers are not led into misjudgments of marginal utility and resulting irrational purchasing decisions. This in turn means that stable money supply contributes to efficient allocation of resources, including labor. By "efficient allocation of resources," we mean allocation to those productive efforts that meet rational rather than irrational consumer demand. Such avenues of production are themselves stable, changing only slowly over time as consumers' *real* (not illusory) purchasing power and their *rational* (not irrational) judgments of marginal utility change. This means that employment in those avenues will be stable.

High, persistent unemployment, in other words, is always caused by inflation.[24] And continuing inflation cannot solve the problem; it can only delay and magnify the pains that will be experienced when reality finally sinks in. This is because there is a middle link in the causal chain between inflation and unemployment: the disruption of rational judgment by buyers (consumers) and sellers (producers) in the market. Unemployment is a *symptom* of a market whose essential information processing mechanism—prices (including wages) determined by supply and demand among free buyers and sellers—has been damaged. The longer inflation continues, the more it damages the price system, and hence misdirects the allocation of resources (including labor).[25] "Any attempt to preserve the jobs made profitable by inflation would lead to a complete destruction of the market order."[26]

THE END OF THE ROAD: PAINFUL ADJUSTMENT,
OR COMPLETE COLLAPSE

This whole process will inevitably end, sooner or later (and the sooner the better), either with a conscious decision to stop money supply growth (inflation), or with the complete disorganization of the economy.[27] Either alternative will mean massive unemployment, tremendous shortages of some (usually the most essential) goods and services and tremendous surpluses of others (usually the least essential),[28] and horrible human suffering. In light doses we call this a recession; in heavy doses (the inevitable result of long-term inflation) we call it a depression. Though either recession or depression is painful, consciously stopping money supply growth is preferable to letting it continue in that it doesn't destroy the whole market mechanism. The market can keep functioning. Steady *real growth* (in contrast with the illusionary growth of inflation) can resume following the adjustments (recession or depression) necessary to stop misallocations of resources and start proper allocations. The unemployment, surpluses and shortages, bankruptcies, and other difficulties inherent to these adjustments will be painful, but they need not be fatal.

In contrast, the chances of solid recovery are very slim after the complete disorganization of the economy resulting inevitably from long-term, unchecked inflation. This is because the natural, fear-generated response to the disintegration of the economy is public pressure for a powerful leader who can solve all problems, regardless of intrusions on civil liberties.[29] This helped to pave the way for Napoleon's rise to power in France in 1799[30] and for the rise to power of the National Socialist German Workers' Party

(Nazis) in Germany following that country's hyperinflation from 1918-1923.[31] Bewildered by the complete confusion of the economy around them, citizens and politicians plead for someone to bring order by controlling production, prices, and consumption. That way lies socialism, a cure worse than the disease.[32] In the words of John Maynard Keynes, "Lenin is said to have declared that the best way to destroy the capitalist system was to debauch the currency. Lenin was certainly right. The process engages all the hidden forces of economic law on the side of destruction, and does it in a manner which one man in a million is able to diagnose."[33]

WHAT HAS ALL THIS TO DO WITH STEWARDSHIP?

We said at the beginning of this chapter that stewardship—the practice studied by economics—is the allocation of resources for the production, distribution, and consumption of goods and services toward the goal of building the Kingdom of God.[34] The more efficiently resources are allocated toward that end, the better the stewardship; the less efficiently resources are allocated, the worse the stewardship.

Inflation must therefore be seen as a serious instance of bad stewardship, because it necessarily causes misallocation of resources, often on enormous scales. It causes people to misjudge the value of their money and hence their ability to afford various goods and services. Those misjudgments translate into unwise consumer choices, the first level of misallocation of resources. Those choices, in turn, cause misjudgments of market demand, which translate into misallocation of productive resources. The result is waste of human labor, raw materials, and capital —resources over which God has given man responsibility for which He will hold man accountable.

All of this means that ending inflation and preventing its return are prime tasks of Christian stewardship. In Chapter Ten, we'll see how these things can be done.

SOUND MONEY FOR
GOOD STEWARDSHIP

*E*nding inflation is technically simple. By definition inflation is growth in the money supply.[1] Thus by definition, stopping inflation means stopping growth in money supply. We will see in a moment how to do that.

But while it may be technically simple, it is politically difficult. Why? Because inflation offers a short-term solution to unemployment and can fuel short-term economic growth. It can solve unemployment short-term by fooling consumers into buying things they really can't afford, and so creating a demand for things, and the workers who produce them, that otherwise would not be demanded. It fuels short-term economic growth by creating the appearance of increasing wealth in a society. Politicians find both of these effects of inflation attractive, because they give voters the illusion of well-being. And by the time the illusion gives way to the hard reality of the recession or depression that must follow it, few voters will understand that it was the inflation several years before that caused the present difficulties.

What is needed to make the technically simple solution to inflation politically feasible is for enough voters to begin to understand the connection between inflation and the boom-and-bust cycle that they begin to vote out politicians who support inflationary policy and replace them with politicians who support stable money policies. This growth in understanding is one of the aims of this and the previous chapters.

Putting a permanent end to inflation by making fiat money creation illegal even by government is crucial not as some esoteric economists' intellectual game, but as a fundamental element in *good stewardship*. Permitting inflation to continue will, as noted at the end of Chapter Nine, eventually disrupt any economy, impoverish its people, and lead to tyranny.

FOUR WAYS OF INCREASING
THE MONEY SUPPLY

How, then, can inflation be stopped? By outlawing money supply expansion except by production of real commodities with real market value.[2] To understand this properly, and to work toward making it a reality, we must first understand the four ways in which new money can be created and how such a law would affect them.

INFLATION BY COUNTERFEITING,
TYPE A: ILLEGAL PRIVATE ACTION

First, new money can be created by private individuals who engrave plates for use on printing presses to print bills that appear just like the money the Federal Reserve System prints.[3] This is called counterfeiting, and it is illegal. It was made illegal because it is a form of theft. It is theft because new counterfeit money devalues all money already in circulation. When a counterfeiter increases the money supply, whether by 2 percent or by .1 percent, he has stolen from all other holders of money an amount equal to the value their money loses.

How can we solve the problem of private counterfeiting? By outlawing it and apprehending, prosecuting, convicting, and punishing counterfeiters. That is what we are doing, and it works pretty well. Private counterfeiting is a tiny drop in the bucket of money supply expansion.

INFLATION BY COUNTERFEITING,
TYPE B: LEGAL GOVERNMENTAL ACTION

Second, new money can be created by civil government when it (or a private entity with which it contracts, in our case the Federal Reserve System) engraves plates for use on printing presses to print bills that appear just like the money the Federal Reserve System prints. There's nothing wrong with this when the new money merely replaces old, worn-out currency that is taken out of circulation. But the Federal Reserve prints far more money than what is required to replace worn-out currency. That excess money expands the money supply. This is called fiscal policy, and it is legal. It is legal despite the fact that it is a form of theft. It is theft because newly printed money devalues all money already in circulation. When the Federal Reserve Board increases the money supply, whether by 2 percent or by .1 percent, it has stolen from all other holders of money an amount equal to the value their money loses.[4]

Counterfeiting is illegal, so it's easy to see how that can be theft. But it's legal for the Federal Reserve Board to print new money. Can that really be theft? Yes, it can. Making something legal doesn't make it right. Witness abortion. Witness withholding standard medical care from handicapped newborns. There is such a thing as a "throne of destruction . . . which devises mischief by decree" (Psalm 94:20). That is, it is possible for God-ordained rulers to declare as law what God declares is wrong; and when they do, they bring destruction on their people and, ultimately, themselves.

Inflation is a particularly clear example of such "mischief by decree." The Hebrew word for "mischief" can be translated "trouble," "labor," or "toil" as well.[5] And that is precisely what happens when inflation occurs. Everyone in the economy experiences the trouble of mistaken consumers' choices, misallocated labor, and confusion of the whole information system that is the market. Civil governments that inflate currency are thrones of destruction: their actions destroy the value of the currency and, if continued long enough, destroy whole market orders.

There is little *ethical* difference *in principle* between private counterfeiting and government money supply expansion, though there is some difference politically:

> What is the difference *economically*? Only the beneficiaries: private counterfeiters who buy up goods and services, or politicians who buy up goods, services, and votes.
> What is the difference *politically*? Private counterfeiters betray people's trust in criminals. Government counterfeiters betray people's trust in the government.[6]

The only significant difference between private counterfeiting and government counterfeiting is that the private counterfeiter acts contrary to the public's will, while the government acts by the consent of the voters, who keep returning inflation-loving politicians to office.

Does this somehow make the government's counterfeiting ethical as well as legal? No, for two reasons: First, there are those who understand that government counterfeiting is a form of theft, and who do not vote for the inflation-loving politicians. Stealing from them is no less theft merely because it is done by the ballot box. Second, inflationary monetary policy is actually a violation of the Ninth Commandment, which prohibits false witness. What is implicit in the expansion of the money supply is the message, "This new money's as good as the old." But the actual fact is that the new money not only isn't as good as the old, but also diminishes the value of the old. If people understood this, they would stop clamoring for money supply expansions as a means of fighting unemployment. The fact that they don't understand it does not excuse the politicians' continuing the policy. It only means that the policymakers are combining false witness with taking advantage of people's ignorance.

How can we solve the problem of government counterfeiting? By outlawing it and punishing those who practice it. But since the people who make our other laws are also the ones who have already passed the laws permitting government counterfeiting, the law probably needs to be passed at a higher level. That is, it needs to be made part of the Constitution, not left up to the legislature.

INFLATION BY COUNTERFEITING,
TYPE C: LEGAL PRIVATE ACTION

Third, new money can be created by private persons or corporations when they are permitted to pretend they have money they don't have and then extend credit based on the pretense. This is done by banks. It is called fractional reserve banking, and it is legal. It is legal despite the fact that it is a form of theft. It is theft because newly created money—loans of money banks don't have—devalues all money already in circulation. When banks increase the money supply, whether by 2 percent or by .1 percent, they have stolen from all other holders of money an amount equal to the value their money loses.

This method deserves a little explanation, because it's something few people understand. American law permits banks to lend more money than they hold in deposits.[7] This is called fractional reserve banking, and its inflationary effects can be awesome.[8]

THE MULTIPLICATION EFFECT

Banks are required to keep in reserve only a small fraction of the money deposited in them—some as low as 5 percent. The rest they can lend. This means there is a multiplying effect on money.

Here's how it works: Suppose you deposit $100 in cash in your checking account in a bank with a 5 percent reserve requirement. Now you can go out and spend that $100 by writing checks. Your bank, meanwhile, can lend $95 to Jennifer, who can deposit that in her checking account in another bank. Jennifer can spend her $95 by writing checks, while her bank lends $90.25 to Mike. Mike can deposit that in his bank and write checks on it, while his bank lends $85.74 to Jim. Jim can deposit that in his bank and write checks on it, while his bank lends $81.45 to Kelly. Kelly can deposit that in her bank and write checks on it, while her bank lends $77.38 to Mary.

This can go on and on until the whole $100 of initial deposit is used up *not in loans but in reserves!* After twenty-five steps the loans against that initial deposit will have amounted to $1,445.15, there will still be another $29.20 to be whittled away, and the borrowers will be able to spend the $1,445.15 as if it were all real cash. Once there was only your little $100 in cash potentially bidding for goods in the marketplace; now suddenly there's that plus $1,445.15 bidding for goods. The law of supply and demand tells us the money price of those goods must go up because the supply of goods has not risen along with the supply of dollars demanding them.

The inflationary element in the process is that *two or more people (or banks) can be using the same money at the same time to demand goods in the marketplace.* That is why fractional reserve banking drives up prices.

The figures based on $100 may not sound too bad in an economy with a gross national product measured in trillions of dollars. But imagine now that you deposit not $100 but $1 million, and the process begins. After twenty-five steps, loans can total $14,451,150. Or suppose you deposit $1 billion. After twenty-five steps, loans can total $14.45 billion. And while loans based on an initial $100 deposit are likely to stop after twenty-five steps because the remaining amount is too small to be very useful as a loan, loans based on $1 billion will go on for scores or hundreds of steps, meaning far greater multiplication and, hence, far more inflation.

LENDING ISN'T THE PROBLEM

The problem is not that banks lend money. It is that they use the same money in two ways that, under certain conditions, can be mutually exclusive. On the one hand, banks promise depositors that their money will be safe and they can get it whenever they wish. On the other hand, they tell borrowers that they can walk away with that same money. They use an item (the money deposited) as collateral to secure a loan from one person (the depositor), and give the same item (the money deposited) to another person (a borrower) as a different loan.

Under ordinary circumstances this pretense doesn't show up. But if enough people demand the return of their deposits at once, and enough loans have been made against those deposits, the banks can come up short of the money needed to pay back their depositors. Banks are not only lenders, but also borrowers. Every time someone deposits money in a bank, the bank is borrowing that money. It issues a receipt, which functions as a promise to return the money on demand. But if it doesn't have enough money on the premises to cover all the outstanding receipts, it cannot fulfill that promise if all the outstanding receipts are presented to it at once.

This is what happens in a "run on the bank," as it did to hundreds of banks during the Great Depression. A few small banks overstretched themselves so far that they weren't able to cover even a few receipts when they were presented, and suddenly people began to mistrust other banks. Not wanting to be caught holding worthless receipts, they hurried to the banks and demanded their money—and one after another the banks folded, unable to meet their obligations to depositors (people who lend their money to the banks).

The problem, then, is not with fractional reserves *as an isolated factor*, but with fractional reserves *coupled with* demand deposits. Fractional reserves are a necessary effect of lending—the opposite side of the coin, so to speak. By definition a bank cannot hold in its vault what it issues as a loan. Lending any part of money in deposit necessarily means the remainder is a fractional reserve.

The problem arises when both lender (depositor) and borrower (who gets the loan *at* the bank but *from* the depositor, since it is not the bank's money but the depositor's) are permitted to *use the money simultaneously*. This is how fractional reserve banking becomes inflationary. This phenomenon can only be avoided, as we will see, by prohibiting the use of demand deposits as lending capital.

ABUSE OF COLLATERAL

Fractional reserve banking, then, is unwise monetary policy. It interferes with good stewardship in precisely the way all inflationary policy does. But is it to be avoided only because it is *unwise*? Or is it something that is *unethical* on Biblical grounds?[9] It is in fact both.

We have already argued that inflation is always unethical, because it devalues money already in circulation. Because of this it is a form of theft—a violation of the Eighth Commandment. Since fractional reserve banking is inflationary, it is therefore unethical. But there is another reason why fractional reserve banking is un-Biblical, and it has to do as much with the Ninth Commandment, against deception, as with the Eighth.

Biblical Law's discussion of loans always assumes that borrowers must provide collateral.[10] This applies even to the poor, who may have nothing more than a cloak to give in pledge (Exodus 22:26, 27). And while, in such instances, Scripture requires the creditor to return the pledge overnight so the poor borrower can use it to keep warm, it also requires the borrower to return it to the creditor in the morning.

The effect of this was to prevent the borrower's using the same item as collateral for more than one loan. Why would that be important? Because using the same item to secure more than one loan is fraudulent: it means promising to two different lenders that they can, if you don't pay them back, recover their loss by taking possession of the same item. But they *cannot* both take possession of the same item.[11]

Fractional reserve banking amounts to the same thing as using one piece of collateral to secure multiple loans. The initial $100 (or $1 million, or $1 billion) deposit is the sole money on which loans amounting to ten or more times the original amount are based.

SOUND BANKING POLICY

How can this problem be resolved without prohibiting banks from lending money? The twofold goal is to prevent inflation and to ensure that two or more simultaneous claims are not admitted to the same resources. Several interrelated steps are necessary to achieve both goals.

First, lending money received as demand deposits must be prohibited.[12] This means that demand deposits—which depositors can remove at any time (for example, by writing checks against them)—would not bear interest, since banks would not be able to lend them to others who would pay interest. They would simply be safe storage, equivalent to putting money in a safety deposit

box. Banks probably would charge a small fee for keeping depositors' money safe—a fee some depositors would willingly pay to
ease themselves of the worry that their money might be stolen if
they kept it in their homes.[13]

Second, interest-bearing accounts, in contrast, must not be
demand deposits, because the interest is earned by lending from the
principal to borrowers who pay interest. They must be withdraw-
able only at the end of a pre-arranged term.[14] During that term, the
banks would act as middlemen between depositors and borrowers,
passing on to depositors a portion of the interest paid by borrowers
and keeping a portion for themselves as an agency fee.[15]

Third, the term of a loan *from* a bank must not exceed the
term of the deposit (or deposits) that fund the loan. In other
words, a two-year term deposit could not fund a three-year term
loan. The necessary effect of this would be that money deposited
to be loaned out again could not circulate in two places simultaneously. The depositor could not use his deposited money to buy
things (for instance, by writing checks against it) at the same time
that a borrower used it to buy things (or to deposit it in another
bank). This would stop the inflationary multiplication effect of
fractional reserve banking.

One more step is necessary. Banks' guarantees to repay
deposits must be based on their own assets and trustworthiness,
or on their participation in a real insurance program in which
they pay premiums to a company that insures their deposits, not
on the civil government's or any quasi-governmental body's
promise to reimburse depositors if the banks go broke.[16] Presently
the Federal Deposit Insurance Corporation (FDIC) and the Federal
Savings and Loan Insurance Corporation (FSLIC) "insure"
deposits in banks and savings and loans in the United States. But
the money with which to pay off members' losses—particularly
when those losses are huge, as they are in a series of runs on
banks—does not come from premiums. Instead it comes from the
Federal Reserve's printing new money, which is inflationary.
Thus this kind of deposit guarantee, when implemented, steals
from everyone in the economy (except those whose deposits they
reimburse) by devaluing money already in circulation.

Those who hope to earn interest on deposits must face the
possibility of real losses, losses that won't be made up by newly
printed money. If they want the chance of profit, they must take
the risk of loss. "The depositor might be given a choice: a higher
rate of interest, but without the bank's guaranteeing repayment

from the lender, or a bank guarantee of repayment, at a lower rate of interest."[17] (This is because the bank would be assuming a greater risk by guaranteeing the deposit than by not guaranteeing it.)

MONEY SUPPLY GROWTH
BY COMMODITY PRODUCTION

The fourth way money supply can grow is by adding new quantities of commodities used as money (media of exchange, stores of value, and units of account) to the market *when those commodities are also valuable as something other than money*. This is what happens when new gold and silver are mined. (In a society that used pearls as money, it would happen when new pearls were harvested.) The differences between this means of expanding the money supply and the others are important: (1) The commodities themselves have value other than as money, and so putting more into the economy adds nonmonetary value to the economy. (2) Adding them requires real labor, not a mere decree. (Workers in government money printing offices labor, but their product would not be money if it were not for the decree that it must be accepted as legal tender.)[18] (3) Adding them is of necessity a much slower process than printing money or crediting balances to bank accounts by writing figures in ledgers or punching computer buttons. Because it is so slow, it tends never to outpace growth of production in the rest of the economy, so money supply doesn't grow relative to the supply of goods and services that can be bought with money.

Money growth by commodity production is not inflationary. It is not theft. Thus it is the only means of expanding money supply that does not violate the Eighth Commandment: "You shall not steal" (Exodus 20:15). Thus it is the only only means of expanding money supply that is consistent with Biblical ethics and, not surprisingly, it is the only means that will not bring about the pernicious effects of inflation.

MAINTAINING THE VALUE OF MONEY

What does this mean practically? It means that money should always be in one of two forms: (1) A real commodity that has real market value and the five essential characteristics of money: divisibility, portability, durability, recognizability, and scarcity; (2) Receipts for such commodities deposited for safekeeping in secure warehouses (banks, savings and loans, etc.).

What role should the civil government play in money? It should not make money (because politicians tend to make deci-

sions based on political, not properly economic, concerns, and
therefore are too vulnerable to the temptation to pursue inflationary policies). Instead it should enforce laws against fraud and theft
by regulating the quality of money in two ways: (1) requiring that
commodities used as money be of the quantity and quality
claimed (for instance, by requiring that a coin claiming to contain
1/10 ounce of pure gold really contains 1/10 ounce of pure gold
and punishing those who misrepresent the quantity or quality of
the commodity); (2) enforcing the limits on banking discussed earlier when we considered how to solve the problems related to
fractional reserve banking.[19] Aside from these two functions, civil
government would have little to do with money. Money would be
like any other commodity in the marketplace, its value determined by the marginal utility judgments of buyers and sellers.

Such a monetary system would rest primarily on the application of the Eighth Commandment,[20] one specific implication of
which is that money must not be debased. Money can be debased
in either of two ways: mismeasurement and impurity. Both are
condemned in Scripture:

> You shall do no wrong in judgment, in measurement
> of weight, or capacity. You shall have just balances,
> just weights, a just ephah, and a just hin: I am the
> Lord your God, who brought you out from the land of
> Egypt. (Leviticus 19:35, 36)

> You shall not have in your bag differing weights, a
> large and a small. You shall not have in your house
> differing measures, a large and a small. You shall have
> a full and just weight; you shall have a full and just
> measure, that your days may be prolonged in the land
> which the Lord your God gives you. For everyone
> who does these things, everyone who acts unjustly is
> an abomination to the Lord your God. (Deuteronomy
> 25:13-16; cf. Proverbs 20:10)

> How the faithful city has become a harlot, she who
> was full of justice! Righteousness once lodged in her,
> but now murderers. Your silver has become dross . . . .
> Therefore the Lord GOD of hosts, the Mighty One of
> Israel declares, "Ah, I will be relieved of My adver-
> saries, and avenge Myself on My foes. I will also turn
> My hand against you, and will *smelt away your*

dross as with lye, and will remove all your alloy.
Then I will restore your judges as at the first. . .; after
that you will be called the city of righteousness, a
faithful city." (Isaiah 1:21, 22, 24-26)

The Bible requires just weights and measures. This means
not only that the butcher shouldn't put his thumb on the scale or
the dairyman water down the milk, but also that a coin represented as bearing 1/10 ounce of silver of .999 fine must really have
that weight of silver at that purity. Corruption of money is an evidence of moral corruption of the society. It is one of the sins for
which God promises to visit judgment (Isaiah 1:21-26).

What would a Biblical system of money look like? Christian
economist Gary North describes it simply:

1. Standard weights and measures, with penalties
imposed by the civil government against those who
tamper with the scales.
2. A prohibition on all forms of multiple indebtedness
by banks, meaning fractional reserve banking.
3. Competitive entry into the silversmith, goldsmith,
or any other smith business. [This means anyone can
make money out of precious metals, so long as he
abides by standards of purity and quantity.]
4. No one is to be compelled by law to accept any
form of money. (This is not stated in the Bible, but it
follows from the first three principles, which are
based on voluntarism.) This means no legal tender
laws (compulsory acceptance).[21]

A key aspect of all of this is that money production would
become the province of the private sector, rather than the civil
government, though civil government would continue to regulate
the quality of money. This is the only way we can keep civil government from resorting again and again to the quick fix of monetary inflation. Karl Marx and Friedrich Engels understood the
destructive effects of inflation on economies. They hoped for the
destruction of non-Communist economies. That is why they
included as the fifth of ten steps toward Communism,
"Centralisation of credit in the hands of the state, by means of a
national bank with state capital and an exclusive monopoly."[22] If
we hope to get off the high road to Communism, we must also
take the money monopoly out of the hands of the state.

THE GOLD STANDARD?

Does this mean the gold standard? Decidedly not. "Gold standard" means backing up paper money with the promise that it can be exchanged for real gold on demand. By itself that is fine, but it must be qualified in two ways. First, the gold standard must not be used as a pretense for keeping civil government in the money-making business; history has proven all too well that political systems cannot long resist the temptation to debase currency.[23] Second, the gold standard must not be understood as meaning that *only* gold or gold-backed notes can be used as money. The Bible leaves people free to use any commodity as money that buyer and seller both accept, the only restrictions being against fraud and theft.[24]

What it does mean is that civil government is to protect people from fraud and theft while they pursue their own ends freely within the limits of God's moral Law.

> What freedom produces is *parallel standards.* Various forms of money compete with each other. The State is to establish no fixed, bureaucratic price between moneys. The decisions of free men can then determine which form or forms of money become most acceptable. There is nothing magic about money. It is simply *the most marketable commodity.* The market establishes this, not the coercive power of the State. *Money is the product of voluntary human action, not of bureaucratic design.* Money is the product of freedom, and it reinforces freedom.[25]

NEEDED: A LITTLE HUMILITY

Fundamentally we are arguing here for a free market in money, just as we would argue for a free market in any other commodity not prohibited by God's Law. (There should be no market, either free or regulated, in murder, adultery, theft, etc.) And this argument flows partly from a growing realization that controlling a market without causing pernicious unintended consequences is simply beyond human ability. The argument for a free market, in money as in anything else, rests on a commitment to humility, as Hayek pointed out in his Nobel lecture "The Pretense of Knowledge":

> There is danger in the exuberant feeling of ever growing power, engendered by the advance of the physical

sciences, which tempts man to try—"dizzy with success," to use a characteristic phrase of early communism—to subject not only our natural but also our human environment to the control of human will. The recognition of the insuperable limits to his knowledge ought indeed to teach the student of society a lesson of humility that should keep him from becoming an accomplice in man's fatal striving to control society—a striving that makes him not only a tyrant over his fellows, but may well make him destroy a civilization that no brain has designed, a civilization that has grown from the free efforts of millions of individuals.[26]

We cannot attempt to control man more minutely than the broad restrictions of God's moral Law without simultaneously exalting some men (the controllers) to a godlike status and debasing all others (the controlled) to the status of animals. C. S. Lewis made the same argument in *The Abolition of Man*: ". . . Man's conquest of himself means simply the rule of the Conditioners over the conditioned human material, the world of post-humanity which, some knowingly and some unknowingly, nearly all men in all nations are at present labouring to produce."[27]

A TIME FOR REPENTANCE, A TIME FOR ACTION
American Christians need to repent for ignoring the moral degradation embodied in an inflationary monetary system, and we need to plead with God to delay His judgment long enough to permit a change in our country's laws. But we need to do more than that. We need to put pressure on our political representatives to restore an honest system of money to this country. And if they don't respond, we need to run for office ourselves and, once elected, do the job ourselves.

If we don't—if we allow continued corruption of our money—we may be sure of ten things: (1) Inflation will continue. (2) Prices will continue to rise. (3) Inflation will continue to engender bad buying choices based on mistaken judgments of money's purchasing power.[28] (4) Producers will continue to get the wrong signals about what consumers most need. (5) Resources of production—capital, raw materials, and labor—will continue to be misallocated. (6) The boom and bust cycle will continue, with continued bouts of high unemployment and high business failure rates. (7) The economy will become increasingly confused until at last it collapses. (8) If God is merciful, the collapse will be minor—a severe depression, perhaps. (9) If God exercises vengeance for our sins of theft by inflation, the economic collapse will be severe, [29] and with it will come the collapse of our whole system of government, which probably will be replaced by a totalitarian system that imposes on us the order of tyranny—in place of the order of justice that we rejected by choosing inflation. [30] (10) If that total collapse occurs, we may bid not only our prosperity but also our liberties good-bye.

PART FOUR

STEWARDSHIP AND GOVERNMENT

STEWARDSHIP AND LIMITED GOVERNMENT

*R*epeatedly the last seven chapters have touched on questions about the role of civil government[1] in the economy. Chapters Nine and Ten examined the impact of governmental control of money supply, and found it to be pernicious whenever it goes beyond regulating the truthfulness of claims of quality and quantity of money—what the Bible refers to as enforcement of just weights and measures (see Proverbs 20:10, 23). Chapter Eight mentioned that some governmental intrusions into the marketplace—for instance, to control prices—have ill results. This chapter considers the nature and proper role of civil government, particularly as it affects the economic sphere of life. The following two chapters will examine whether certain governmental regulations of the marketplace fit within that proper role and what happens when government pursues them.

THE ROLE OF CIVIL GOVERNMENT
The key Biblical text on the nature and functions of civil government is Romans 13:1-7:

> Let every person be in subjection to the governing authorities. For there is no authority except from God, and those which exist are established by God. Therefore he who resists authority has opposed the ordinance of God; and they who have opposed will receive condemnation upon themselves. For rulers are not a cause of fear for good behavior, but for evil. Do you want to have no fear of authority? Do what is good, and you will have praise from the same; for it is *a minister of God to you for good.* But if you do what is evil, be afraid; for it does not bear the sword for

> nothing; for it is *a minister of God, an avenger who
> brings wrath upon the one who practices evil.*
> Wherefore it is necessary to be in subjection, not only
> because of wrath, but also for conscience' sake. For
> because of this you also pay taxes, for rulers are ser-
> vants of God, devoting themselves to this very thing.
> Render to all what is due them: tax to whom tax is
> due; custom to whom custom; fear to whom fear;
> honor to whom honor.[2]

Proper government is a good thing, and normally those who
govern deserve the utmost respect. A Christian understanding of
economics—or of any other aspect of life affected by civil government—cannot be anti-government in principle. It cannot dispar-
age the importance of government within its proper sphere of
authority.[3] Governing authorities are ministers of God. For this
reason, wrote John Calvin, "civil authority is a calling, not only
holy and lawful before God, but also the most sacred and by far
the most honorable of all callings in the whole life of mortal
men."[4]

The two key clauses on the functions of government tell us
that it is both "a minister . . . for good" and "a minister . . . who
brings wrath upon the one who practices evil." These are the
chief purposes of government: to do good, and to restrain evil (by
threat and use of punishment). This is not to imply that restraining evil is not good. Rather, doing good and restraining evil are
viewed as opposite sides of a coin, the one positive and the other
negative. How is government to do good and restrain evil? The
text itself tells us.

DOING GOOD AND RESTRAINING EVIL

Look first at how government is to do good: "Do you want to
have no fear of authority? Do what is good, and you will have
praise from the same. . . ." Government is to do positive good by
praising people who do good. It should point to righteous people
as examples for others to follow. It should reward them with
recognition. But that is all. The text never hints that government
should do more than that—say, give them some kind of financial
remuneration for doing good[5]—and we find no such instruction
elsewhere in Scripture, other than that a good government puts
good people rather than bad in positions of authority (Psalm 101;
Proverbs 29:2).

Now look at how government is to restrain evil: ". . . if you do what is evil, be afraid; for it does not *bear the sword* for nothing; for it is a minister of God, an *avenger* who brings *wrath* upon the one who practices evil." Punishment—including capital punishment when warranted—is the way in which government is to restrain evil. Government should be so adept at apprehending, trying, convicting, and punishing those who do evil that those who contemplate it will be deterred by fear of punishment.[6]

These considerations naturally lead to another question: If government is to praise those who do good and punish those who do evil, it must have some standard, some definition of good and evil. Otherwise it cannot determine whom to praise and whom to punish. What is that standard?

Defining Good and Evil

The Apostle Paul answers that question in the same context: "Render to all what is due them ....." This, we saw in Chapter Four, is what it means to do justice: to render impartially to each his due according to a right standard. Paul then goes on to look at this from a different perspective—the perspective of love:

> Owe nothing to anyone except to love one another; for he who loves his neighbor has fulfilled the law. For this, "You shall not commit adultery, You shall not murder, You shall not steal, You shall not covet," and if there is any other commandment, it is summed up in this saying, "You shall love your neighbor as yourself." Love does no wrong to a neighbor; love therefore is the *fulfillment of the law.* (Romans 13:8-10)

Justice and love are, in Biblical perspective, two sides of the same coin—just as restraining evil and doing good are. The standard of justice, we saw in Chapter Four, is the Decalogue. It is the standard of love, too.[7]

Where love and justice differ is that justice is the minimum requirement of the Law, and love the drawing out of the positive principles underlying the negative commandments.[8] Justice is what is *due* another, what to fail to render is to violate his rights. Love not only does not violate another's rights, but also builds him up (1 Corinthians 8:1b). Justice refrains from stealing, but love goes farther and gives (notice the frequent coincidence of love and giving in Scripture: John 3:16; Galatians 2:20; Ephesians 5:25).

When Paul wrote in Romans 13:3 that governing authorities are to praise those who do good, he had in mind not those who merely do what is just by observing the minimum requirements of the Law, but those who love others by going beyond (but never against) the minimum requirements and sacrificing for the good of others. Thus when a mayor, governor, or president singles someone out for special recognition for heroism, self-sacrifice, or "going above and beyond the call of *duty*," he is praising one who has done good. And when Paul wrote in Romans 13:4 that a governing authority is to be "an avenger who brings wrath upon the one who practices evil," he had in mind not those who fail to love, but those who, by falling short of the minimum requirements of the Law, practice injustice. When the state tries, justly convicts, sentences, and executes just punishment on a criminal, it brings wrath on the one who practices evil.

These recognitions lead to another important—indeed an essential—distinction between love and justice. Justice can be enforced, while love can only be urged and praised. Government can—and must—punish those who do injustice. But it can only pity those who fail to love, and try to lead them to change by praising those who do love; it cannot punish them for lovelessness. This is what moral philosopher Adam Smith was driving at when he wrote that justice may be enforced and injustice punished by civil government, but love may only be praised and its lack grieved.[9] Government may bemoan the stinginess of someone who refuses to give to the poor, and it may try to persuade him to do it by praising those who do. But it may not punish him for for his lack of love, or force him to give by taking his wealth and giving it to others.[10] To do so would be both to attempt to enforce love, which cannot be done, and to violate his own right to property, which would itself be an injustice.[11]

THE ROLE OF COERCION

What all of this points to is a very strict limitation, from a Biblical perspective, on the coercive power of the state. Civil government may use its power of persuasion to urge people to love others, but it may not use its power of coercion to force them to do so. It may praise a generous, self-sacrificing person and urge others to follow his example. But it may not force others to give generously (indeed it is not possible to force generosity) or to sacrifice themselves.[12]

What, then, is the proper role of governmental coercion? It is to restrain citizens from violating each other's rights and to punish those who do. In the words of one group of evangelicals who examined Biblical teaching on the nature and functions of civil government, "civil government has the responsibility of administering justice, which includes and is limited to the commendation of those who do right, the punishment of evildoers by restitution and retribution, and the preservation of peace against domestic and foreign oppressors. . . ."[13] Civil government must use force only to enforce justice by punishing those who do injustice.[14]

It is essential at this point that we recall precisely what justice is, for it is possible, if we do not insist on a clear and strict definition of the term, to defend almost any governmental action in the name of "justice." We saw in Chapter Four that justice means rendering impartially to each his due in accord with the right standard of God's Law. And because justice recognizes that different people, in different circumstances, are due different things, it recognizes that people are not due equal things. Justice must not be confused with any preference for economic equality or any other particular relative distribution of wealth among men.[15]

PROTECTING RIGHTS

But this is to put the matter negatively. It is to speak of what government ought to do *to* people who do injustice. The opposite side of that coin is that government is to *protect rights*. And those rights are spelled out in the same Law that is the standard of both justice and love. They are the rights to life (Sixth Commandment), sanctity of the marriage bond and of the family (Seventh and Fifth Commandments), property (Eighth Commandment), and truthful dealing (Ninth Commandment).[16] For a government to restrain injustice is for it to restrain violations of these rights.

Let's see what some of the implications of these rights are for governmental regulation of the marketplace.

THE RIGHT TO LIFE

In enforcing the Sixth Commandment, "You shall not murder," government rightly uses its coercive power to restrain people from killing or injuring others unjustly, and to punish those who do.[17] For economics, this means of course that government must prohibit—and punish—paying people to kill or injure others unjustly. It may properly prohibit and punish the threat or use of violence to achieve economic ends—practices common to some employers resisting unionization of their employees, but also to unions trying to force employers to meet their demands.

This also means that government properly restricts or prohibits the sale of products that are inherently dangerous to life and health even in their proper use, and exacts retribution on and restitution from those who violate those restrictions. Product safety laws—insofar as they truly protect people[18]—exemplify the legitimate use of the coercive power of the state to protect Sixth Commandment rights. Negligence liability laws also fall under this heading (Exodus 21:28-36).

THE RIGHT TO FAMILY INTEGRITY

In enforcing the Seventh Commandment, "You shall not commit adultery," government properly prohibits rape, incest, and other sexual relations outside marriage and protects the sanctity of the family.[19] In economic application, this means government may properly use its coercive power to prohibit and punish prostitution, the production and distribution of pornography, and employers' demands for sexual favors from employees in exchange for promotion or higher wages. Laws restricting divorce also fall under this commandment. And in enforcing the Fifth Commandment, "Honor your father and your mother. . .," government may uphold legitimate parental authority over dependent children.[20]

Government protection of the family is of tremendous economic importance, because the integrity and longevity of a family are key elements in economic prosperity. The family, with its concern for the welfare of spouse, children, and grandchildren, is the most important factor in imparting to individuals the future orientation that must replace insistence on present gratification in order for people to prosper.[21]

THE RIGHT TO PROPERTY

In enforcing the Eighth Commandment, "You shall not steal," government rightly uses its coercive power to restrain people from taking from others anything of value—physical goods, time, energy, even ideas—forcibly, i.e., without their free and informed consent.[22] This means government properly "provides that each man may keep his property safe and sound," as Calvin put it.[23]

This is a matter of fundamental economic importance. A society that does not respect property will not—indeed cannot—prosper, for property will be cared for and enhanced only to the extent that anyone recognizes a benefit from it, and when it can be taken at random by others no one will be able to foresee such benefit.[24] Much of our discussion of the justice (or injustice) of economic regulation in the next chapter will rest heavily on this commandment.

Ownership and Control

A common misunderstanding is that property rights are respected when ownership remains in private hands even though authority to control use and exchange is claimed by the state. The Bible cannot countenance this idea, for it sees control as fundamental to ownership; deny the former and you have denied the latter. Thus, for instance, the landowner in Jesus' parable of the laborers in the vineyard equates control with ownership when he says, "Is it not lawful for me to do what I wish with what is my own?" (Matthew 20:15).[25] Peter emphasized the same point when he told Ananias that a field, while it was unsold, remained Ananias' own possession, and that its price, after the sale, was under Ananias' control (Acts 5:4).

Property Rights Are Human Rights

Property is essential to human life and to the exercise of all other human rights. Thus property rights and human rights are not contrary to each other. Property rights are simply the rights of humans to property. No one can live without property in food, or be warm and modest without property in clothing, or earn a living without property in his labor. "We emphasize that property rights are *not* rights *of property*; they are rights *of people* to [the] use of goods. . . . It is silly to speak of a contrast or conflict between human rights and property rights. Property rights *are* human rights to the use of economic goods."[26]

The human right to private property is part of the foundation of human freedom—whether of religion, expression, or association.[27] Someone without property must be wholly dependent on others for maintenance of life and health. That dependency can be a strong disincentive to his thinking and acting contrary to the will of his patrons.

This is why life, liberty, and property so frequently appear together as a triad of rights. Thus the Fifth Amendment to the United States Constitution provides that no person shall "be deprived of life, liberty, or property, without due process of law; nor shall private property be taken for public use without just compensation."[28] In the United States this aspect of property rights has been buried in recent decades by mountains of laws controlling private property—zoning, eminent domain, public access, and many other regulations.[29] Many of these laws are clearly contrary to the intent of the authors of the Fifth Amendment, who recognized that ownership and control—within the limits of others' rights—are inextricably intertwined. Happily recent court decisions indicate a growing recognition of this principle.[30]

THE RIGHT TO TRUTHFUL RELATIONS

Finally, in enforcing the Ninth Commandment, "You shall not bear false witness. . .," civil government rightly uses its coercive power to restrain people from defrauding one another. Laws against false advertising and false labeling are good examples of this exercise of civil government's power. So, too, are laws against "bait-and-switch" sales tactics.[31] By the same principle, government should forbid and punish the debasing of money (or any other commodity) either by mixing impurities with precious metals (or other commodities) or by using false weights and measures (Proverbs 20:10, 23).[32]

The coercive power of the state, then, may properly be used to enforce justice by upholding the Fifth through Ninth Commandments. Beyond this it must not go—and when it does go beyond it, it becomes a tool of injustice rather than of justice.[33]

CIVIL GOVERNMENT IS NOT ABOVE THE LAW

Respect for property must exist not only on the private but also on the governmental level. This is equally true in respect to all other rights. Government exists to enforce, not to violate, God-given rights. Just as civil government may not require people to violate the First Commandment by requiring them to worship false gods or disobey God (Acts 5:29), so it may not require people to violate the Fifth Commandment by teaching children in public school classes to ridicule their parents' values.[34] Neither may it require anyone to take another's life unjustly, in violation of the Sixth Commandment; or to commit adultery, in violation of the Seventh; or to bear false witness, in violation of the Ninth.

The Eighth Commandment does not say, "You shall not steal unless you are a king," or "You shall not steal unless you are a legislator," or "You shall not steal except by popular vote." It says simply, "You shall not steal." As Old Testament scholar J. Barton Payne put it, "Israel's judges were warned not to permit economic need to influence their decisions (Lev[iticus] 19:15); for in the distribution of property the standard, 'Thou shalt not steal,' includes stealing, even by society as a whole."[35] Or, in the words of Christian philosopher R. C. Sproul, "When people use the power of the ballot box to vote for themselves largess or subsidies from the general coffers, it is a sophisticated form of stealing. . . . Christians need to be sensitive about how they use the power of the ballot."[36]

The Eighth Commandment protects property against all coercive expropriation other than as punishment for a crime (both retribution and restitution; see Exodus 22:1-15) or tax support (Romans 13:7; cf. Matthew 22:21) of government's *legitimate functions* (praising the good, restraining injustice). In no other instance does Scripture permit coercive taking of property. A king may not even force a subject to sell property, much less take it by force without payment (1 Kings 21).[37]

No "Divine Right of Kings"

For centuries throughout the world it was assumed that kings—thought to be divine, or semi-divine—had legitimate authority (or "divine right") to do whatever they pleased, including taking anyone's property at will. This idea is contrary to the Biblical understanding of kingly authority limited by the Law of God.[38] Even the highest civil authorities are subject to God's Law. Their violation of it is as much an injustice as that by any private individual. That is why God required even a king to read His Law "all the days of his life, that he may learn to fear the Lord his God, by carefully observing all the words of this law and these statutes, that his heart may not be lifted up above his countrymen and that he may not turn aside from the commandment, to the right or the left; in order that he and his sons may continue long in his kingdom in the midst of Israel" (Deuteronomy 17:19f). Justice is the same for the great as for the poor, and must be set aside for neither (Leviticus 19:15).

The prevalence of Christianity in the West up through the late Middle Ages resulted in hitherto unheard of limitations on kingly power. With the coming of the Renaissance and its rejection of Biblical authority, however, many kings claimed to be above law; limited monarchies began to turn into absolute monarchies.[39] The Reformation, insisting on the authority of Scripture over every man, resisted that turn. When King James I of England, followed by his son Charles I, attempted to assert the divine right of kings, the English people—led by the Puritans —responded by overthrowing the monarchy.[40] When, after the monarchy was restored, King James II attempted to assert the divine right of kings anew, the English people rebelled again.

The result was the "Glorious Revolution" of 1688, in which the people fought again to defend the protection of property against kingly usurpation that they had won 473 years before when King John had been forced to sign the Magna Charta.[41] The American Revolution eighty-eight years later was fought largely over the same principle: that civil rulers—whether kings or parliaments—cannot take property from people, but that taxation must be levied by the people on themselves.[42]

Vox Populi, Vox Dei?

But what of a government in which "the people" rule? If kings and parliaments have no authority to take property except in punishment for crime (retribution and restitution) or taxation to fund legitimate functions of government, might "the people" have such authority?

Certainly not. That would be to substitute for God's Law a new standard of justice. It would be to claim that the voice of the people is the voice of God.[43] Justice is not defined by majority vote, which is why God expressly warned, "You shall not follow a multitude in doing evil, nor shall you testify in a dispute so as to turn aside after a multitude in order to pervert justice . . ." (Exodus 23:2). Granted the prevalence of so-called "concern for the poor" as an excuse for forced redistribution of property, can it be accidental that the words immediately following these are, ". . . nor shall you be partial to a poor man in his dispute" (Exodus 23:3)? When a majority votes to take from the rich in order to give to the poor, is that not "a multitude" being "partial to a poor man in his dispute" for another's property?

Representative democracy, founded on Biblical as well as classical notions,[44] can remain a system of justice and liberty only so long as it avoids the temptation to claim for itself the unjust powers claimed by the kings and parliaments it replaces. When the voice of the people begins to be considered the voice of God, true justice is denied.[45] When a representative democracy throws off the shackles of justice, claiming authority to run rampant over the rights protected by God's Law, it takes upon itself new shackles in which, as John Stuart Mill put it in his autobiography, the central government—by popular demand—becomes a despotism ". . . over a congregation of isolated individuals, all equals but all slaves."[46] Perversely, a people quick to deny the tyranny of king and parliament can be equally quick to assert its own.[47]

How strange that many Christians, who see clearly that

civil government must not force people to violate the other commandments, believe it can require violation of the commandment, "You shall not steal," and that their own receipt of property taken unjustly by government is excused because government did the taking. When Christians quietly consent to forced redistribution of wealth, whether from poor to rich or from rich to poor, we unintentionally become partners in crime. We become beneficiaries of legalized theft by accepting government subsidies,[48] whether student financial aid, or welfare, or Social Security beyond the return of what we pay into the system.[49]

LAW, LIBERTY, AND ECONOMIC REGULATION

Time and again in our consideration of the role of civil government in economic (and other) affairs, we have noticed the tight connection between law and liberty. Laws that violate the fundamental, God-given rights enumerated in the Ten Commandments (for economics, specifically the Fifth through Ninth Commandments) necessarily infringe on God-given liberties. A government that places itself above God's Law, taking upon itself the authority to steal property (or to take lives unjustly, or to break up families, or to deceive citizens), attacks its people's freedom.

This is because law—particularly God's Law—stands at the very root of liberty. It is the fence that guards liberty. That is why God introduced the Ten Commandments with this reminder to Israel: "I am the Lord your God, who brought you out of the land of Egypt, *out of the house of slavery*" (Exodus 20:2). It is why James refers to the commandments as "the perfect law, the law of liberty," and as "the royal law" (James 1:25; 2:8; note that here again the Law is summed up in the command to love). The purpose of law—particularly God's Law—is to preserve human liberty within its bounds. Thus the ultimate purpose of civil government in enforcing law is to preserve that same human liberty within the bounds of God's Law.[50]

The degree of justice in economic regulation, therefore, is the degree to which it respects and protects the liberty of those it affects, within the bounds of God's Law. To the extent that economic regulation impairs that liberty, it is unjust. God's Law is the ultimate and infallible standard of justice, and so also the standard of judgment for any man-made law: "To the law and to the testimony! If they do not speak according to this word, it is because they have no dawn" (Isaiah 8:20).

STEWARDSHIP AND ECONOMIC REGULATION: PRICE CONTROLS

God holds Christians, especially those who have a voice in shaping public policy (as we all do in democratic governments), accountable for working to ensure good stewardship not only in our private lives but also in society (Philippians 2:4). We ought, therefore, to work to persuade our legislatures to enact only those economic regulations that meet the test of good stewardship, and to rescind those that don't.

The chief criterion for judging economic regulation must be God's Law as the standard of justice. But laws can also be tested for stewardship by observing their actual effects. This is not to adopt a utilitarian ethic. If an act is contrary to God's Law, it is wrong regardless of its effects, long- or short-term. The end does not justify the means,[1] but a demonstrably nasty end ought to incite us to consider anew whether the means to it were just. Frequently the ends brought about by economic regulations are, despite legislators' best intentions, exceedingly nasty. That is why, as economist Walter Williams put it, ". . . truly compassionate policy requires dispassionate analysis."[2]

Henry Hazlitt, in *Economics in One Lesson*, wrote, "The art of economics consists in looking not merely at the immediate but at the longer effects of any act or policy; it consists in tracing the consequences of that policy not merely for one group but for all groups."[3] Good intentions alone, as long-term effects of using inflation to fight unemployment demonstrate,[4] do not make good economic policy. Warm hearts with foolish heads are a recipe for disaster. Because real compassion requires not only feeling but also understanding, there is no excuse in Christian stewardship for zeal without knowledge.

CRITERIA FOR TESTING ECONOMIC REGULATIONS

These things said, let's test several common types of economic regulation by these two criteria: (1) Is it just? That is, is it consistent with God's Law revealed particularly in the Fifth through Ninth Commandments? Does it involve rendering impartially to each his due according to the right standard of God's Law? (2) Is it good stewardship? Are its long-term, population-wide consequences beneficial? Does it contribute to the fundamental goal of stewardship, the increase of man's dominion over the earth as God's viceregent? Does it work? Because moral and physical reality are consistent, the answer to both of these questions will be the same for any given law. A just law will have good consequences; an unjust law will have bad consequences.

This chapter will examine one common type of economic regulation, price controls. The next will examine two more types, access controls and subsidies.[5] Space doesn't permit examining any specific examples of government regulation of the economy in great detail. The aim is to establish basic principles and methods of analysis that apply equally to any examples of each type.

Two rules of thumb will simplify matters a little: (1) Any regulation that restricts or prohibits an owner's use or exchange of his property is *unjust* (a violation of the Eighth Commandment) unless it can be proved beyond reasonable doubt that the regulation is necessary to prevent violations of people's God-given rights outlined in the Ten Commandments.[6] (2) Any regulation that makes goods and services more scarce than they otherwise would be is *bad stewardship* unless it can be proved beyond reasonable doubt that the benefits of the regulation[7] outweigh the harm entailed by the increased scarcity.[8]

PRICE CONTROLS

There are two fundamental, and opposite, kinds of price controls: maximum prices and minimum prices. When a government attempts to enforce either of these, it violates the Eighth Commandment's prohibition of theft by prohibiting people's using their property in voluntary, nonfraudulent exchanges. These controls cannot be justified by an appeal to some notion of a "just price," for the only just price is that at which buyer and seller freely arrive in nonfraudulent negotiations.[9]

Besides being unjust in principle, price controls also disrupt the information processing mechanism of the market. In other words, they result in inaccurate signals regarding consumers' and producers' judgments of marginal utility. As a result, resources are misallocated from producing goods consumers would ordinarily value more highly to producing those they would ordinarily value less highly. Thus price controls are also bad stewardship.

Yet people argue for price controls on two primary bases: (1) Minimum prices are necessary for the welfare of sellers and, through them, of buyers. (2) Maximum prices are necessary for the welfare of buyers (but without regard to the welfare of sellers). How do these arguments measure up to analysis of consequences?

MAXIMUM PRICES

If maximum prices—rent controls, natural gas price controls, and the controls on gasoline prices that were imposed during the Arab oil embargo of the 1970s—are set higher than the market price established by marginal utility and supply and demand, they will have no effect. They will therefore be useless. But if they are set lower than the market price, they must cause shortages.

Why? Because in a market where buyers compete against buyers and sellers against sellers for the opportunity to exchange, price naturally tends toward the lowest point that will bring sufficient returns to cover the costs of production and render a profit high enough to attract producers. The market price of any good is always determined by consumers' judgments of marginal utility—what they are willing to pay for that unit of the good that they value least.[10] If it becomes illegal to sell a good at a higher price, producers will stop producing it, and consumers' demands will go unmet.[11] Let's look at rent control as an example, remembering that precisely the same effect must occur no matter what product is regulated by a maximum price.

RENT CONTROL

Rent control is defended as a way to make housing affordable to the poor. The argument runs that if maximum rents are not set by law, rental housing will become so expensive that the poor will be left homeless. A fair test of the legitimacy of the argument, then, would be to see whether there are more or fewer homeless in cities with rent control than in those without it.

William Tucker's research shows conclusively that cities with rent control have significantly higher homelessness rates than those without it—and no other factor accounts for the difference. Of the seventeen of America's fifty largest cities with the highest rates of homeless persons, nine have rent control. Of the remaining thirty-three with lower rates of homelessness, not one has rent control. No other plausible factor—percentage of population in poverty, unemployment rate, availability of public housing, total population, climate, or rental housing vacancy rates—showed significant statistical correlation.[12]

Why does this unintended consequence of rent control occur? Because putting maximum prices on rental housing —unless those prices are above the going market rate anyway, in which case they are irrelevant—makes production and maintenance of much rental property uneconomical. That is, it makes it so that fewer producers can meet the costs of building and maintaining apartment buildings and rental houses. As a result, fewer rental properties are available.[13]

And who gets hurt the most by the shortage in rental housing? Remember that the market price of any good is always set by *marginal* buyers' ability to pay and the *marginal* producers' ability to produce.[14] That is, for any good in a competitive market in which buyers compete freely against buyers and sellers against sellers, the market price will be that at which buyers with the least ability to pay can still afford to buy, and at which producers with the least efficient (most costly) production can still afford to produce. What this means is that the buyers (renters) who will be shut out of the housing market under rent control will be the poor—the very people the legislators intended to protect from high rents—and the sellers (landlords) who will be shut out of the market will be those least able to afford to provide rental housing.[15] Rent control laws, in other words, hurt the most vulnerable people on both sides of the rental exchange,[16] and they do this *necessarily* because of the action of the economic laws of marginal utility and supply and demand.[17]

The real impact of rent control is to reduce the availability of housing in a rental market.[18] Rather than suffer losses by renting property at prices below construction or maintenance costs, property owners will choose other uses for their property. They may turn it into expensive condominiums or office space. Or they might even find it most economical to let it stand vacant and deteriorate—hence the block upon block of empty, dilapidated buildings in New York City and many other major cities with rent control, unmatched by any cities without rent control (except those that have just been bombed in war and haven't had time to rebuild; this ought to say something about the destructiveness of rent control).

The ill results of rent control should have been predicted. Rent control violates the Biblical principle that people are free to use their property as they wish so long as they do not harm others (Matthew 20:15; Acts 5:4). As such it is unjust. And in God's unified creation, in which moral and physical laws are intertwined, immoral actions must have bad physical results.[19]

MINIMUM PRICES

At the opposite end of economic regulation from maximum prices are minimum prices—prices below which no one is legally permitted to buy the regulated good or service. As we might expect by now, minimum prices will have precisely the opposite effect from maximum prices. If set *lower* than the market price, they will be useless. But if set *higher*, they will cause a *surplus*.

Why? Because the higher minimum price will cause the *marginal* units of the good or service (the ones that, under the market price, just barely got sold) to go unbought.[20] That is, those units of the good or service that consumers judge to have a utility (expected satisfaction value) below that represented by the minimum price will remain on the shelf. Let's look at two examples—minimum dairy prices and minimum wages—remembering that precisely the same unintended consequence will derive from any application of minimum prices.

MINIMUM DAIRY PRICES

At typical hearings before state dairy commissions, dairy farmers contend that they are losing money and that, if a minimum price of milk is not set, many farmers will go out of business, diminishing the supply of milk and so forcing consumers to pay even higher prices in the future.[21] If the dairy commission accepts the farmers' arguments and sets a minimum price significantly higher than the market price (as many do, year after year in state after state), what will happen?

Some producers, present and potential, who can't meet costs of production by selling at market prices and still gain a profit adequate to justify staying in the dairy business, will stay in (or enter) the business instead of leaving it (or staying out of it).[22] As a result, more milk will be produced than consumers are willing to buy at the high fixed price. Then the state will need to either buy up the surplus, let it go to waste, or lower (or remove) the minimum price so that all the milk can be sold at the lower market price.

Bureaucracies being what they are, the dairy commission won't likely admit its mistake and lower or remove the minimum price. But if the state refuses to buy the surplus, marginal dairy farmers (those whose costs of production only permit them to stay in business at the legislated minimum price, not at the lower market price) will go out of business. And that is precisely the reason the minimum price was adopted in the first place. Hence the commission will choose to buy the surplus—or pay farmers to destroy it or not to produce it, either of which is the same thing viewed a little differently.

Consumers thus get hit coming and going. They pay higher prices for milk (or wheat, or sugar, or corn, or steel, or textiles—whatever is affected by a minimum price) than they would if the price were determined by the natural functions of marginal utility and supply and demand, and they get taxed to finance the state's buying the surplus. And those who suffer most can least afford it: the poor, who are badly hurt by the increased tax burden and also have to reduce their consumption of milk at the higher-than-market price.[23] These are the very consumers the law was intended to protect from a shortage of milk that was predicted to occur if the market price were allowed to reign.[24] They end up able to buy less milk while spending more money.[25]

All of this adds up to *misallocation of resources*. And since good stewardship (good economics) is defined as wise allocation of scarce resources, it adds up to *bad stewardship* (or bad economics). Without the minimum dairy price, farmers who couldn't produce profitably at the market price would have to pursue some other kind of enterprise—perhaps trying several before they found one at which they could meet a consumer demand and still make a profit. With it, they are permitted to pursue an enterprise that consumers would otherwise have told them they did not value highly enough to make it profitable.

There is yet another negative and unforeseen result of minimum product prices when coupled with government buy-outs of the necessarily resultant surpluses. By permitting people to continue in a business that is not, by the judgment of the market itself, efficiently meeting others' needs, they cater to self-serving, rather than other-serving, activities. Thus they also undercut the basic Biblical value of self-sacrifice for others discussed in Chapter One (cf. Matthew 20:28; John 12:24).

There is no reason why a farmer who cannot make a profit by raising and selling milk (or corn, wheat, cotton, sugar, peanuts, tobacco, or any other product) at the market price should be supported in his inefficient activity by the forcible expropriation of wealth from others through taxation. The same holds true for steel makers, automobile manufacturers, textile manufacturers—anyone. If someone chooses to continue in a business despite his inability to make profits, he should bear the loss himself rather than forcing others to bear it for him. If he's not willing to do that, he should find another business in which he can make a profit, or avoid the risk of business loss altogether by working for someone else.

Some people, acknowledging that minimum prices are detrimental to the domestic economy, defend the practice on the grounds that the surpluses can be sent to foreign countries as aid. Not only does this still fail the test of justice (the price control and the taxation to buy the surplus both violate the Eighth Commandment), but also—naturally since moral and physical reality are one—it still has bad consequences. Most food shipped to foreign countries as government-to-government aid never reaches the poor for whom it is intended. Most goes to government officials and other wealthy persons, and a significant portion is resold on the world market to finance costly government projects that don't serve the interests of the people.[26] Further, foreign aid reinforces the idea that poor countries cannot solve their problems internally but must depend on outside help—a notion that many economists and others have argued stands in the way of their climbing out of poverty.[27]

MINIMUM WAGE

Perhaps the most pernicious of price controls is the minimum wage law—and it was adopted by legislators who probably had the best of motives.[28] They intended to help the poor by ensuring that everyone received a "livable wage." What is the actual effect?

Anyone can predict it by applying the economic law of marginal utility: an increase in price creates a decrease in consumption. If the price of labor rises, the consumption of labor must fall. In other words, minimum wage laws—unless the minimum is set below the market rate, in which case it will be useless—must produce unemployment.[29] The people forced out of work by the minimum wage law *must* be those with the least valuable skills—marginal workers. The very people the legislators hope to help by raising their wages will instead become unemployed because the minimum price employers may legally pay will be higher than the marginal utility value of their labor.[30]

This prediction holds true in the real world. A study of

changes in unemployment rate, correlated with changes in the federal minimum wage rate, shows that unemployment among low-skilled workers increases right along with increases in the minimum wage.[31] As minimum wages rise, employers hire fewer unskilled (and hence low-paid) workers. If one worker paid $9 per hour can do in one hour what it would take three paid $3.35 per hour to do, the employer will use the one instead of the three. But if the three could be paid $2.50 per hour, the employer would hire the three instead of the one. Or if an employer can buy and maintain a machine to do a job for $3 per hour, but would have to pay an unskilled worker $3.35 for the same production, he will buy the machine instead; but if the worker can underbid the machine, by working for just $2.95 per hour, the machine will be unemployed instead of the worker.

This is not all. The unemployment caused by minimum wage laws is not general across the board for the poor. It not only hurts less skilled workers more than more skilled workers, but also hurts certain segments of less skilled workers more than others: namely, targets of racial (or other) bias. Why? Because it removes economic incentive to hire across barriers of bigotry. (This is not to excuse racial discrimination, which the Bible condemns. It is simply to acknowledge what happens in the real world.)

If a black person can offer his services for 30 cents an hour less than a white person, a white bigot might employ him, choosing to maximize his profit rather than to express his racism. But if the bigot is forced to pay the same minimum wage to either the white or the black person, he has no economic incentive to act against his bigotry. Hence the black person will go unemployed.[32]

This prediction is borne out precisely by unemployment statistics for the United States, where blacks more frequently are targets of racial discrimination in hiring than whites. In 1948, before the minimum wage reached a level that was significantly higher than the market rate for unskilled labor, black and white unemployment rates for youths aged sixteen to seventeen were almost identical (9.4 percent and 10.2 percent, respectively). Indeed, black youths had a slightly lower unemployment rate than white youths, presumably because they were willing to work at slightly lower wages. Aside from a temporary rise in the ratio of black to white youth unemployment in 1949, this pattern continued until 1955.

But with the rise in the minimum wage in 1956, black unemployment in that age group rose to 1.4 times white unemployment. It rose fairly steadily from then until 1967, when another hike in minimum wage brought about a jump in the ratio of black sixteen- to seventeen-year-old unemployment to white from 1.8 to 2.26 times that of white. Since then black unemployment in that age group has rarely dipped below twice that of white unemployment in the same age group; in 1980 the figure for whites was 18.5 percent, while for blacks it was 37.7 percent.[33]

Although minimum wage laws have effects opposite those hoped for by legislators, they work exactly as those who lobbied for them hoped: "The source of pressure for them is demonstrated by the people who testify before Congress in favor of a higher minimum wage. They are not representatives of the poor people. They are mostly representatives of organized labor, of the AFL-CIO and other labor organizations. No member of their unions works for a wage anywhere close to the legal minimum. Despite all the rhetoric about helping the poor, they favor an even higher minimum wage as a way to protect the members of their unions from competition."[34] Organized labor favors high minimum wages because they make it uneconomical for employers to hire several low-skilled workers to do what one high-skilled—and highly paid—worker can do instead.

STANDARD PRICES:
EQUAL PAY FOR EQUAL WORK

There is a third kind of price control, one that sets neither a maximum nor a minimum price but, for want of a better name, a *standard price*. This price control is known as "equal pay for equal work" or, in a recent variant of the idea, "comparable worth."[35] Surely this concept is just, particularly in the sense of justice as "equal things for equals and unequal things for unequals in proportion to their relevant inequalities"?

Surprisingly—or perhaps not so surprisingly in light of the law of marginal utility—the answer is "No" again. Why? There are two fundamental reasons. First, requiring equal pay for equal work[36] violates the Biblical understanding of property rights by prohibiting the *free use* of property by its owners (employers using their money to buy services, employees using their labor to buy wages) so long as that use does no actual harm to another (Matthew 20:15; Acts 5:4).

Second, paradoxically,[37] mandating equal pay for equal work actually violates the principle of justice as equal things for equals and unequal things for unequals in proportion to their relevant inequalities. Why, when the pay is equal and the work is equal? Because neither the affected employers need be equal to each other, nor the affected employees equal to each other *in the sense of the marginal utilities that they attach to the job in question* (though of course they are morally equal before the law).

DIFFERING MARGINAL UTILITIES

Any two employees and any two employers may be, and often are, unequal in the most economically relevant sense of all: the marginal utility (subjective value) that they attach to the same job. One employer often values the same job (wage paid for service) differently from another at the same time, and one employee often values the same job (service paid for wage) differently from another at the same time. Not only that, but a single employer may value the same job differently at different times, and a single employee may value the same job differently at different times. Furthermore, the different values they attach need have nothing to do with fraud or exploitation; they may stem instead from objective differences in circumstances. How can this be? An example from my own life will help make this clear.

A year ago I was working half-time as editor of a small weekly newspaper at a generous wage (in comparison with wages for similar positions in this geographical area). I was also getting fairly steady work on independent contract editing, and my family had significant savings. At that time it would have taken quite a high wage offer to persuade me to take a new job.

Now things are different. Four months ago the newspaper was sold and the new owner took over my job. Since then my family has lived off of our savings plus rather meager independent contract income, while I have finished one book and nearly finished another. By the time I finish this book, our savings might be exhausted. With our third child due in a month, and all the costs of childbirth, it probably won't be long before we'll be scraping the bottom of the barrel.

Consequently, I now judge the marginal utility (subjective value) of any given wage for any given job much more highly than I did a year ago. In other words, a far lower wage will be sufficient to persuade me to take the job a month from now than would have been necessary a year ago. And it will not be because some nasty capitalist is exploiting me; it will be because my objective circumstances have changed, and with them the subjective value[38] I place on a given job.

Marginal utility—the value we place on *one more unit* of a given good—is the key to all of this. For all economic goods —including jobs—the degree of satisfaction we expect from each additional unit, and hence the economic value we place on it, diminishes as the number of units already possessed increases, and vice versa.[39]

This constant variability of economic value—for particular individuals and among different people—explains why mandating equal pay for equal work is in fact unjust. The same pay (say, $10 per hour) might not be equally valuable to the same individual at different times, or to different individuals at the same time.

VOLUNTARY PRIVATE POLICY

Private persons may of course adopt the policy of equal pay for equal work without government requirement. The Bible insists that anyone may do what he wishes with what is his own so long as he doesn't actually harm someone (Matthew 20:15). But even a voluntary, private policy of this sort may have unforeseen consequences for the needy that call the policy into question.

Suppose, for instance, that your company employs five drill press operators, each at $7.50 per hour. Now a well-qualified person applies for a job of the same classification. He badly needs the job, and you'd like to hire him because you do have a little more work than the five can handle without working overtime. But you can't quite afford him at $7.50 per hour because you don't have enough extra work to employ someone full-time, and he says he can't accept part-time. So, you reluctantly turn him down. Then he tells you he'd gladly accept the job at just $6.50 per hour in hopes of being raised to $7.50 later. At that rate, you figure you can afford to hire him.

But your equal pay for equal work policy stands in the way. Should it? Why should he be left without that income, and you without his production, simply because you've decided to pay everyone the same amount for the same work? Is that really justice? Or is it arbitrary policy? Might the unequal pay (equal pay for unequal amounts of the same work) to the laborers in Jesus' parable of the vineyard (Matthew 20:1-15) indicate that unequal pay for equal work can, under certain circumstances, be both just and economically beneficial? Wouldn't both he and you be better off if you hired him at $6.50 per hour and raised his pay when you were able to?

This is not to argue that employers should try to get workers as cheaply as possible. Out of concern for others' needs, they should pay as well as they can (Philippians 2:4). But the best they can pay is not always equal pay for equal work. Furthermore, even employers who don't have employees' best interests in mind are ill advised to be stingy with wages. In a competitive labor market, employees can be attracted to other jobs by higher wages. That turnover costs employers dearly in employee training that can be avoided only by paying employees well enough to keep them from leaving.

COMPARABLE WORTH

A variation on the equal pay for equal work law is the so-called "comparable worth" law. This would require equal pay for different jobs that are judged of "comparable worth" in the marketplace. The idea is fraught with internal inconsistencies.

First, if the jobs are truly of comparable worth in the judgment of freely competing employers and employees, the actual wages paid for them will be equally comparable.[40] Hence the law would be irrelevant unless it set a wage different from what the market would set, i.e., a wage contrary to the marginal utility judgments of buyers and sellers. Second, the law would require bureaucratic classification and valuation of jobs that almost certainly would vary considerably from the marketplace's own classification and valuation of them (and the difference between the two would grow over time). Third, the law would violate the Eighth Commandment's protection of free use of property so long as no one is harmed.

THE LITTLE GUY LOSES

And once more, who suffers most from equal pay for equal work and "comparable worth" laws? The *marginal* employees and employers—employees who most need the wages and employers who most need the services.[41]

If Fred, who already employs Mary to wait tables in his restaurant, must pay Sam the same wage for more of the same work, the marginal utility theory of value makes it likely that, under many circumstances, Fred won't hire Sam, because the value Fred will place on *more* of something will be less than what he placed on what he already has of it. As a result, Fred will be denied Sam's services (and so might Fred's customers, whose lunches won't be served faster after all), and Sam will be denied Fred's wages—that is, the law will have prevented the exchange.

But if Sam, who really needs a wage, is legally permitted to do the same work for a lower wage, and if Fred is legally permitted to pay him that wage, Sam will enjoy a wage and Fred (and his customers) will enjoy a service.

What does this mean in terms of stewardship—the allocation of God's resources in a world of scarcity? It means that equal pay and comparable worth laws are bad stewardship, because they must cause unemployment, i.e., misallocation (waste) of resources. Voluntary equal pay policies, while not strictly contrary to justice, still have negative effects on the needy in at least some instances. In light of these facts, the Biblical standard should be freedom for individuals to reach mutually satisfactory agreements with each other, and for others to withhold judgment in the humble recognition that they may not know all the facts of the situation.

ENVY AND EQUALITY
When the landowner in the parable of the laborers in the vineyard (Matthew 20:1-15) gave equal pay for unequal work (which is the same thing as unequal pay for equal work), those who were paid less protested, "These last men have worked only one hour, and you have made them equal to us who have borne the burden and the scorching heat of the day" (v. 12). Their complaint is equivalent to that of someone who says, "We both did the same job, but you paid him more. That's not fair!"

To the laborers the landowner—who in the parable represents God—replied, "Take what is yours and go your way, but I wish to give to this last man the same as to you. Is it not lawful for me to do what I wish with what is my own? *Or is your eye envious because I am generous?"* (vv. 14, 15). Despite protests to the contrary, fallen man's real motive in demanding equal pay for equal work, or "comparable pay for comparable worth," is envy, a violation of the Tenth Commandment. No doubt employers ought to pay all employees generously—and both smart ones and loving ones do. But the demand for equality is covetous.

JUSTICE AND PRICE FLEXIBILITY
The inherent inequalities among employers, employees, and circumstances (buyers, sellers, and needs) necessitate varying economic values of the same jobs. Therefore, justice demands price flexibility in all jobs (and all other goods).[42]

The degree of flexibility the market produces will depend largely on the competitiveness of the market for that job (or other good). The more prospective buyers and sellers there are for a given good, the more narrow will be the price range. The fewer competitors there are on both sides, the wider will be the price range.[43] But flexibility must be permitted in order for people's wants and needs to be served. Anything else is both unjust and uneconomical, because moral and physical reality are one.

THE VERDICT ON PRICE CONTROLS

Price controls, whether maximum, minimum, or "standard," violate the Biblical principle of liberty under God's Law. They violate the Eighth Commandment by removing control of property from owners. They are thus unjust by comparison with the ultimate standard of justice.

They also have bad consequences on the economy and hence on the physical welfare of those affected by them. The shortages and surpluses they cause are the necessary effect of the working of fundamental economic laws of marginal utility. Those laws can no more be denied than can the law of gravity.

Price controls are injustice and bad stewardship, and Christians have a responsibility to work through the political process to rescind them as part of our role as stewards of the resources God places at man's disposal for the fulfillment of the dominion mandate of Genesis 1 and 2 and for the service of our fellowmen.[44]

STEWARDSHIP, ACCESS CONTROLS, AND SUBSIDIES

*T*wo other prevalent types of economic regulation attempt to control access to various types of occupations and markets, on the one hand, and to transfer wealth from one segment of a population to another,[1] on the other hand. In this chapter we'll see how these two types of regulation stand up to the tests of Biblical justice and stewardship.

ACCESS CONTROLS

There are four major kinds of access controls: (1) occupational licensure, (2) trust and antitrust, (3) quotas, (4) zoning. Each of these kinds of laws is defended on the grounds that it protects people, whether from poor quality and perhaps even dangerous goods or services, from "unfair" competition, or from loss of property value due to the proximity of less valuable property. Do such laws meet the standards of justice and stewardship? We'll look closely only at licensure, but in principle the same kind of analysis applies to all four.

OCCUPATIONAL LICENSURE

Ostensibly to ensure quality and safety, many states require people to get licenses to provide certain kinds of services. In a state that requires licensure for a given occupation, no one can perform that service legally without the license.

How do such laws stand up to the test of justice? A person's capacity to work is part of his property. Any law that restricts his use of that property other than to prevent or punish actual violations of others' rights[2] is unjust because of the Eighth Commandment's prohibition against stealing (see also Matthew 20:15). Laws that prohibit people from injuring or killing each other unjustly, violating the sanctity of the family, stealing from each other, and defrauding each other—and exact retribution and restitution when they do—such laws, and only such laws, are proper restrictions on property use.

Do licensure laws meet this test? No one argues for licensure on the basis that it prevents outright murder, rape, theft, or fraud. Holding a license to perform a service does not render anyone immune to the temptation to sin. Instead, arguments for licensure typically rest on appeals to competency.[3] According to such arguments, requiring a license to practice a profession and requiring proof of competency for acquisition of the license minimize the entry of incompetent practitioners into the profession.[4] This, in turn, minimizes the risk of accidental injury to persons and property from incompetence or negligence.

This argument clearly applies more readily to some sorts of occupational licensure than to others. It's easy to see how requiring licensure of doctors, pharmacists, dentists, and lawyers, for instance, might be defended on this basis. These fields are complex and often have enormous implications for the life, health, and—in the case of lawyers—liberty of customers. But will the argument apply as readily to taxi drivers, psychologists, librarians, threshing machine operators, dealers in scrap tobacco, egg graders, guide dog trainers, pest controllers, yacht salesmen, tree surgeons, auctioneers, well diggers, tile layers, potato growers, professional boxers and wrestlers, piano tuners, and hypertrichologists (who remove excessive and unsightly hair)?[5] If someone can be trusted to drive safely when not being paid for driving, why can't he be trusted to drive safely when being paid? In which case, why require more than a driver's license for operating a taxi service?[6] While we can all decry the loss of time that might be occasioned by a librarian's misfiling or miscataloging a book, can we really argue that public health and safety are endangered by unlicensed librarians?

WHO PAYS? WHO BENEFITS?

One good sign of the legitimacy of arguments based on public health and safety is the historical background of the licensing legislation. Who proposes it?[7] While avoiding the genetic fallacy—judging truth or justice by origin rather than by objective correlation with reality and God's Law—it never hurts to ask, "*Cui bono?* For whose good?"[8] Does the call for licensure arise from public outcry against charlatans and incompetents? Almost never. Instead, those who suggest it almost invariably are already in the occupation.[9] Rarely is there any measurable improvement in health and safety effects in any given occupation from before to after the start of licensure, and even when there is it would be difficult to argue that the change arose from licensure rather than from advances in the tools and methods of the trade that would have effected the same improvement regardless.

Indeed, licensure often keeps incompetents in a trade by enabling them to attract business by display of a license rather than by recommendation of satisfied customers.[10] The very fact that they hold a license gives consumers the impression that they must be competent. If the profession weren't licensed, consumers would rely more heavily on recommendations from past customers. That method of evaluating the quality of products works quite well in ensuring that few cars are sold that blow up when you turn the key, or that fall apart after ten thousand miles. Why shouldn't it work equally well with most—if not all—of the occupations presently licensed?

Licensure also often protects members of a profession from effective liability suits by injured consumers. Frequently the only "experts" courts recognize for testimony in liability cases involving licensed occupations are other members of the licensed occupation. Often fellow members have strong influence over each other's access to lucrative markets. Concern about possible future loss of business therefore can keep some professionals from testifying against their peers, though they would be more willing to testify if that concern did not exist. [11]

TECHNICAL AND ECONOMIC EFFICIENCY

Finally, even if licensure did increase the quality of service by those practicing a particular occupation, it would not follow that it actually increased the average quality of service received by the public. It could instead *decrease* it. This point rests on the distinction between technical and economic efficiency.[12] Undoubtedly Magic Johnson shows tremendous technical efficiency as a basketball player. But it would be economically inefficient for the Podunk, Iowa, semi-pro basketball team to hire him. Better to hire Jim Johnson, owner of the hardware store. He might not dazzle the crowds, but he won't bankrupt the team either.

Suppose that the minimum qualifications for medical licensure were revised to the level of skill of the Surgeon General of the United States, and that he were an exceptionally skillful physician. No doubt it would be nice if all doctors were that skillful. No doubt it would be nice if all sick people could get care from such skillful doctors. But in reality few doctors are that skillful, or ever will be. If his skills were among the top 10 percent of doctors now practicing, revising qualifications to that level would put 90 percent of doctors out of business.

Obviously the medical care that was given after the revision would be, on the average, of much higher quality than that given before it. But just as obviously, the total amount of medical care given would fall drastically. And because supply would fall drastically relative to demand, price would rise drastically. Only the rich would get medical care; everyone else would go without. Thus at the same time that the average quality of medical care *given* would rise, the average quality of medical care *received* by all persons in the population would drop dramatically at the same time that its price rose dramatically.

But we *don't* set such a high standard for medical licensure. Okay, suppose the Surgeon General's skills were rated, on a scale of 0-100, at 90, and the licensure minimum were 50. Could anyone rationally argue that someone with skills rated at 49 could not treat a common cold as well as someone rated at 50? (Be careful how you answer if you've ever advised a friend to take some aspirin, eat chicken soup, run a humidifier, stay warm, and get some bed rest.) If a 49 could do it, why not a 48? A 30? Could a 45 treat a second-degree burn, or acne, or an ingrown toenail? Isn't it just possible that someone with an overall skill rating of 35 could treat one or two particular problems, in which he specialized, better than could someone with an overall rating of 75 who didn't specialize in those problems? Why should he be kept from treating them—or, more pertinently, why should sufferers of those problems be kept from benefiting from his specialized expertise?

SHORTAGES AND HIGH PRICES

The point is that licensure, because it diminishes the number of practitioners of any occupation from what it would be under free entry, automatically increases the price, since price must rise when supply falls relative to demand. When price rises, marginal buyers are pushed out of the market. Thus even if those who can still afford to get medical care (or any other licensed service) *might* get technically better service than they otherwise would,[13] those pushed out of the market get *no* service instead of poor service. It is difficult to see how that result benefits them or the public as a whole.[14]

This leads back to the earlier question: *Cui bono?* Clearly the only group that consistently benefits from occupational licensure is the licensed members of the occupation. They can charge higher prices because there isn't enough competition to force prices down. Everyone else necessarily loses: consumers pay higher prices, potential providers who can't afford to pay the licensing fee or receive the requisite training are kept out of the occupation, and people who can't afford the artificially high price must go without the service.

THE FAILURE OF LICENSURE

Occupational licensure, then, fails both tests of government regulation: it is unjust because it violates the Eighth Commandment's implied prohibition on controlling another's property beyond the point of preventing or punishing violations of rights, and it is bad stewardship because it diminishes the amount (and perhaps also the quality) of goods and services available to the public. Also, like price controls, it burdens the poor more than anyone else, for they are least able to absorb the higher costs necessitated by the diminished supply of the affected good or service.[15]

The fundamental problem with licensure is that it puts a prior restraint on trade. An alternate method of weeding out incompetents from trades would add a combination of registration and banning for cause to the possibility of civil liability suits for malpractice.

Under this arrangement, anyone could register to practice a trade, but incompetency or gross negligence proven in a civil liability suit could result in revocation of his registration and his being banned from the trade. Display of valid registration, then, would not imply endorsement of competency by the registering agency, as a license does. It would mean simply that the agency has not had cause to ban the holder from the trade. Someone who continued to practice despite revocation of registration could be held criminally, and not only civilly, liable for any injury he caused to another's life, liberty, or property.[16]

OTHER ACCESS CONTROLS

The other three kinds of access controls—trust and antitrust laws, quotas, and zoning—all are susceptible to similar criticisms on the basis of both Biblical justice (particularly property rights protected by the Eighth Commandment) and stewardship (economic efficiency).

TRUST AND ANTITRUST LAWS

Laws that create monopolies where none would naturally exist artificially limit the supply of goods and services and so raise prices. Laws that prohibit natural monopolies artificially force inefficiencies of resource allocation and so both raise prices and cause waste of factors of production.[17] Compulsory trade union laws not only violate Biblical liberty of property and association, but also prevent low-skilled workers from competing for jobs by offering to work for lower wages than high-skilled workers can command.[18] Service area restrictions—limiting providers to competing only within specific geographic boundaries—infringe on Biblical property rights, diminish supply relative to demand and so drive up prices, and cause inefficiencies of resource allocation.[19] Restrictions on advertising[20]—other than prohibitions of false and misleading advertising—violate Biblical property rights by prohibiting exchanges between potential advertisers and the media that would carry their messages, and drive up prices by reducing competition and consumer access to information about supply.[21]

QUOTAS AND TARIFFS

Quotas and tariffs on imports, if they have any effect at all, diminish the supply of goods relative to demand and so drive up prices.[22] This hurts consumers in two ways. First, and obviously, by reducing supply relative to demand, it means they must pay more for both imported and domestic goods of the kind controlled by the quota.

Second, it also means consumers must pay more for other goods not controlled by, but influenced by, the quotas and tariffs. For the only reason imports would outsell domestically produced goods if not limited by quotas and tariffs is that the imports could be produced and brought to market at a lower cost than the domestics. This means that foreign producers have a *comparative advantage*[23] in that field over domestic producers. By restricting imports, quotas and tariffs override the economic information generated by that comparative advantage. As a result, domestic producers focus more productive resources than they otherwise would on a field in which they are at a comparative disadvantage. This in turn means that domestic production of still *other* products, at which domestic producers would have a comparative advantage over foreign producers, is curtailed. That results in two forms of bad stewardship: higher prices for the other domestically produced goods than would prevail in a free market (one without quotas and tariffs), and misallocation of resources to inefficient activities.

Import quotas and tariffs typically are supported on the grounds that they protect domestic jobs, preventing unemployment. But their real effect is simply to shift employment from fields in which domestic producers would have a comparative advantage to those in which they have a comparative disadvantage. If imports drove some domestic producers out of business, the resources those producers would have used would be invested elsewhere, creating jobs to replace those lost. But this is not all. The Christian especially, who recognizes that God requires that we care for foreigners as truly as we do for citizens of our own nation, must see that domestic jobs can be protected only by taking away foreign jobs. Many who lose those foreign jobs will be low-income earners of Third World countries who may then be hard pressed to survive. How, in light of the Biblical standards of impartiality and concern for the poor, can we justify that?[24]

ZONING

Laws restricting the geographic placement of certain kinds of structures and enterprises frequently violate the Biblical principle of freedom of property use within the limits of neighbors' rights as defined in the Ten Commandments. The reduction in exchange value of one piece of property because of the erection of another nearby is no more a violation of Biblical property rights than the reduction in exchange value of one truck-load of oranges because someone else ships another truck-load into the same market. The Bible protects property itself from actual damage or destruction by another, not property's market exchange value.[25]

It could be argued that zoning laws do not violate property rights when they apply only to future changes of use. A law that permitted present nonconforming uses to continue so long as the property continued under the same owner might be seen as satisfying the Biblical principle of free use of property. However, even this limited restriction might violate property rights, for it prohibits future sale of property to anyone who might want to continue—or even initiate—a nonconforming use. It appears that such laws could meet the Biblical requirements only if *everyone* affected by them at the time of enactment approved of them and if *every* future buyer were adequately informed of the restrictions before completion of sale. Under these conditions the restrictions would be voluntarily self-imposed.

Zoning laws run afoul not only of the Biblical principle of justice, however, but also of concern for the needs of the poor. Economist Walter Williams points out that zoning laws, by requiring minimum residential or commercial lot sizes and minimum square footages for structures and by prohibiting multiple occupancy, effectively prohibit entry into zoned areas by low-income people (or low-income businesses). Without the zoning, several poor families might pool their resources to buy a single house or store space and split it into several residences or stores. With the zoning, they can't. Hence the zoning laws become a barrier to upward economic and social progress.[26]

Zoning, like licensure, trust and antitrust laws, and quotas and tariffs, reduces the supply of goods (in this case real properties) relative to the demand for them. It therefore necessarily increases the price of the remaining goods. That increase in price hurts the poor more than anyone else. Thus both in the simple sense of diminished total goods and services, and in the sense of adverse effects on the poor, zoning is bad stewardship.

THE VERDICT ON ACCESS CONTROLS

Access controls, like price controls, violate the Biblical principle of private property rights. They also create shortages, and hence artificially high prices, in the goods and services they affect. Hence they are both unjust in principle and bad stewardship in practice, particularly in that they put disproportionate burdens on low-income earners. Christians need to work through the political process to rescind these controls in order both to restore the liberty of property use protected by the Eighth Commandment and to pursue good stewardship (optimal allocation of scarce resources for the production, distribution, and consumption of goods and services) toward increasing our fulfillment of the dominion mandate of Genesis 1 and 2.

GOVERNMENT SUBSIDIES

In the United States, and in many other nations as well, a wide variety of economic activities are *subsidized* by the state: agriculture, manufacturing, education, medical care, and poverty.[27] Subsidies are defended on the ground that they protect jobs in the subsidized activities.[28]

Do subsidies stand up to the Biblical test of justice? Because the state cannot *produce* the wealth that it gives to the subsidized activities,[29] subsidies require taking something from someone by means of the taxing power of the state and giving it to someone else. As such they are not free exchanges but coerced. They are, in fact, a form of theft, a violation of the Eighth Commandment.[30]

What are the economic (stewardship) effects of subsidies? They are the same as those of minimum prices. They create *surpluses* of the economic activities and products subsidized. A subsidy of cotton farming, for instance, creates the impression of a greater consumer demand for cotton than in fact would exist at a market price. In response to that apparent demand, more cotton will be produced than can be sold at the market price. Just as we saw in our analysis of minimum dairy prices, the resulting surplus will have to be bought by the state, allowed to go to waste, or sold on the market at lower prices than are necessary to sustain production without losses. If the state buys the surplus, it must get the money to do so by taxing consumers (directly or indirectly through inflation). Allowing the surplus to go to waste adds new waste to the initial waste of the subsidy. And allowing the surplus to be sold at lower prices will drive some producers out of business unless subsidies not only continue but are increased.

Subsidies, in other words, not only are unjust but also add up to misallocation of resources, which is bad stewardship.

Rather than analyzing a wide variety of subsidies, let's look at just one type here: subsidies to the poor. If it can be shown that these subsidies fail the tests of Biblical justice and good steward-ship, it will be clear by implication that any other subsidies must as well, and for similar reasons.

SUBSIDIES TO THE POOR
A moment ago I said that there are such things as subsidies to pover-ty, and that poverty is an economic activity.[31] How can that be?

An economic activity is any that has to do with the alloca-tion of scarce resources to the production, distribution, and con-sumption of goods and services. Clearly poverty is such an activi-ty. The labor potential of the poor is a scarce resource that could contribute to production or distribution of goods and services, and the poor do consume goods and services. State transfers of wealth to the poor, therefore, are subsidies of poverty.

DEMAND ELICITS SUPPLY
This ought to indicate what will come of income transfers to the poor: they will cause a surplus of poor people—that is, more poor people than a free market without the income transfers would naturally produce. The subsidies will create the appearance of a

demand for poor people (people who depend on subsidies for subsistence rather than on the income they could earn through their
own productive labors). That appearance of demand will draw
people to supply it. If a poverty subsidy is available, more people
will choose poverty than would otherwise.

It may sound strange to think of people "choosing poverty."
On the surface that doesn't appear to be what they're doing, and
probably no one consciously chooses *poverty*.[32] Instead people
choose the necessary and sufficient conditions of poverty: lack of
work, lack of learning, lack of saving, and lack of personal responsibility. That is really what poverty subsidies subsidize: not poverty itself, but its necessary and sufficient conditions. The poor
receive subsidies because they are unemployed, don't have significant savings, and aren't supporting themselves.

CHOICES AND CONSEQUENCES

Choosing and attaining the conditions necessary to be non-poor
are not easy; they require self-sacrifice (hard work), study to gain
wisdom and skill, self-restraint (saving), and postponement of satisfaction (self-denial). Many people consider it easier and more
pleasant not to work than to work, not to save than to save, not to
learn than to learn, not to delay gratification than to delay it.[33]
One thing that helps people to choose the hard way instead of the
easy way is awareness of consequences. Unless there are clearly
visible costs to choosing the easier way, people will choose it.[34]
This is why, in the Book of Proverbs, God so frequently uses
warnings about future unpleasant consequences for the lazy and
foolish, and promises of future enjoyments for the hard-working
and wise, to motivate people to work: [35]

> I passed by the field of the sluggard, and by the
> vineyard of the man lacking sense; and behold, it
> was completely overgrown with thistles, its surface
> was covered with nettles, and its stone wall was
> broken down. When I saw, I reflected upon it; I
> looked, and received instruction. "A little sleep, a
> little slumber, a little folding of the hands to rest,"
> then your poverty will come as a robber, and your
> want like an armed man. (24:30-34; cf. 13:18; 21:5;
> 22:29; 24:3, 4, 27; 27:23-27; 28:19)

> The hand of the diligent will rule, but the slack hand
> will be put to forced labor. (12:24; cf. 12:11)

He who loves pleasure will become a poor man; he who loves wine and oil will not become rich. (21:17)

The desire of the sluggard puts him to death, for his hands refuse to work; all day long he is craving, while the righteous gives and does not hold back. (21:25, 26; cf. 19:15; 14:4, 23; 15:19; 20:4, 13; 23:17-21)[36]

AVOIDING A PAINFUL CHOICE?

Transfer payments to those who choose the conditions of poverty eliminate many of the most important costs associated with laziness, rejection of discipline, overspending, and irresponsibility. They appear to permit people to avoid the choice (based on marginal utility) between enjoying idleness, overspending, foolishness, and irresponsibility on the one hand, and enjoying the food, clothing, shelter, and other goods and services they would like on the other hand. They therefore significantly diminish the apparent (and real) costs of choosing the conditions of poverty, and in fact put positive economic incentives on those choices. In so doing, they offer people the illusion that they can get around the fundamental principle expressed in Proverbs 16:26: "A worker's appetite works for him, for his hunger urges him on." If someone's appetite will be sated regardless whether he works, it no longer "works for him" or "urges him on." Hence he more readily chooses the conditions of poverty than he would otherwise.

PREDICTION AND FULFILLMENT

All of these things could have been predicted by any decent economist when subsidies to the poor were first considered by legislatures—and they were, time and again. Does history bear out the predictions?

The evidence is overwhelming. Subsidies to the poor increase their numbers rather than decreasing them. Charles Murray, in *Losing Ground*, has documented thoroughly and incontestably the fact that in program after program of transfer payments to the poor, the more money spent on behalf of or given directly to the poor (either in cash or in free or reduced-price commodities or services), the more poor there have been to receive the subsidies.[37]

The number of poor people in America fell rapidly throughout the two decades before the "Great Society" programs of the Lyndon Johnson presidential era. During that time, government

expenditures on aid to the poor were extremely low in comparison with later standards. The number of the poor continued to fall
during the Johnson years, when government spending on the poor
began to rise. But spending didn't reach historically high levels
until *after* 1968. Then, when government expenditures began to
skyrocket, the drop in the number of the poor stopped—and
reversed itself. Since then, the more money that has been spent
on the poor, the more poor there have been.[38] Far from being the
cure to poverty, government subsidies have stopped and reversed
its cure.

The historical facts bear out in brutal reality the predictions
economists have made for years that governmental transfers of
wealth to the poor will increase, not decrease, the number and
proportion of poor among us. Poverty subsidies foster poverty, just
as dairy subsidies foster the production of dairy products. What is
amazing is that so many sensible people see so easily how the latter happens, but are bewildered at the reality of the former.[39]

ELIMINATE POVERTY SUBSIDIES

The same things are true of subsidies to the poor as of subsidies to
dairy farmers, automobile manufacturers, and professional athlet-
ic teams.[40] They violate the Eighth Commandment by forcibly
taking property from some people and giving it to others, and so
are unjust. And they cannot be justified on the grounds that they
are approved by a democratic process, or that their recipients are
poor, for justice neither is defined by popular vote nor permits
violations of the principle of impartiality toward rich and poor:

> You shall not follow a multitude in doing evil, nor
> shall you testify in a dispute so as to turn aside after a
> multitude in order to pervert justice; nor shall you be
> partial to a poor man in his dispute. (Exodus 23:2, 3)

Furthermore, far from helping the poor, subsidies invariably
hurt them. Because God's creation is consistent, ethical evil must
cause physical evil. That has been true of every regulatory violation of Biblical property rights surveyed before, and it is no different with subsidies to the poor. Despite subsidy proponents'
declared intention to help the poor, the subsidies, consistent with
their violation of Biblically defined justice, hurt them. The only
proper conclusion for the Christian who understands the ethical
principles and the economic and historical facts is to oppose government transfer payments to the poor, to seek to have them

abolished, *and then to learn and practice Biblically just and economically effective ways of helping the poor instead.*

Charles Murray, after showing that subsidies to the poor increase rather than diminish the incidence of poverty, stepped for a moment out of the cool, calculating role of the sociologist to pose a powerful dilemma for those who persist in favoring the subsidies anyway:

> Let us suppose that you, a parent, could know that tomorrow your own child would be made an orphan. You have a choice. You may put your child with an extremely poor family, so poor that your child will be badly clothed and will indeed sometimes be hungry. But you also know that the parents have worked hard all their lives, will make sure your child goes to school and studies, and will teach your child that independence is a primary value. Or you may put your child with a family with parents who have never worked, who will be incapable of overseeing your child's education—but who have plenty of food and good clothes, provided by others. If the choice about where one would put one's own child is as clear to you as it is to me, on what grounds does one justify support of a system that, indirectly but without doubt, makes the other choice for other children? The answer that "What we really want is a world where that choice is not forced upon us" is no answer. We have tried to have it that way. We failed. Everything we know about why we failed tells us that more of the same will not make the dilemma go away.[41]

We cannot have our cake and eat it too. We can continue to subsidize poverty, and so to perpetuate and increase it, along with all its harmful side effects like dependence, envy, and oppression; or we can stop subsidizing poverty and turn to Biblical responses instead, responses that can both deliver the poor from poverty and uphold the Biblical standard of justice. The final three chapters are devoted to the latter choice.

STEWARDSHIP AND POVERTY

THE NATURE AND CAUSES OF POVERTY

*F*red—cold, crippled, and nearly blind—hobbles along the
street in Los Angeles, desperately seeking charity from anyone who notices him. He cannot work. If he has relatives, he
doesn't know where they are, and if they even know where he is,
they do nothing for him. He has no income, and no prospect of
ever earning one. He is one of the people who have fallen through
the cracks in the vaunted American social welfare safety net.
Each day is his last, unless someone takes pity on him.

Steve, a robust twenty-five-year-old, sits before his televi-
sion set in public housing in Chicago on a Friday afternoon in
1979, wondering where he's going to go cruising that night.
Diana, his live-in, calls him to a lunch cooked on an electric
stove. The food, preserved anywhere from three days to six weeks
in a refrigerator and freezer, was bought with food stamps, and
there's enough still in the refrigerator and cupboards to last five
days before the next shopping trip. Diana's two children are at
school, where they've just eaten their federally paid for lunches.
Steve has tried to hold down a job a few times, but he just doesn't
seem to have the psychological makeup of a good worker.
Nonetheless he and his makeshift family have about $18,000 in
income that year in federal (and a few state) subsidies, and anything Steve and Diana earn with odd jobs is icing on the cake.[1]

Frank, forty-five and slim, hopes no one will recognize him
in the unemployment line in Pittsburgh. He's as ashamed to be
here as he was to be in the food stamps line yesterday, and to go
to the church-operated secondhand store last week. But somehow
he's got to make ends meet, despite having been permanently laid
off from the steel mill eighteen months ago. He sold the house a
year ago to get out from under mortgage payments, and now the

family's renting a duplex in a run-down part of town. Union leaders keep telling him to hang on, that new jobs will open up soon.
But how long can a man wait? And what can he do if he doesn't?
Any job he could get now would pay less than he's qualified for in
federal aid—and he'd lose part of that earned income in taxes, too.
Why, when he'd taken that night watchman's job at the mill a
few months ago, he'd lost more in benefits than the job had paid,
even before taxes! Climbing back into the car after the humiliat-
ing interview, he thinks for the hundredth time, "I guess you can
swallow a lot of pride to keep your family fed and clothed."

DEFINING POVERTY

In contemporary language, we call Fred, Steve, and Frank all poor.
But somehow we wonder whether that makes sense. The common dictionary definition of the poor as "lacking material possessions; having little or no means to support oneself; needy," and of
poverty as "indigence, lack of means of subsistence";[2] or the common encyclopedia definition of poverty as "an insufficiency of the
material necessities of life";[3] or the older dictionary definition of
poverty as "need or scarcity of means of subsistence; needy circumstances; indigence; penury"[4]—these traditional definitions
force us to conclude that Steve and Frank—and the millions like
them who comprise the average persons on federal subsidies to
the poor in the United States—are not poor, while Fred is.

But by modern sociologists' relative definition of poverty,
individual poverty in America might be defined as money income
of about two-thirds, and family poverty about one-third, the
national average.[5] And those with such "low" money income
might still be defined as poor even if they receive in-kind income
worth enough to make their aggregate income substantially higher than the national average.[6] Using this definition, Steve and
Frank and their families are poor.

POVERTY IS DESTITUTION

Which definition shall we use?[7] The traditional one seems, at
least at first glance, more sensible than the modern one. And it
is, for in its emphasis on the bare means of survival it is parallel
to a Biblical definition of the poor as ". . . persons who do not
have and are unable to obtain the means for sustaining life. If
they are to survive they are thus dependent upon the resources
of other people."[8] For the Bible, poverty—at least the sort that
makes someone the appropriate object of charitable giving
specifically because he is *poor*—has to do not with relative

incomes or possession of relative proportions of total wealth in a
society, but with bare survival.

There is a distinction in Scripture among three sorts of people. The rich, for whom the Greek word is *plousios*, need not
work to survive, or even to thrive, but can live entirely on the
earnings of their investments in others' labor.[9] A second sort consists of those who lack none of their daily necessities, but who do
not have sufficient wealth to hire others to do their work for
them. These people, the *penes*,[10] may be identified with those
today who must work for a living rather than living on the interest and dividends of savings and investment.[11] The third group
consists of people so destitute that they must depend on charity
for survival. They cannot sustain themselves, usually because
they are too old or young or handicapped to work.[12] These, for
whom the Greek word is *ptochos*, are the truly poor.[13] They alone,
in the New Testament, are objects of charitable giving simply
because they are poor.[14]

POVERTY IN HISTORY

Poverty is nothing new. Rooted in God's curse of the ground and
the consequent frustration of work subsequent to the fall (Genesis
3:17-19), it was the normal state of the vast majority of the
world's people in every part of the world throughout the history of
the human race, until the late eighteenth century in Europe and
North America. Then the Industrial Revolution, spurred by the
adoption of various new liberties in economic activity, substantially brought famine—the most horrible sort of poverty—to an
end for the Western world.[15]

For example, famine occurred in England prior to the
Industrial Revolution an average of seven times per century, lasting an average of ten years per century.[16] The rest of the world suffered about the same fate.[17] But as a result of the tremendous
changes in the economies of the West, no famine has struck a
country in the now-industrialized world since 1700 other than in
wartime, with two exceptions: the Irish Potato Famine of 1846-
1847 in which two to three million people died, brought on by a
widespread blight to the potato crop,[18] and several in Communist
lands where the political system has stifled productivity.[19]

In contrast, a third of the population (ten million) in the
Indian province of Bengal died in the great famine of 1769-1770,
and there were two more severe famines in India in 1783 and
1790-1792. Later India suffered eight famines in the sixty-three

years from 1838 to 1901, with estimated deaths of over 9.3 million, and a famine in Bengal took about 1.5 million lives in 1943. In a single famine in north China in 1877-1878, 9.5 million are estimated to have died, and China suffered severe famines again in 1887-1889 and 1916.[20]

What brought the West out of pandemic poverty? It was the adoption of the kinds of economic understandings discussed in Chapters Six and Seven of this book—working harder and working smarter.[21] Ultimately, if the rest of the world is to follow the West out of poverty, it must follow the West's example in these factors.

The key question then, when confronted by the disparity between rich and poor individuals and societies, is, "How did this man, or this society, become rich?" It is not, "How did this man, or this society, become poor?" Poverty is the natural condition of mankind, a condition from which some have risen from time to time, from which many have yet to rise, and into which any will fall back if they ignore, misunderstand, or fail to apply the causes of wealth.

WHAT CAUSES POVERTY?

R. C. Sproul distinguishes four causes of poverty: sloth, calamity (earthquake, war, etc.), exploitation, and personal sacrifice.[22] Scripture teaches that the slothful must suffer the consequences of their sin: "[I]f anyone will not work, neither let him eat" (2 Thessalonians 3:10). The poor by calamity are appropriate recipients of charity, though the aim is to help them become self-supporting again. The poor by exploitation need both charity to meet immediate needs and justice in the form of restitution from those who exploited them; the former is the work of private individuals and churches, the latter the work of the state.[23] The poor by personal sacrifice have, of course, chosen their lot and do not (or at least should not) ask for relief from others. [24]

These distinctions undermine the mistaken notion that God is somehow "on the side of the poor" simply because they are poor.[25] God is on the side of the righteous and just, against the unrighteous and unjust, regardless whether they are poor, middle-class, or wealthy (Exodus 23:2, 3, 6).

Types of poverty can also be divided into two chief categories: self-caused and imposed. In this case, Sproul's categories of sloth and personal sacrifice would be included under self-caused poverty, while calamity and exploitation would be included under imposed poverty.

SELF-CAUSED POVERTY

Carl F. H. Henry points out that material and spiritual poverty are closely related: "For one thing, moral poverty often dooms its victims to ongoing material poverty. . . ."[26] Scripture reveals four primary roots of self-caused poverty: laziness (Proverbs 10:4; 19:15, 24; 20:13; 21:17, 25, 26; 22:13; 24:30-34; 26:13; 6:6-11), greed (Jeremiah 6:12, 13), foolishness (Hosea 4:6; Psalm 106:13-15; Proverbs 11:14; 10:14-16; 13:18), and shortsightedness (Proverbs 21:5; Matthew 7:24-27; Luke 14:28-30). Each of these is a symptom of rebellion against the Law of God, which sets forth a pattern of life that is both naturally fruitful and supernaturally blessed by God (Deuteronomy 8:11-20; 11:18-32; 28:1-68; 30:1-20).

> All combined, these sayings could be summed up in the axiom, "A poor man has poor ways." While the truths of these verses may be unsettling and unwelcome, the cause of self-induced poverty always leaves open the possibility for change. Movement toward prosperity can begin the moment the cause of poverty is weakened. Before poor people in the negligent, foolish category can really overcome their poverty, they must first overcome the causes of their poverty.[27]

IMPOSED POVERTY

There are two chief sorts of imposed poverty, oppression and religious error. Oppression consists in violating others' God-given rights, whether to life (the Sixth Commandment), to family integrity (Fifth and Sixth Commandments), to property and liberty (Eighth Commandment), or to truthful relations (Ninth Commandment). It takes the forms of fraud, theft, and violence. Anything that prohibits people from enjoying freely the fruits of their labors, or that prohibits their exchanging them freely with others for mutual benefit, is oppression, whether perpetrated by individuals or governments.[28]

TWO SOURCES OF OPPRESSION

On the one hand, oppression may be practiced primarily by individuals, usually the wealthy oppressing the poor. Sometimes the wicked mock the poor (Proverbs 17:5), or the greedy hates his neighbor (Proverbs 14:20, 21) and oppresses him for money (Proverbs 22:16). Always oppression involves violating clear provisions of God's Law. The prophet Amos, for instance, sees oppression as a pattern of violation of the Law (Amos 2:4): selling the righteous into slavery (2:6; 8:6), oppressive lending conditions to the poor (2:8), unbridled pursuit of wealth (4:1), cheating in weighing money and products (8:1), and passing off poor quality goods as high quality (8:5f).[29]

On the other hand, oppression often is the act of civil rulers who refuse to defend the rights of the poor in courts of justice (Job 24:1-12; Isaiah 1:21, 23) or violate them themselves: "Like a roaring lion and a rushing bear is a wicked ruler over a poor people. A leader who is a great oppressor lacks understanding, but he who hates unjust gain will prolong his days" (Proverbs 28:15, 16).

Usually oppression is domestic. A people's own rulers are more likely to oppress them economically than people from other countries. Historically, in fact, it appears to be the exception rather than the rule that oppression in one society is imposed on it by another. Much more frequently it is the work of unjust rulers who transgress their subjects' God-given rights, sometimes through outright extortion, often through confiscatory tax rates, strict controls on all economic activity, and insistence on building impressive cities, monuments, and industrial complexes with foreign aid and domestic revenues rather than channeling that capital into enterprises more useful to the domestic population.[30] The instances in which Third World poverty might have been caused by oppression by the West are rare. Instead, Third World nations and regions tend to prosper in direct ratio to the extent of their economic interactions, past and present, with the industrialized West. Even colonization, on the whole, has contributed more to economic development than to underdevelopment.[31]

Leaders may cause poverty not only by their own direct injustice, but also by the judgment God brings on a whole people because of their sin (2 Samuel 21:1). Nonetheless the defense and ultimate delivery of the oppressed from their oppressors is in the hands of God (Isaiah 3:14, 15; Ezekiel 22:12-14; Amos 5:11, 12; Jeremiah 5:26-29). He may bring a foreign nation to crush the wicked rulers, or raise up new rulers from within (Psalm 94).

RELIGIOUS ERROR

A second major source of imposed poverty is a society's fidelity to a religious view of world and life that is inconsistent with the revelation of God in Scripture. Like oppression, this has both direct and indirect results. Religious error's direct result is the adoption of economically and culturally harmful patterns of thought and action. Its indirect result is the judgment of God.

God promises prosperity and blessing to societies that abide by His Law (Exodus 23:24-26; Deuteronomy 28:1-14; 30:19, 20). But He warns of misery and judgment on those who reject it (Deuteronomy 11:26-28; 28:15-68; 2 Chronicles 24:20; Isaiah 65:11-14). The prosperity and blessing, on the one hand, and the misery and judgment, on the other, are not solely caused by God's response to our actions. They are also the natural, cause-and-effect results of behavior consistent or inconsistent with the moral and physical laws God has woven into the fabric of creation. The Biblical worldview, by recognizing these laws and teaching people to operate consistently with them, underlies the prosperity of the West.[32] Un-Biblical worldviews, seeing reality as disjointed, the gods as capricious, and power and wealth as achievable through luck or magic or karma rather than through hard and wise labor and cooperation, underlie the poverty of the Third World.[33]

Christian missionary E. Stanley Jones, who spent much of his life in India, attributed that nation's economic difficulties to its religious culture:

> In the mind of the Mohammedan there is gripping him in the inmost place the thought of Kismet— everything is predestined by the sovereign will of Allah. When he gets under difficulties the tendency is to tap his forehead and say: "What can I do? My Kismet is bad." It is more or less fatalistic. On the other hand the Hindu has lying back in his mind the thought of Karma—that we are in the grip of the results of the deeds of the previous birth. When the Hindu runs against difficult situations he usually says: "What can I do? [M]y Karma is bad." It too is more or less fatalistic and consequently paralysing.[34]

For Hinduism and Buddhism the material world is not real; it is mere *maya*, illusion. Man's greatest virtue is denial of the illusion, abandonment of the material. Thus the truly orthodox Hindu or Buddhist who not only professes but also lives his faith cannot be a productive member of society.[35] Similarly, animists and spiritists think the world controlled by spirits whose joy often is to trick or surprise them.[36] Such a worldview cannot be conducive to economic productivity. Planning becomes impossible.

Superstition, not wise labor, rules. Sprites and fairies, not cause and effect, make the world go 'round.

This is why, when asked why he didn't just give the starving Indian people bread instead of preaching the gospel to them, Jones replied: "India does need bread and needs it desperately. . . . [But] I believe that the best way to give India bread is to give her Christ."[37] Culture—not raw materials, not population density, not even the structure of government[38]—is the most powerful influence on economic productivity. And religion is the most powerful influence on culture.[39]

Detailed study of the correlations between religious preference and per capita income in most of the nations of the world indicates that, in general, the poorest nations are those least Christian and most spiritist, animist, Buddhist, Confucianist, and Hindu—the worldviews most radically inconsistent with Christianity. Of those few highly Christian but quite poor, most are recently Christianized. Of those wealthy but generally non-Christian, most are primarily Islamic, the religious worldview closest to Christianity (aside from Judaism, which is the majority only in Israel); and wealth in those countries is generally of recent origin, coming from oil, and very unevenly distributed. In general, the most productive, and therefore the wealthiest, nations tend to be Christian and primarily Protestant.[40]

This doesn't mean that Christians may sit smugly in warm houses and say to the poor, "Ha, ha! You brought it on yourselves!" No, God has made us ambassadors to reconcile to Him alienated sinners presently under His curse (2 Corinthians 5:9-20).[41] That ministry includes both preaching the gospel to reconcile sinners with God, and teaching converts the Biblical world-and life-view, with all its moral and practical principles, so that they can be reconciled also with the reality God has created (Matthew 28:19; 2 Corinthians 10:5). It also includes ministering to immediate and long-term needs through charitable giving and life-changing teaching (James 1:27; Ephesians 4:28; 2 Thessalonians 3:6-15). The next two chapters will explore how churches, families, and individuals can help the poor through both charity and Biblical evangelism and discipleship.

FIFTEEN

HOW CHURCHES CAN HELP THE POOR

*R*ecent chapters have implied that helping the poor through charity is not civil government's job.[1] Now let's answer a common objection to that idea and look at specific ways churches and (in Chapter Sixteen) families and individuals can help the poor and why they can be more effective than government.

The chief objection to the idea that civil government should not be involved in poor relief is that the problem is too enormous to be tackled by any other entity.[2] But this is not true, for two reasons. First, when measured by Biblical rather than relative notions of poverty and of the proper levels of support through charity, the problem, though vast, is not so enormous as many people think. Second, church and private resources are considerably larger than many people think, particularly considered in comparison with the real size of the problem.

HOW BIG IS THE PROBLEM?

Deciding, in Chapter Fourteen, whether to use the Biblical or the relative definition of poverty to determine recipients of charitable giving was not a matter of merely academic interest. In part, it was a matter of fidelity to Scripture, which defines only the destitute as truly poor and eligible for systematic charitable support. In part, too, it was a matter of great practical consequence. It made a tremendous difference in estimating the magnitude of the problem. Similarly, hard statistical study related to poverty in America is not just academic exercise; it, too, renders information essential to determining the real extent of the problem and the resources necessary to address it.[3]

How Many Poor Are There in America?

Despite the hundreds of billions of dollars spent in recent years in America's "war on poverty,"[4] official poverty estimates, based on relative rather than absolute (Biblical) definitions of poverty, continue to run around 13 to 15 percent of the population, or thirty-one to thirty-six million people assuming current population of 240 million.[5] But the proportion of our population that is truly destitute—fitting the Biblical definition of poverty—is much smaller, certainly not over a tenth of those presently defined as poverty-stricken.

A rough estimate may be made in terms of the number of homeless persons in America. Homelessness is a good measure of poverty because people tend to forego housing before they forego food and clothing, the real essentials of survival.

While some advocates cite figures of two to three million homeless nationwide, or about 1 percent of the American population, Anna Kondratas, administrator of the Food and Nutrition Service at the federal Department of Agriculture, says, "The idea of 2 to 3 million homeless is totally preposterous. There is absolutely no data, no study, no report that would indicate anything of that magnitude." Instead, the advocates' figures are based more on guesses that "are often inflated by including such groups as 'hidden homeless' who cannot be located or 'borderline homeless' who are doubled up with relatives," reports journalist Carolyn Lochhead. She adds, "Richard Freeman, a Harvard economist with the National Bureau of Economic Research, in 1986 estimated the national homeless population to have been about 279,000 in 1983. . . . By 1985, he estimated, the population had grown as high as 363,000. 'While our figures are to be viewed as rough orders of magnitude only,' Freeman wrote, 'it is important to recognize that they are strongly inconsistent with the claim that 1 percent of Americans are homeless.'"[6]

Part of the problem with exaggerating the numbers of the homeless and other poor is that the seemingly astronomical figures can discourage private individuals, families, churches, and voluntary associations, making them think the problem is simply too big for them to respond to effectively. But approaching the problem with a Biblical definition of poverty in mind and sticking with hard statistical information rather than guesses can give us a whole new picture in which we see that the problem is much smaller than it first appeared. In fact, we can even compromise with the exaggerations and still find the problem readily manageable.

Assume for a moment that the true number of the homeless in America is roughly halfway between the high figure cited by advocates (three million) and the high figure cited by statisticians (363,000), or 1.68 million. Then double that figure to account for those who might be truly destitute but not homeless (a gratuitous assumption since most people give up housing before food and clothing). The result is a rough estimate of 3.36 million poor people in America, only about 10.8 to 9.3 percent of the number of poor defined by the official poverty rate of 13 to 15 percent of the population.

This makes quite a difference in the extent of the burden facing those who hope to help the poor. If the poverty rate in America were only about 1.4 percent (3.36 million) based on the Biblical definition of poverty as true destitution, instead of the 13 to 15 percent based on the relative definition, then there would be about 9.8 poor people for each of America's roughly 344,000 churches[7] to care for instead of 91 to 105. This is something probably all but the smallest churches could do, and many larger churches could care for many more. Churches alone, with no help from civil government at any level, could provide for all of these poor with little difficulty. (Of course this means that if we limited our estimate of the real poverty rate in America to the number of homeless [about 363,000] estimated by hard studies instead of guesses, the rate would be only about .15 percent of the population instead of 1.4 percent. There would then be not 9.8 poor persons for every church, but 1.05.)

Another way of looking at churches' ability to meet the needs of the poor is to compare total church membership with the number of poor people. In 1985 there were roughly 142 million church members in the United States.[8] If the Biblically defined poverty rate at the time was 1.4 percent of a population of 240 million (3.36 million), then there were about 42.3 church members to every poor person in America. The number of poor persons in the U.S., then, was about 2.37 percent of the number of church members. Assuming that church members' disposable (after taxes) per capita annual income was equal to the nation's average,[9] or about $11,820,[10] this means total disposable income of about $499,986 was available from which donations could be made to support one poor person. Even if the goal were to provide federally defined "poverty level" income—$5,469 per year per person[11]—not just what was necessary for subsistence, and to provide *all* of that income, not just the shortfall after the person's earned income, only about 1.1 percent of the $499,986 available would need to be given to each poor person. This means that barely a tenth of church members' tithes on disposable income would have been more than sufficient to take care of the poor in America. (Again, if the real poverty estimate were the 363,000 verifiably homeless, we would conclude that only about .12 percent of churchgoers' disposable incomes, or just over one one-hundredth of their tithes, would have been more than sufficient.)

Now, for the sake of argument, let's accept the federally defined poverty level and the 13 to 15 percent poverty rate. Do churches still have the resources needed to care for the nation's poor?

Consider the year 1985 again.[12] In that year there were about 7.2 million poor families in the United States, based on the federal poverty definition.[13] The aggregate shortfall of their total *money income* below poverty level was about $55.4 billion, or an average of about $7,692 per family[14] (about half the total actually spent on direct poverty relief by civil governments that year).[15]

At the same time there were about 35.5 million families in churches in the United States—five church families for every poor family.[16] To raise the $55.4 billion needed to bring all the poor families up to the poverty level, each church family would have to have contributed about $1,560. Median family disposable (after-tax) income in 1985 was about $29,600,[17] and in the Bible the general (and probably minimum) standard of giving to the church is the tithe, 10 percent of income.[18] Assuming that church families were average in income,[19] a tithe on disposable income would have been about $2,960 per family, almost twice (1.9 times) the amount needed to raise all of the poor to the poverty level.[20]

In fact, slightly under 5.3 percent of church families' after-tax incomes in 1985 would have been sufficient to have brought all of the governmentally defined poor up to the governmentally defined poverty level. That would have left slightly over 4.7 percent of church families' after-tax incomes—or 47 percent of their tithes—for other uses by their churches, *if* churchgoers had tithed. Taking care of the poor in America—even the poor defined by government standards—would, then, require roughly half of church families' tithes.[21]

Indeed, if all church families had tithed in 1985, giving churches total donation income of $105.08 billion, and if $55.4 billion of that had been given to the poor, churches would have been left with about $49.68 billion in their coffers—nearly four times their actual donation income for that year.[22]

By either definition, then—whether the Biblical definition of poverty as actual destitution, or the modern relative definition of poverty as earnings below a pre-defined percentage of the national average—the actual number of the poor in America and the extent of their need are such that Christian individuals and churches can meet the needs with their own resources, without turning to civil government for help.

THE STANDARD OF CONTENTMENT

Another way of viewing the Biblical criterion of whether someone is eligible for systematic charitable aid[23]—rather than in need of opportunities to work to improve his economic welfare—and the extent of the aid for which he is eligible, is to consider the Apostle Paul's teaching about the church's charitable giving and contentment in 1 Timothy 5 and 6.

WHO IS ELIGIBLE FOR SUPPORT?

Addressing economic difficulties in the congregation over which Timothy was pastor, Paul explains that the church is to "Honor widows who are widows indeed" (1 Timothy 5:3)—that is, who are truly without any other means of support. If a widow has able children or grandchildren, she must depend on them for provision, not on the church (v. 4).[24] Only if a widow "has been left alone" and "has fixed her hope on God, and continues in entreaties and prayers night and day" (v. 5) is she eligible to be cared for by the church. In other words, she must be in desperate straits.

Even then, she is only eligible for the church's charity if she is frugal (v. 6), lest the fellowship be reproached for supporting someone in prodigality (v. 7). She must be at least sixty years old, "having been the wife of one man, having a reputation for good works; and if she has brought up children, if she has shown hospitality to strangers, if she has washed the saints' feet, if she has assisted those in distress, and if she has devoted herself to every good work" (vv. 9, 10). She must, in short, serve her fellow believers in every way she can if she is to be supported. Younger widows are to "get married, bear children, keep house, and give the enemy no occasion for reproach" (v. 14; cf. vv. 11-15). They are not to be supported by the church (v. 11), presumably unless they are physically disabled.[25] Paul is determined that the church should not be burdened with supporting those for whom other support is available (v. 16).

Next Paul explains that "elders who rule well" are "worthy of double honor, especially those who work hard at preaching and teaching. For the Scripture says, 'You shall not muzzle the ox while he is threshing,' and 'The laborer is worthy of his wages'" (vv. 17, 18; cf. Deuteronomy 25:4; Leviticus 19:13; Deuteronomy 24:15; Matthew 10:10; Luke 10:7). In other words, those who labor diligently for the church are eligible for its financial support. Then, after warning against entertaining accusations against elders too quickly, but also against elevating anyone too quickly to the office (vv. 19-25), Paul instructs slaves to respect their masters and serve them heartily, especially if their masters are believers (6:1, 2). Apparently, then, slaves were not to appeal to the church for financial support or liberation merely because of their slavery.

In sum, Paul considers eligible for systematic financial support by the church only those who (1) have been left alone, unable to care for themselves and depending solely on God (5:5), or (2) are rendering service to the church, whether preaching and teaching (5:17, 18), or providing personal services like cooking or housecleaning to members (5:10). "If anyone advocates a different doctrine," he adds, "and does not agree with sound words, those of our Lord Jesus Christ, and with the doctrine conforming to godliness, he is conceited and understands nothing; but he has a morbid interest in controversial questions and disputes about words, out of which arise envy, strife, abusive language, evil suspicions, and constant friction between men of depraved mind and deprived of the truth, who suppose that godliness is a means of gain" (6:3-5).[26] Connection with the church must be seen not as a means of financial gain, but as an opportunity for service.

HOW MUCH SUPPORT IS NEEDED?

Finally, he concludes, "But godliness actually is a means of great gain, when accompanied by contentment. For we have brought nothing into the world, so we cannot take anything out of it either. *And if we have food and covering, with these we shall be content.* But those who want to get rich fall into temptation and a snare and many foolish and harmful desires which plunge men into ruin and destruction. For the love of money is a root of all sorts of evil, and some by longing for it have wandered away from the faith, and pierced themselves with many a pang" (6:6-10).

The standard of contentment is "food and covering." Adequate nourishment plus clothing and shelter adequate to protect us from the elements are sufficient to make any godly person content.[27] Whoever can obtain these through his own labor, or has family members able and willing to provide them, is ineligible for financial aid from churches. Only those who neither can obtain these things themselves nor have relatives to provide them have a claim on the church's charitable giving. And basic survival and health—not some predetermined level of wealth relative to the surrounding society—are the goal of the church's charitable help to the poor. Arguing that people have a right to anything more merely stirs up envy, strife, argument, evil suspicions, and interpersonal friction (1 Timothy 6:4, 5), encouraging people to chase harmful desires and be plunged into ruin and destruction (v. 9).

The standards of churches' charitable giving, then, are three: (1) It should go only to those who cannot support themselves and cannot be supported by their families. (2) Its aim is to provide food and covering sufficient for basic survival and health.[28] (3) Recipients must serve the church in return for charity insofar as they are able.

CHURCHES CAN MEET THE NEED

The problem of poverty and the resources needed for relieving it are, then, considerably smaller than many people think. Churches and their members undoubtedly have all the economic resources needed. Whether we have the will is another question. God warns that failure to give to meet the needs of the poor is sin, and that He will hear the cry of the neglected poor (Deuteronomy 15:7-11).

HOW CHURCHES CAN HELP THE POOR

What are some actual steps churches can take to help the poor? How can they best use their resources to lift the poor out of poverty and help them to bear their own burdens (Galatians 6:5) afterward? Let's look at the answers to these questions in terms of three major categories of work: (1) evangelism and discipleship, (2) charitable giving, (3) political action.

EVANGELISM AND DISCIPLESHIP

Frequently the root causes of poverty, for individuals and families as well as for whole societies, are an un-Biblical world- and life-view and the behavior patterns it engenders.[29] The crying need of such people is for their whole way of thinking and living to be changed from the ground up. That can come only with their adoption of Christian faith and their consequent regeneration. "Salvation, in this world and the next, is not found in economics. Regeneration is the only foundation for social stability and growth."[30]

Christian churches must see evangelism and discipleship as the most important steps toward helping the poor. But evangelism cannot stand alone. New converts must be trained to think and act consistently with Scripture in every aspect of life. Quiet, private piety that makes no difference in outward behavior and society is not the goal of the Christian life. Our goal is obedience to all that Christ commands in Scripture (Matthew 28:20). Every aspect of life needs to be brought under His Lordship (2 Corinthians 10:5).[31]

Many people object to evangelism as "pie in the sky by-and-by" when theologically conservative Christians insist that it take a higher priority than giving charitably to the poor. No wonder! Typically our evangelism has been truncated, divorced from the true discipleship that must follow if we are to obey the Great Commission (Matthew 28:18-20). As a result we have seen "conversions" that made no difference in how people lived. But if thorough Biblical discipleship were to follow upon evangelism—discipleship that includes teaching people Biblical principles and practices of justice, economics, personal financial management, work, saving, staying out of debt, and caring for one's family—then we would see wholesale changes in converts' thinking and behavior that would do more than anything else could to lift them, and keep them, out of poverty.

Particularly, churches need to make personal and family financial counseling a part of their regular ministry. If no qualified financial counselor already is a member of a congregation, the congregation should assist a deacon in getting the training he needs to become qualified.[32] Then, both as part of his normal ministry to members and as part of his ministry to the poor who come for help, he should teach people about hard work, budgeting, saving, comparative shopping, tithing, staying out of debt, and contentment.

One other important part of churches' discipling ministry must be helping people to understand that they cannot prosper over the long haul, either materially or spiritually, by accepting handouts, particularly if the handouts are taken coercively from some by government and given to others. Proponents of an equalitarian notion of "social justice" have worked hard to create the impression that people have a right to basic sustenance provided by others regardless of their own productive activities.[33] The Bible condemns such thinking (2 Thessalonians 3:10). When people accept charity without rendering service in return, to whatever extent they are able, they choose a life of dependency that will impede their spiritual and economic growth. They need to be taught that it is a part of basic Christian maturity to be as self-supporting as possible, and that they share in government's violation of the Eighth Commandment when they accept government subsidies—whether to the poor or to the rich.[34]

CHARITABLE GIVING

The ways churches can give charitably to help the poor are almost unlimited. Every local situation offers different possibilities from every other, and careful study of local areas is necessary to match methods with needs.[35] However, the methods chosen need to be consistent with some fundamental Biblical principles.

GLEANING

One important charitable measure of Old Testament Law was gleaning:

> Now when you reap the harvest of your land, you shall not reap to the very corners of your field, neither shall you gather the gleanings of your harvest. Nor shall you glean your vineyard, nor shall you gather the fallen fruit of your vineyard; you shall leave them for the needy and for the stranger. I am the Lord your God. (Leviticus 19:9, 10; cf. 23:22)

> When you reap your harvest in your field and have forgotten a sheaf in the field, you shall not go back to get it; it shall be for the alien, for the orphan, and for the widow, in order that the Lord your God may bless you in all the work of your hands. When you beat your olive tree, you shall not go over the boughs again; it shall be for the alien, for the orphan, and for the widow. When you gather the grapes of your vineyard, you shall not go over it again; it shall be for the alien, for the orphan, and for the widow. And you shall remember that you were a slave in the land of Egypt; therefore I am commanding you to do this thing. (Deuteronomy 24:19-22)

In *Bringing in the Sheaves*, his outstanding book on how churches and individuals can minister to the poor, George Grant describes three principles of giving that these laws, in light of their application in Ruth, teach. First, ". . . recipients of Biblical charity must be diligent workers, unless entirely disabled (Ruth 2:2-7)."[36] Because gleaners had to look for and harvest only what was left behind by the main harvesters, their work was difficult.[37] Second, ". . . Biblical charity is privately dispensed by the landowners, not by an overarching state institution (Ruth 2:4-16)."[38] Third, ". . . Biblical charity is discriminatory (Ruth 2:7). Biblical charity knows nothing of promiscuous handouts to sluggards."[39] Landowners were responsible for permitting or prohibiting prospective gleaners in their fields, orchards, and vineyards; if they knew someone to be a drunken sluggard, for instance, they did not have to let him glean in their fields. Biblical Law required them to welcome gleaners; it did not require them to welcome everyone who wanted to glean (Ruth 2:1-7).

In addition, Biblical Law placed a limit on what gleaners were supposed to take: "When you enter your neighbor's vineyard, then you may eat grapes until you are fully satisfied, but you shall not put any in your basket. When you enter your neighbor's standing grain, then you may pluck the heads with your hand, but you shall not wield a sickle in your neighbor's standing grain" (Deuteronomy 23:24, 25). Gleaners were not to harvest a surplus above their own immediate needs that they might sell at profit; that would be theft. This agrees with the principle in 1 Timothy 5 and 6 that the aim of charitable giving should be to meet people's needs for basic survival and health, but nothing more.

Is gleaning a viable method of charity today? Yes, says John Naisbitt:

> Americans, especially senior citizens, are helping themselves by salvaging the vast food resources usually wasted in production and harvesting (about 20% of all food produced, according to the United States Agriculture Department). Gleaners groups in Arizona, California, Michigan, Oregon, and Washington State go into the fields and find food passed over by the harvest, then distribute it in community groups. St. Mary's Food Bank in Phoenix, Arizona, which collects cast-aside and gleaned food, sent two million pounds of food to schools and social service groups and fed 48,000 emergency victims for three days during 1979. Now St. Mary's helps other groups all across the country to learn the self-help approach to cutting waste and feeding the poor.[40]

One thing that hampers the effectiveness of gleaning in modern America is the concentration of many poor people in large cities. This happens primarily because many government poverty programs aim specifically at the urban poor, which means that for people to receive their aid they must be or become urbanites. If the government programs were abolished, the concentrations of the poor in cities would diminish.

Even in cities, however, a form of gleaning is possible. Supermarkets and restaurants daily throw away tons of food that has outlived its "shelf life" but is still nutritious and safe.[41] In many cities, churches and private relief agencies have enlisted the cooperation of stores and restaurants. They collect the unsalable food and distribute it to the poor. Not only food but also clothing and many other items are available to watchful gleaners, including manufacturers' seconds that never get from factory to retailer.[42]

Churches have available, in the form of members' tithes, sufficient financial resources to handle the problem of poverty in the United States, with a great deal left over (if members will tithe). To those can be added the resources available by gleaning, and they are enormous. According to one experienced organizer of community gleaning efforts, "If even one-fourth of the edible food disposed of each day in the United States could be saved, hunger would be, for all intents and purposes, conquered. Unfortunately, charities haven't yet learned how to utilize the resources around them. More often than not, they'll go looking for some kind of federal grant instead of just checking in with the guy down the street."[43]

THE THIRD-YEAR TITHE

A second important Old Testament charitable provision for the poor was the third-year tithe: "At the end of every third year you shall bring out all the tithe of your produce in that year, and shall deposit it in your town. And the Levite, because he has no portion or inheritance among you, and the alien, the orphan and the widow who are in your town, shall come and eat and be satisfied, in order that the Lord your God may bless you in all the work of your hand which you do" (Deuteronomy 14:28, 29; cf. 25:12-15).[44]

Like gleaning, the third-year tithe was locally controlled. While no explicit requirement of work accompanied it, the town elders, who administered the fund, could distinguish local "deadbeats" from those who were unable to support themselves. While the New Testament does not mention the specific idea of a third-year tithe, it does include examples of regular, systematic giving to the congregation to meet the needs of the poor (Acts 4:35; 1 Corinthians 16:2; 2 Corinthians 8—9; 1 Timothy 5—6). And interestingly, roughly a third of the tithe of all American churchgoers' income would be sufficient to meet the needs of all the nation's poor, even using the government's relative definition of poverty. If the poverty rate were really only about a tenth of the government's estimate, then only a thirtieth of members' tithes would be necessary, and if the goal were food and covering adequate to life and health rather than income equal to a certain percentage of national average, the amount needed would be even less.[45]

TEACH A MAN TO FISH

The old saying goes, "Give a man a fish and you feed him for a day. Teach him to fish and you feed him for a lifetime." The goal of Biblical charity to all but the totally disabled is to teach them to support themselves and, later, their families and others. Discipleship should work a transformation as radical as that in which someone who once stole begins to work instead so that he can have something to give to others (Ephesians 4:28).

Churches can take effective steps to help the poor learn to help themselves. Beyond the fundamental points of discipleship, they can help them acquire specific job skills by matching low-skilled people with more highly skilled church members willing to teach them. They can operate job placement services for their charity recipients, teach them interviewing skills, and introduce them to prospective employers.

Sadly, however, the minimum wage law currently stands in the way of many low-skilled workers getting their first jobs. Their skills simply aren't worth the minimum wage plus all the additional costs their employers incur in hiring them (worker's compensation payments, unemployment compensation, employer's share of Social Security tax, plus added capital investments needed to employ new personnel).[46] As a result, many low-skilled workers simply cannot be profitably employed. Hence they never learn the skills they need to gain higher paying jobs. At the same time, many people—especially heads of households—would find living on minimum wage extremely difficult even if they could get it.

Churches could change much of this. They could cooperate with local businesses to make low-skilled workers employable in either of two ways. First, for someone whose skills were not worth the minimum wage, a church could agree to pay a business, for a limited time, to hire the worker anyway. During the set time, the worker could gain the skills to render his employer an adequate return for his wage and other costs. Second, for someone whose skills were already worth the minimum wage, who couldn't support his family on it and could find no work at a higher wage, churches could agree to supplement the worker's minimum wage with charity sufficient to meet his family's basic needs until he was able to find a higher paying job. Third, churches could conduct their own job training programs in which people could be apprenticed to church members to learn a trade, and then helped to find their own jobs.[47] In either case, the charity is consistent with the Biblical principle that those able to work must do so (2 Thessalonians 3:10), even in return for charitable aid (1 Timothy 5:3-6:10).[48]

The great challenge for churches in dealing with the poor is not so much finding enough money. That is available, if members will comply with the Biblical standard of the tithe—or even at current levels of giving, if poverty and the goals of caring for the poor are defined Biblically. The challenge is for churches to practice charity without repeating government's mistakes. Handouts create dependency. Biblical charity creates responsibility. Applying the principles and methods of gleaning, tithing, and discipleship can "create self-sufficient, productive workers."[49]

POLITICAL ACTION

While civil government is not the proper vehicle of charitable aid to the poor,[50] there are things it can do to help them, and churches can influence it to do those things.

The most important thing government can do is to fulfill its role as a minister of justice, protecting people's rights to life, liberty, property, family integrity, and truthful relations. If it will do this, and allow people to act freely in cooperation with each other within the limits of God's Law, it will have gone a long way toward removing many barriers to the poor's rising out of poverty.

Government can also rescind many regulations that hurt the poor. None of these criticisms of employment regulations implies that it is ethically acceptable for employers to be stingy with wages or to discriminate on such grounds as ethnicity or sex when such distinctions are economically irrelevant. The Biblical definition of justice as rendering *impartially* to each his due in conformity to the right standard of God's Law condemns such bias. Nevertheless, the way to end such bias appears not to be by government regulation, which inevitably results in violations of other rights and in destructive disruptions of the economy that hurt low income earners more than anyone else, but by ethical instruction by the church and other institutions.

Some regulations, for instance, diminish opportunities for the poor to help themselves. Minimum wage laws,[51] occupational licensure laws—especially for such common-skill occupations as taxi services—and restrictive trade laws (e.g., regulated taxi and truck routes) frequently keep the poor from entering employment to support themselves.[52]

Legally enforced union pay scales and equal pay for equal work laws have the same effect as minimum wage laws, impeding the acquisition of new skills by poor workers and so slowing or completely stopping their economic advance.[53] Tight immigration restrictions make it difficult for the foreign poor to come to America to enjoy the greater liberty and opportunity available here.[54]

Other regulations raise the cost of living for the poor. Inflation rapidly eats away at their money's purchasing power, causing a loss that low income earners can least afford to suffer.[55] Import quotas and tariffs, domestic commodity price supports (including legally enforceable union pay scales), and occupational access impediments (high licensure costs and restrictions on service areas)—all forms of trade restriction—artificially raise prices of many goods and services.[56] Those high prices hurt the poor far more than they do the middle-class and the rich. Rent control laws cause housing shortages, the burden of which falls mainly on the poor, whether renters or landlords.[57] Similarly, zoning laws that require large residential or commercial lots, minimum square footages, and other expensive factors reduce opportunities for the poor to rise by small increments from dilapidated, inner-city housing or business property to much better suburban locations.[58]

If government ceased both kinds of regulations—those that impede upward mobility for the poor and those that raise costs of living—we would see simultaneous rapid increases in the skills and earnings of the poor and rapid declines in the costs of living. Those changes would help the poor more than anyone else in society, and would help them more than anything else society can do.

Church leaders and members need to grasp these economic facts and to recognize that they are consistent with the Biblical standard of justice.[59] Then we need to work to influence legislators accordingly. But if we want to be taken seriously, we must first make sure our own poverty relief programs are in place. Otherwise our calls for elimination of governmental programs and regulations ostensibly designed (however mistakenly) to help the poor will be seen as self-serving and callous.

Churches, then, can take powerful steps to help the poor. They can combine evangelism with whole-life discipleship that includes application of Biblical principles of stewardship and economics, helping believers to live new and more productive lives spiritually and materially. They can practice charitable giving consistent with the principles of gleaning, the third-year tithe, and the standard of contentment (1 Timothy 5—6). And they can influence political leaders to diminish governmental intrusion in the economy that harms the poor.

SIXTEEN

HOW INDIVIDUALS AND FAMILIES CAN HELP THE POOR

*W*hat can private individuals and families do to help the poor? More than anyone else in society! All the wealth in society, other than the raw, undeveloped wealth of nature, comes from the actions of private people working individually and cooperatively. There is no wealth to share unless they produce it through their diligent and wise efforts. Churches can't give to the poor if members don't earn and contribute money. Governments can't enforce justice unless private people earn money so they can pay taxes.

How can we turn some of our great energy and productive capacity toward helping the poor directly? Let's look at basic principles and motives first, then at specific actions.

PRINCIPLES FOR PRIVATE ACTION
Our actions as stewards of God's gifts in service to the poor need to be rooted in four principles: justice, charity, contentment, and devotion to God.

First, justice—rendering impartially to each his due in accord with the right standard of God's Law—teaches respect for the rights of the poor. Scripture clearly prohibits cheating the poor, something that is tempting because they are vulnerable targets, and warns that God will punish those who oppress them (Exodus 22:21-24; 23:9; Leviticus 19:33-37). "Cursed is he who distorts the justice due an alien, orphan, and widow" (Deuteronomy 27:19; cf. Proverbs 14:31; 22:22f; 23:10f; 29:7; 31:8f). Justice forbids profiting from the misfortunes of the poor by charging them interest on charitable loans (Exodus 22:25-27;

Leviticus 25:35-38). Whoever shows partiality to the rich over the poor has done a grave injustice, particularly culpable in the congregation of believers (James 2:1-9).

Second, God commands His people to be charitable to the poor, promising blessing on those who are, but threatening His judgment on those who are not:

> If there is a poor man with you, one of your brothers, in any of your towns in your land which the Lord your God is giving you, you shall not harden your heart, nor close your hand from your poor brother; but you shall freely open your hand to him, and shall generously lend him sufficient for his need in whatever he lacks. . . . You shall generously give to him, and your heart shall not be grieved when you give to him, because for this thing the Lord your God will bless you in all your work and in all your undertakings. For the poor will never cease to be in the land; therefore I command you, saying, "You shall freely open your hand to your brother, to your needy and poor in your land." (Deuteronomy 15:7, 8, 10, 11; cf. Proverbs 22:9; Luke 12:33f; 14:12-14)

> He who shuts his ear to the cry of the poor will also cry himself and not be answered. (Proverbs 21:13)

Real love always produces service to those in need (1 John 3:16-18; cf. James 1:27; 2:14-17). The love of Christ naturally evokes in His disciples an overflowing generosity in imitation of Him who for our sakes became poor, that we through Him might be made rich (2 Corinthians 8–9).

Third, God instructs believers to be content regardless of circumstances. They are not to succumb to envy and covetousness (Exodus 20:17), but are to imitate Paul, who wrote, ". . . I have learned to be content in whatever circumstances I am. I know how to get along with humble means, and I also know how to live in prosperity; in any and every circumstance I have learned the secret of being filled and going hungry, both of having abundance and suffering need. I can do all things through Him who strengthens me" (Philippians 4:11-13). With King Agur we should be willing to pray, "Keep deception and lies far from me, give me neither poverty nor riches; feed me with the food that is my portion, lest I be full and deny Thee and say, 'Who is the Lord?' or lest I be in want and steal, and profane the name of my God" (Proverbs 30:8, 9). So long as we have food and covering adequate to survival and health, we are to be content (1 Timothy 6:8).

Fourth, Christians are to love and serve God above all other things, including riches: ". . . seek first His kingdom and His righteousness; and all these things shall be added to you," Jesus said (Matthew 6:33). "[T]he love of money," Paul warns, "is a root of all sorts of evil . . ." (1 Timothy 6:10). When God does bless His people with riches—something He often does in response to their obedience to the whole of His Law (Deuteronomy 28:1-14)—they must resist the temptation to credit their prosperity to themselves:

> When you have eaten and are satisfied, you shall bless the Lord your God for the good land which He has given you. Beware lest you forget the Lord your God by not keeping His commandments and His ordinances and His statutes which I am commanding you today; lest, when you have eaten and are satisfied, and have built good houses and lived in them, and when your herds and your flocks multiply, and your silver and gold multiply, and all that you have multiplies, then your heart becomes proud, and you forget the Lord your God who brought you out from the land of Egypt, out of the house of slavery. . . . And it shall come about if you ever forget the Lord your God, and go after other gods and serve them and worship them, I testify against you today that you shall surely perish. (Deuteronomy 8:10-14, 19)

RIGHT MOTIVES FOR GIVING

What are proper Biblical motives for giving to the poor? Some say the main motive should be justice—that the poor have a right to charitable gifts, and that people violate their right by not giving.[1] In one sense this is true: Biblical Law commands charitable giving to the poor, and those who refuse to do it are violating God's command.

But in another sense it is false. It is false insofar as it implies that any human institution should enforce the right of the poor to charity by forcibly taking from some to give to others. Nowhere in Scripture is enforcement of God's command to give to the poor committed to any human institution.[2] It, like the Tenth

Commandment's prohibition of coveting, has to do with attitudes of the heart into which no human agency can pierce. Just as there is no civil penalty for coveting in Scripture, so there is no civil penalty for stinginess—though there are warnings of divine judgment for both. God commits to civil and ecclesiastical government jurisdiction to punish violations of outward actions; He reserves to Himself all judgment of sins of the heart. Charity can no more be forced by state or church than can contentment, and laws that attempt to force it, because they transgress the jurisdictional boundaries God has ordained for government, invariably violate other rights (particularly the right to property secured in the Eighth Commandment).

The more powerful Biblical motives of charitable giving are love, joy, and grace, all expressing gratitude for God's prior blessing. After instructing Israel to provide liberally for the poor, Moses summed up the motive of all charity when he told Israel, "And you shall remember that you were a slave in the land of Egypt, and the Lord your God redeemed you; therefore I command you this today" (Deuteronomy 15:15). When Zaccheus excitedly decided not only to pay restitution to whomever he had defrauded, but also to give half what he owned to the poor, he expressed gratitude for the love Jesus had shown him (Luke 19:8).

The Christians in Macedonia gave sacrificially to poor believers in Jerusalem out of grace (2 Corinthians 8:1) and joy (v. 2). Paul urged the Corinthians, too, to give as a matter of grace (v. 7) and love (v. 8), following the gracious example of Christ (v. 9). Their giving was to be not reluctant (9:6, 7), but generous, bountiful, and cheerful (vv. 5-7) in response to God's gracious provision for them (v. 8). For He had indeed already scattered His seed abroad, giving to them so that their seed in turn might multiply, so that they in turn might be "enriched in everything for all liberality . . . producing thanksgiving to God" (vv. 9-11)—that is, so that they might give liberally to the poor in Jerusalem.[3]

Generous giving to those in need is a "proof of . . . love" (2 Corinthians 8:24) and of genuine confession of the gospel (2 Corinthians 9:13). Love and giving go hand in hand: "We know love by this, that He laid down His life for us; and we ought to lay down our lives for the brethren. But whoever has the world's goods, and beholds his brother in need and closes his heart against him, how does the love of God abide in him? Little children, let us not love with word or with tongue, but in deed and truth" (1 John 3:16-18). Indeed, charity is even a proof of faith: "What use is it, my brethren, if a man says he has faith, but he has no works? Can that faith save him? If a brother or sister is without clothing and in need of daily food, and one of you says to them, 'Go in peace, be warmed and be filled,' and yet you do not give them what is necessary for their body, what use is that? Even so faith, if it has no works, is dead, being by itself" (James 2:14-17).

Charitable giving, then, should be motivated by gracious, joyful love in obedience to God, expressing gratitude for His great gift of salvation.[4]

PRIVA'. E HELP FOR THE POOR

Poverty relief begins at home. The first and probably the most important thing anyone can do to help the poor is to make sure he and his family aren't poor. Only someone with a surplus over his own basic survival needs can give enough to help others out of poverty. Gaining sufficient wealth to give abundantly to the needy requires working harder, longer, and smarter than we otherwise might,[5] and living frugally and avoiding debts except in emergencies (Proverbs 22:7; Leviticus 25). It means foregoing present pleasures and saving and investing for the sake of future gain and security (Proverbs 6:6-11).

Paul insists that whoever refuses to work should not even be allowed to eat (2 Thessalonians 3:10). Anyone who refuses to support his own family has denied the faith (1 Timothy 5:8)—and Paul had in mind by "family" not just husband and wife and children, but the extended family. Brothers, uncles, cousins, indeed any blood relatives should consider it their duty to look after each other (Leviticus 25:47-49).

HELP BY INVESTING

Investing is one of the best means of helping the poor. It automatically incorporates three of the principles of gleaning identified in Chapter Fifteen: recipients of charity should be hard workers, charity should be privately dispensed, and charitable givers should distinguish between worthy and unworthy recipients. Investments benefit those who work for companies they fund, and wise investors distinguish carefully between good and bad stewards of their capital.

The parable of the talents illustrates the importance of investment (Matthew 25:14-30). Without the capital entrusted to them by the master, none of the three servants could have produced much. But with his capital, two were able to multiply the investment; as a result they were entrusted with greater responsibilities. The fruitfulness of labor is closely related to the amount of capital available for its use in the form of resources, buildings, tools, and other mechanisms.[6] One man working with a mule and plow cannot hope to produce as much wheat as another working with tractor, combine, irrigation equipment, and chemical pesticides. But those tools, like tools in any other trade, cost money. That is why investment is so essential to increased productivity, higher wages, and decreased product prices—all of which help the poor.

Christians who want to help the poor should, therefore, consider investment one way of doing it. They need to ask three questions about each investment opportunity:

(1) Will it be profitable? If it loses money instead of gaining, the investor will soon have nothing left to invest. Profit is not, in and of itself, a sign of greed; it is a sign of effective service to consumers. This doesn't mean the Christian will always choose the *most profitable* investment. He might, for various reasons, choose less profitable investments.[7] But it does mean that he will invest in enterprises that prove by profitability that they are serving people.[8]

(2) Will it create needed goods and services? In particular, will it create goods and services needed by the poor? It might be more profitable to invest in a luxury health spa or a retail store that specializes in selling fur coats to movie stars than in a supermarket or discount department store chain, but the benefits of the latter will accrue far more to the poor.

(3) Will it enable employers to employ more people? Particularly, will it enable employers to employ more poor people, who usually are low-skilled workers? One effective way for Christians to help the poor in underdeveloped countries is to invest in companies that do business in those countries, either directly employing workers there or buying their products and so indirectly employing the workers who produce them.[9]

Now let's look at three more ways private persons can help the poor: evangelism and discipleship, political action, and charity.

HELP BY EVANGELISM AND DISCIPLESHIP

Individuals and families can help the poor by sharing the gospel with them and teaching converts to understand and live by Biblical values. Preaching the gospel to the poor is one of the primary activities in the Messianic Kingdom (Luke 4:18). The gospel and Biblical values impart to people a new understanding of all of life.

Just as churches' discipleship needs to include teaching converts about Biblical principles of stewardship and economics, so does personal discipling. An effective disciplemaker will learn what new knowledge and habits young believers need in order to become more productive and self-supporting. He might teach his charge how to make and live with a budget, balance a checkbook, do comparison shopping to keep food and clothing costs down, or even read. Some people need to learn to be content so that they don't always overspend to satisfy their covetousness or greed.

Many poor people have never been taught the habits necessary to get and hold jobs. The disciplemaker might need to teach someone how to find a job, how to dress for work, how to be sure to get there on time. He might volunteer to give his friend a wake-up call or even to drive him to work to be sure he won't be late.

The most effective teaching will always be by example. When the Christian disciplemaker exemplifies a life of hard work, personal responsibility, contentment, thrift, and generous charity, those he disciples will follow in his footsteps. The Apostle Paul was himself a model of personal discipline, hard work, and responsibility:

> For you yourselves know how you ought to follow our example, because we did not act in an undisciplined manner among you, nor did we eat anyone's bread without paying for it,[10] but with labor and hardship we kept working night and day so that we might not be a burden to any of you; not because we do not have the right to this, but in order to offer ourselves as a model for you, that you might follow our example. For even when we were with you, we used to give you this order: if anyone will not work, neither let him eat. For we hear that some among you are leading an undisciplined life, doing no work at all, but acting like busybodies. Now such persons we command and exhort in the Lord Jesus Christ to work in quiet fashion and eat their own bread. (2 Thessalonians 3:7-12)

HELP BY POLITICAL ACTION

Just as churches need to influence legislatures to end government regulations that hamper economic productivity and hurt the poor, so do individuals and families. Christians need to learn the Biblical principles of limited government and economics and then urge their political representatives—not only in Congress but also in state legislatures, county boards of commissioners, and city councils—to govern in accord with them. When we find books or articles that express Biblical positions on public policy issues, we can send copies of them to representatives.

We can learn about proposed legislation and compare it with Biblical standards of justice and stewardship, then let legislators know, by phone calls and letters, how we think they should vote on it. We can decide on the basis of past voting records whether to vote to reelect past representatives or try to replace them. And many more Christians need to seek political office, beginning at local levels. Once in those offices, they need to apply Biblical justice and stewardship to every decision about proposed legislation or regulation.

HELP BY CHARITABLE GIVING

The third way private persons and families can help the poor is charity. In part they can do this by complying with the Biblical standard of tithing,[11] a third of which churches might dedicate to the poor.[12] They can also serve as deacons or on church poor relief committees, give individual gifts and no-interest loans to the poor, help facilitate gleaning efforts, and take the homeless into their own homes.

Charity does not always mean giving something for nothing. Individuals' charitable giving, just like churches', needs to be governed by the four principles connected with gleaning: (1) if they are able, recipients should work in return for aid; (2) giving should be privately controlled and as direct as possible so that givers can know well the needs of recipients; (3) givers should distinguish worthy from unworthy recipients (2 Thessalonians 3:10); (4) the main goal of charitable gifts should be to meet basic survival and health needs.[13] Private givers need to be as careful as churches not to foster dependency or pander to sloth or prodigality in recipients. At the same time, they need to be ready to give generously where needs are real and recipients are willing to do all they can to comply with Biblical patterns for living.

The early Christians took their responsibility to care for poor fellow believers so seriously that they were even willing to sell houses and lands to do it (Acts 4:32-37).[14] Though no one would have excused taking another's property without permission by appealing to the needs of the poor,[15] still believers considered their property entrusted to them by God for the good of the whole Body of Christ (Acts 2:44-46). Their great generosity contributed to the credibility of the gospel so that preaching was fruitful (Acts 2:47), confirming Christ's prediction, "By this all men will know that you are My disciples, if you have love for one another" (John 13:35).

What can you do, individually or with your family, to help?

SERVICE IN THE CHURCH

You can serve as a deacon or on your church's poverty relief committee.[16] In that capacity, you can help your church do demographic studies of your community to identify how many poor people are around you, where they are, what their needs are, what kinds of job opportunities there are, and what other resources are available in the community to help the poor.[17] Or you might help start and operate a church food pantry, job placement and training service, or gleaning ministry.

Many churches already operate food pantries from which they can dispense emergency food to the poor. Any church could do it and, following the example of the towns in Israel that were instructed to keep a special fund to care for orphans and widows (Deuteronomy 14:29), probably should. But it's hard work. Someone needs to monitor the stock and ensure that packages with appropriate assortments of foods are available at all times. One good way to do this, without requiring heavy investment of administrative time, is to prepare a menu for a balanced diet sufficient for a family of four for several days, give copies of the menu to church members, and ask them to fill one or two bags periodically with the complete menu.[18] Churches can also collect similar stocks of clothing and basic household utensils, dishes, and supplies. Whether stocking food or other items, though, much of the needed supplies can be found by gleaning, and one individual can do a lot to help his church locate and obtain discarded items.[19]

Some churches operate job placement and even training services. You might volunteer to clip the help wanted ads from the local newspaper every week and post them on a church bulletin board. Or you might help locate jobs for specific unemployed people in your church or community, actually contacting prospective employers and helping to set up interviews.[20]

SERVICE OUTSIDE THE CHURCH

Christians don't have to wait until churches develop poor relief programs. Individuals and families can help the poor on their own initiative.

Give Someone a Job

One way is to help finance the start of a small family business for an unemployed person in your church or community by extending a loan.[21] Trash collection using a pickup truck, door-to-door sales, janitorial services, gardening, and many other kinds of family businesses can start with very small capital investments. They're ideal for teaching budgeting, thrift, hard work, planning, and saving to every member of a family old enough to assist.

Don't fool yourself, though, into thinking all the family will need from you is money for the initial tools. At least during the first few months they probably will need your careful supervision. That will take time. But it will also bear some wonderful benefits. The family will learn diligence from your example. You'll help to ensure the success of the business, which means ensuring that your investment won't be wasted and the family will be provided for in years to come. And in the process, you and that family can build a lasting friendship based on mutual respect and cooperation.[22]

If you don't have enough capital to help start a family business, you can still give someone at least temporary work around your own home. Like most families, you're bound to have odd jobs that you've put off for months because you haven't had time for them. Or maybe you want a tool shed built in the back yard, or a garden plot spaded in the spring. And when the jobs at your house run out, call your friends and encourage them to use your new friend's services, too.

What if someone refuses to work? The Bible is clear: you may urge him to change, but you must not give him a handout. Paul's instruction, ". . . if anyone will not work, neither let him eat" was not a suggestion but an "order" (2 Thessalonians 3:10). Because men bear God's image, they are workers by nature.[23] The fall obscured that image and brought laziness—along with other things—into the world. God's curse on the earth was one way of ensuring that man would work despite his sin (Genesis 3:17-19). Thus when a "worker's appetite works for him, for his hunger urges him on" (Proverbs 16:26), it urges him to work. To give to the sluggard, requiring nothing in return, is to subvert human nature. It is to tell him not only that he need not work to survive, but also that he need not work to be spiritually fulfilled.

Give Outright Gifts

This doesn't mean we ought never to give without requiring something in exchange.[24] Those destitute and unable to support themselves need direct gifts, no strings attached.

Jesus told the rich young man to give to the poor (Matthew 19:21; cf. Mark 10:11; Luke 18:22). He told believers to invite the poor to banquets with the explicit understanding that "they do not have the means to repay" (Luke 14:13, 14), and illustrated that by telling the parable of the dinner to which the host had his servants bring "the poor and crippled and blind and lame," depicting God's gift of salvation by pure grace (Luke 14:15-24). He commended Zaccheus for his decision to give half his possessions to the poor, saying that that was a sign of his salvation (Luke 19:8, 9). Apparently the disciples were accustomed to Jesus' instructing them to give to the poor, for they thought He sent Judas on such an errand (John 13:29). And the huge, international collection Paul administered was for the destitute in Jerusalem (Romans 15:26).

In each instance, the recipients of outright gifts, from whom nothing was expected in exchange, were the *ptochos*, the truly destitute who could not provide for themselves.[25] Just as Jesus called Zaccheus' generous giving to the poor a sign of salvation, He also counted stingy withholding of gifts from the poor a sign of damnation, a point He made in the story of Lazarus (the poor man) and the rich man (Luke 16:19-31). And in the chilling parable of the sheep and the goats, Jesus explicitly taught that, after the final judgment, those who have fed the hungry, given drink to the thirsty, sheltered homeless strangers, clothed the naked, or visited the sick and the imprisoned will inherit the Kingdom, but those who have neglected the needy will be cast away into eternal punishment (Matthew 25:31-46).

Every Christian, then, needs to be willing and ready at every opportunity (Galatians 6:10) to do good to everyone, including giving outright gifts to the poor. Indeed, believers need not only to give when opportunity stumbles upon us, but also to *make* opportunities to give. We are not to wait until the "poor and crippled and blind and lame" come knocking at our doors. We are to "Go out at once into the streets and lanes of the city" and bring them in (Luke 14:21). That means going out of our way to find the poor who cannot help themselves, and helping them. It means taking the homeless into our own homes, clothing the naked with our clothes, feeding the hungry at our tables, giving drink to the thirsty from our cups. It means making them part of our families just as, when we were spiritually poor and crippled and blind and lame, God adopted us as His children (Romans 8:15).

METHODOLOGICAL NOTE ON THE USE OF BIBLICAL LAW

*I*n Romans 2:15 Paul writes that Gentiles who lack the inscripturated Law of God have "the work of the Law written in their hearts." For centuries Christians have believed that even those who do not have the Bible know innately the rights and wrongs implicit in God's moral character. However obscured and twisted this knowledge might be by original sin, cultural customs, personal habits, or familial tradition, it remains. Through moral training under the tutelage of Scripture, in which God's moral character is perfectly and clearly revealed, the law in the heart can be made clear and straight.[1] This underlies the general (though sometimes not particular) agreement on moral issues among the world's major religions.[2] It is why sinners convicted by the Holy Spirit readily recognize the righteousness of God's moral standards in Scripture and desire to repent and be converted.

Moses told the Israelites, "See, I have taught you statutes and judgments just as the Lord my God commanded me, that you should do thus in the land where you are entering to possess it. So keep and do them, for that is your wisdom and your understanding in the sight of the peoples who will hear all these statutes and say, 'Surely this great nation is a wise and understanding people'" (Deuteronomy 4:5, 6). At the very least Moses was asserting that the moral (including civil but excluding ceremonial) Law revealed in the Ten Commandments and throughout the rest of Exodus, Leviticus, Numbers, and Deuteronomy was so perfectly suited to the needs of fallen human beings made in the image of God that even those outside the Covenant would recognize and admire its wise moral instruction. All men today remain fallen human beings made in God's image and have the same needs for moral instruction. Therefore the moral Law of the Bible remains perfectly suited to their needs for moral instruction.

This approach purposely does not attempt to answer the question whether all men have the same juristic, or legal, obligation before God to obey the moral Law that the Jews had prior to Christ. Instead it simply asserts that conformity to that Law remains the way of wisdom (Psalm 119; 111). Just as many things are not legally required but we still recognize them as wise and prudent, so regardless of whether we are legally obligated to obey God's moral Law today, it still is the perfect revelation of the wisest patterns of life for fallen bearers of the image of God, and so may be applied helpfully to concrete situations today. It may even, on that basis, be used as a model for civil legislation adopted through the political processes of a given State.[3]

In this book I often cite Biblical Law to support my arguments. Because some Christians who call themselves Reconstructionists[4] and are committed to what they call "theonomy" do the same, and because their system of thought has become controversial in evangelical circles, I thought it best to explain here why I do so even though I am neither part of that movement nor convinced that theonomy is right.[5] Theonomy, according to its chief expositor, is the doctrine "that the Christian is obligated to keep the whole law of God as a pattern of sanctification and that this law is to be enforced by the civil magistrate where and how the stipulations of God so designate."[6]

Unlike theonomy, my use of Biblical Law presupposes simply that the same moral Law that was perfectly suited to mankind's need for moral instruction four thousand years ago is perfectly suited to mankind's need for moral instruction today. It imparts wise, important, and clear instruction for the economic activities of individuals, families, churches, societies, States, and the whole human race.[7] Of course, the Law is *not* the way of salvation; its role in salvation is to reveal to fallen people their sin so that they will seek salvation by faith in God's gracious atonement in Christ Jesus, who for our sake became poor that we through Him might become rich (2 Corinthians 8:9).

BIBLIOGRAPHY ON
A CHRISTIAN PHILOSOPHY
OF CIVIL GOVERNMENT

*F*our good introductory analyses of the nature and functions of civil government, from a Christian perspective, are:

Calvin, John, *Institutes of the Christian Religion*, ed. John T. McNeill, trans. Ford Lewis Battles (Philadelphia: Westminster, 1977), Book IV, Chapter xx; Vol. 2, pp. 1485-1521.

DeMar, Gary, and Doner, Colonel, eds., *The Christian World View of Government* (Mountain View, CA: The Coalition on Revival, 1986). Available from The Coalition on Revival, 89 Pioneer Way, Mountain View, CA 94041.

Kuyper, Abraham, *Christianity as a Life-System: The Witness of a World-View* (Memphis, TN: Christian Studies Center, 1980). This is an abridgment of the Stone Lectures given by Kuyper at Princeton Theological Seminary in October, 1898. They have recently been reprinted by Eerdmans.

Rose, Tom, and Metcalf, Robert, *The Coming Victory* (Memphis: Christian Studies Center, 1980).

Following are some good general studies of the nature and functions of civil government, particularly from an American perspective. An asterisk (*) after an entry indicates that the authors approach the subject from an avowedly Christian position.

Breen, T. H., *The Character of the Good Ruler: Puritan Political Ideas in New England, 1630-1730* (New York: W. W. Norton & Co., 1970).*

Brownson, Orestes, *The American Republic: Its Constitution, Tendencies and Destiny*, ed. Americo D. Lapati (New Haven, CT: College & University Press, 1972).

Calvin, John, *On God and Political Duty*, ed. John T. McNeill (Indianapolis & New York: Bobbs-Merrill, 1956).*

Cole, Franklin P., ed., *They Preached Liberty* (Indianapolis: Liberty Press, n.d.). This is an anthology of New England ministers' statements on the American Revolution.*

Dietze, Gottfried, *The Federalist: A Classic on Federalism and Free Government* (Baltimore, MD: Johns Hopkins Press, 1960).

Eidsmoe, John, *Christianity and the Constitution: The Faith of Our Founding Fathers* (Grand Rapids, MI: Baker, 1987).*

Hamilton, Alexander, and Madison, James, and Jay, John, *The Federalist Papers* (New York: New American Library, 1961). This is the classic statement of the political philosophy underlying the American Constitution, available in many editions.

Kirk, Russell, *The American Cause* (Chicago: Regnery, 1966).*

————, *The Conservative Mind from Burke to Eliot*, 7th revised ed. (Chicago: Regnery, 1987).*

————, *The Roots of American Order* (Malibu, CA: Pepperdine University Press, 1978).*

Maine, Sir Henry Sumner, *Popular Government* (Indianapolis: Liberty Classics, 1976).

McDonald, Forrest, *Novus Order Seclorum: The Intellectual Origins of the Constitution* (Lawrence, KS: University of Kansas Press, 1985).

Morley, Felix, *Freedom and Federalism* (Chicago: Regnery, 1959).

Rushdoony, Rousas John, *The Foundations of Social Order: Studies in the Creeds and Councils of the Early Church* (Philadelphia: Presbyterian & Reformed, 1975).*

—————, *Law & Liberty* (Fairfax, VA: Thoburn Press, 1977).*

—————, *The Nature of the American System* (Fairfax, VA: Thoburn Press, 1978).*

—————, *The One and the Many* (Nutley, NJ: Craig Press, 1971).*

—————, *This Independent Republic* (Fairfax, VA: Thoburn Press, 1978).*

Van Til, L. John, *Liberty of Conscience: The History of a Puritan Idea* (Nutley, NJ: Craig Press, 1972).*

Walton, Rus, *One Nation Under God* (Old Tappan, NJ: Revell, 1975).*

N O T E S

INTRODUCTION

1. Walter Williams, *The State Against Blacks* (New York: McGraw-Hill, 1982), p. 49.
2. "Properly understood [stewardship] includes all of life; all men's actions and attitudes; personality and personal influence; in money matters, the acquisition, handling, spending, saving, investing, giving, and final disposition; use of the land, resources, and tools; one's profession, job or place of service; education and the use of education; one's worship, the witness of his life, his personal testimony, his purpose and goals in life." Merrill D. Moore, "Stewardship," in Carl F. H. Henry, ed., *Baker's Dictionary of Christian Ethics* (Grand Rapids: Baker, 1973), p. 649.
3. People do value inherently immoral things, and economic principles apply equally to them. Biblical stewardship is concerned with finding ways to *minimize* rather than to *maximize* their production, distribution, and consumption.
4. The verb *oikonomeo*, to "be a manager" or to "manage, regulate, administer, [or] plan"; the noun *oikonomia*, "management" or "direction" of a household or office, or "arrangement, order, plan"; and the noun *oikonomos*, "(house)-steward, manager." Walter Bauer, *A Greek-English Lexicon of the New Testament and Other Early Christian Literature*, 2nd ed., trans. William F. Arndt and F. Wilbur Gingrich, rev. F. Wilbur Gingrich and Frederick W. Danker (Chicago: University of Chicago Press, 1979), pp. 559f.
5. Though even this is impossible in practice. Every person answers constantly to others as they decide whether to respond positively or negatively to each of his choices.
6. A good secular book on the subject is Julian L. Simon and Herman Kahn, eds., *The Resourceful Earth: A Response to Global 2000* (New York and Oxford, England: Basil Blackwell, 1984).
7. Lord Peter T. Bauer, of the London School of Economics, has done outstanding work in this field. See his *Dissent on Development* ([1971] 1976), *Equality, the Third World, and Economic Delusion* (1981), and *Reality and Rhetoric* (1984) (Cambridge, MA: Harvard

University Press). Also valuable is *Freedom, Justice and Hope: Toward a Strategy for the Poor and the Oppressed*, by Marvin Olasky, Herbert Schlossberg, Pierre Berthoud, and Clark H. Pinnock (Westchester, IL: Crossway Books, 1988).

8. See Ronald H. Nash, ed., *Liberation Theology* (Milford, MI: Mott Media, 1984), for a good selection of short essays by Roman Catholic, Anglican, Lutheran, Presbyterian, Reformed, and Baptist writers. Michael Novak's *Will It Liberate? Questions About Liberation Theology* (New York: Paulist Press, 1986) is a powerful philosophical work but lacks the exegetical basis needed to persuade many evangelicals. The same can be said of James V. Schall's *Liberation Theology in Latin America* (San Francisco, CA: Ignatius Press, 1982).

CHAPTER ONE: You Cannot Serve God and Mammon

1. The word "complete " (Greek *teleios*) is also translated "perfect" or "mature," and refers especially to spiritual maturity.

2. Chapter Fourteen will examine precisely who are "the poor" (Greek *ptochos*) to whom Scripture commands charity. Suffice it here to say that they are those actually destitute.

3. Historic pietism taught that faith must be shown by works. Pietist leader August Hermann Francke (1663-1727), e.g., started a school for the poor. James D. Mosteller, "Pietism," in Carl F. H. Henry, ed., *Baker's Dictionary of Christian Ethics* (Grand Rapids: Baker, 1978), pp. 510f.

4. Sinclair B. Ferguson, "Being Like Jesus," *Discipleship Journal* 4:6 (November 1, 1984), p. 20; emphasis original.

5. Wealth has this danger not only for the rich but also for the poor, who may long for it instead of trusting God. First Timothy 6:3-10 concerns people who try to use religion to get rich, not so much those who already are rich.

6. "Mammon" is not merely money but "everything that has value equivalent to money." Cf. Colin Brown, "*mamonas*," in "Possessions," in Colin Brown, ed., *The New International Dictionary of New Testament Theology*, three vols. (Grand Rapids, MI: Zondervan, 1979), Vol. 2, p. 837.

7. *Ibid.*, p. 838.

8. Cf. Peter C. Craigie, *The Book of Deuteronomy* (Grand Rapids, MI: Eerdmans, NICOT, 1976), pp. 36-45, 79-83.

9. Excellent books on steps to maturity are Jerry Bridges' *The Pursuit of Holiness* and *The Practice of Godliness* (Colorado Springs, CO: NavPress, 1978 and 1983).

10. Henry George Liddell and Robert Scott, *A Greek-English Lexicon* (Oxford, England: Clarendon Press, 1968), p. 362.

CHAPTER TWO: Working as a Servant of God

1. We will discuss Biblical principles of rest—the other aspect of the Fourth Commandment—in Chapter Three.

2. See Udo Middelmann, *pro•exist•ence* (Downers Grove, IL: InterVarsity Press, 1974), p. 23.

3. Cf. John Calvin, *Commentaries on the First Book of Moses Called Genesis*, two vols. in one, trans. John King (Grand Rapids, MI: Baker Book House, 1984 rpt.), Vol. 1, p. 94.
4. Calvin, *Genesis*, Vol. 1, p. 125.
5. "The classic definition of economics is that it is the study of the allocation of scarce resources which have alternative uses." Thomas Sowell, *Economics: Analysis and Issues* (Glenview, IL: Scott, Foresman, 1971), p. 2. See also the discussion of supply and demand in Chapter Eight.
6. Calvin, *Genesis*, p. 125, emphases added. Calvin's insights into Scripture's teaching on stewardship became key elements in the transformation of the Western world, enabling it to become more productive—and so to alleviate poverty more fully—than any other civilization in history. Building and conserving an inheritance for descendants, an idea Calvin stressed, was particularly important. See Nathan Rosenberg and L. E. Birdzell, Jr., *How the West Grew Rich: The Economic Transformation of the Industrial World* (New York: Basic Books, 1986), pp. 129f, 62, 70 n. 26, and 88.
7. C.F. Keil and Franz Delitzsch, *Commentary on the Old Testament, Volume I: The Pentateuch*, three vols. in one, trans. James Martin (Grand Rapids, MI: Eerdmans, 1976 rpt.), Vol. 1, p. 84.
8. George Grant, *In the Shadow of Plenty: The Biblical Blueprint for Welfare* (Ft. Worth, TX: Dominion Press, and Nashville, TN: Thomas Nelson, 1986), pp. 50ff.
9. Calvin, *Genesis*, Vol. 1, p. 125.
10. David Chilton, *Paradise Restored: An Eschatology of Dominion* (Tyler, TX: Reconstruction Press, 1985), p. 43. Citations in this book from writers who identify with the Reconstructionist movement or books published by presses identified with the Reconstructionists should not be interpreted to imply that I endorse all of the tenets of Reconstructionism. See "Appendix One: Methodological Note on the Use of Biblical Law."
11. Rousas John Rushdoony, *The Institutes of Biblical Law* (Nutley, NJ: Craig Press, 1973), p. 146; cf. Gustave Friedrich Oehler, *Theology of the Old Testament* (Grand Rapids, MI: Zondervan, 1983), pp. 332f; see also Chapter Three.
12. Grant, *In the Shadow of Plenty*, p. 52.
13. The three primary economic factors of production are land, labor, and capital, though others—like freedom and incentive—also contribute and can make the difference between bare subsistence and great prosperity. See Sowell, *Economics: Analysis and Issues*, Chapter Four, "The Use of Resources."
14. Grant, *In the Shadow of Plenty*, p. 54.
15. See E. Calvin Beisner and Daryl S. Borgquist, eds., *The Christian World View of Economics* (The Coalition on Revival, 89 Pioneer Way, Mountain View, Ca., 94041, 1986), p. 4, and Ronald H. Nash, *Poverty and Wealth: The Christian Debate Over Capitalism* (Westchester, IL: Crossway, 1986), Chapter Two, "What Is Economics?"

CHAPTER THREE: *Resting in the Providence of God*

1. Possessions do not become Mammon until owners idolize them. See Nash, *Poverty and Wealth*, p. 162.
2. See Chapter One.
3. That no particular weekday must always be the sabbath, see Romans 14:4-6 and C. C. Ewing, *Israel's Calendar and the True Sabbath* (Los Angeles: National Message Ministry, n.d.), summarized in Rushdoony, *Institutes of Biblical Law*, pp. 134-136.
4. For more on the Biblical requirement of work, see Chapters Two, Six, and Seven.
5. A. Wetherell Johnson, *Created for Commitment* (Wheaton, IL: Tyndale House, 1982), p. 202.
6. Cf. John 5:17, where Jesus proclaimed His deity by claiming that He, like His Father, worked unceasingly, even during the unending sabbath that began at the completion of God's creative work.
7. Rushdoony, *Institutes of Biblical Law*, pp. 141f, nicely applies the sabbatical year's requirement of letting land rest to modern discoveries about soil conservation, a fundamental element of stewardship over the earth.
8. We will examine the sabbatical and jubilee year regulations briefly here and return to them at greater length in Chapters Four and Five.
9. For a study of Biblical inheritance law, see Rushdoony, *Institutes of Biblical Law*, pp. 328ff. For the economic importance of inheritance, see Rosenberg and Birdzell, *How the West Grew Rich*, pp. 61f, 70 n. 26, and 88.
10. But even in Galatians 4:21—5:5 Paul does not endorse antinomianism or fruitless faith, for in 5:6, after rejecting *ceremonial* works, he endorses "faith working through love"; and love he defines in part as fulfilling the moral Law in relation to others (Romans 13:10).
11. We will see in Chapter Five that these limits on debt also protected lenders from loss of property to borrowers who defaulted on loans.
12. See the extensive discussion of this in Chapter Five.
13. Debts were terminated at jubilee not to redistribute wealth, despite the claims of some "Christian socialists," but because by definition they must be paid off by then, having been secured by either productive capital or indentured labor. See Chapter Five.
14. See Rushdoony, *Institutes of Biblical Law*, pp. 144f, and Gary North, *Honest Money: Biblical Principles of Money and Banking* (Ft. Worth, TX: Dominion Press, and Nashville, TN: Thomas Nelson, 1986), pp. 110f.

CHAPTER FOUR: *A Christian View of Economic Justice*

1. This chapter is adapted from a speech delivered at the Second Continental Congress on the Christian World View, Dallas, Texas, July 22-25, 1985, sponsored by The Coalition on Revival, 89 Pioneer Way, Mountain View, California, 94041.
2. The implications against fiat monetary inflation and false advertising by businesses should be obvious. See Chapters Nine and Ten for more on inflation.

3. St. Thomas Aquinas, *Summa Theologica*, cited in Peter Witonski, ed., *The Wisdom of Conservatism*, four vols., (Mars Hill, NC: Institute for Western Values, 1971), Vol. 1, p. 449.

4. John Calvin, *Institutes of the Christian Religion* (III.vii.3), two vols., ed. John T. McNeill, trans. Ford Lewis Battles (Philadelphia: Westminster, 1977 rpt.), Vol. 1, p. 692.

5. Russell Kirk, *A Program for Conservatives*, revised ed. (Chicago: Regnery, 1962), pp. 166f.

6. Calvin, *Institutes* (IV.xx.16), Vol. 2, p. 1504.

7. For a defense of this idea, see C. S. Lewis's discussion of "The Tao" in *The Abolition of Man* (New York: Macmillan, 1947).

8. "References to natural law in [Calvin's] *Institutes* are usually . . . associated with conscience, frequently also with civil positive law and equity, and the Christian's duties to society. Cf. II. ii. 22, where the key Pauline passage for natural law, Rom. 2:14-15, is employed: see also II. vii. 3-4; II. viii. 1-2, 53; III. xix. 15-16; IV. x. 3; IV. xx. 11 ('natural equity'); IV. xx. 15 (the rule of love); IV. xx. 16 ('the moral law . . . a testimony of natural law'). Calvin's view of the Commandments as a divinely authorized text expressing and clarifying the natural law engraved on all hearts is the traditional one. . . . Aquinas treats natural law with some fullness, e.g., in *Summa Theol.* I IIae, questions xci. 1-3; xciv; c. 1-5, where the principles of the Decalogue are identified with those of natural reason. . . . [Calvin in his *Harmony of the Four Books of Moses, 'Praefatio in legem'* again speaks of the Decalogue] as a specially accommodated restatement of the law of nature for the chosen people, and the entire body of 'Mosaic' legislation is classified under the ten laws." See John T. McNeill's note in Calvin's *Institutes*, Vol. 1, pp. 367f, n. 5. On Luther, see McNeill's "Natural Law in the Thought of Luther," *Church History* X (1941), pp. 211-227.

9. See Forrest McDonald, *Novus Ordo Seclorum: The Intellectual Origins of the Constitution* (Lawrence, KS: University of Kansas Press, 1985).

10. Kirk, *A Program for Conservatives*, p. 167.

11. *Ibid.*

12. I use "equalitarianism" to mean "economic egalitarianism." *Legal* egalitarianism—equality before law—is Biblical. The next chapter will examine arguments for equalitarianism drawn from Biblical passages.

13. Kirk, *A Program for Conservatives*, p. 167.

14. The Puritan Stephen Charnock points toward this principle when he writes, "The goodness of God could not be equally communicated to all, after their settlement in their several beings,—because they have not a capacity in their natures for it. . . . God doth not do good to all creatures according to the greatness of his own power, and the extent of his own wealth, but according to the capacity of the subject; not so much good as he can do, but so much good as the creature can receive." *The Existence and Attributes of God*, three vols. (Grand Rapids, MI: Baker, 1980 rpt.), Vol. 2, p. 234.

15. William Bradford, *Of Plymouth Plantation, 1620-1647*, ed. Samuel Eliot Morison (New York: Alfred A. Knopf, 1952), pp. 120, 121.

16. William Aylott Orton, *The Economic Role of the State* (Chicago:

University of Chicago Press, 1950), p. 123.
17. Kirk, *A Program for Conservatives*, pp. 168, 169. See Chapter Eight for an explanation of why free, non-fraudulent exchange benefits both parties.
18. See Chapters Nine and Ten for further discussion of inflation's violation of the Ninth Commandment's prohibition of false witness.
19. Kirk, *A Program for Conservatives*, p. 169.
20. Edmund Burke, *Reflections on the Revolution in France*, in *The Writings and Speeches of the Right Honourable Edmund Burke*, twelve vols., Beaconsfield Edition (Boston: Little, Brown and Company, 1902), Vol. 3, pp. 308, 309, emphases added.
21. See the discussions of socialism in Chapters Seven and Eight.
22. See Chapter 5 below for answers to claims that the New Testament denies the right to private property, and Chapter Eleven for discussion of infringements of property rights.
23. Ronald Sider, *Rich Christians in an Age of Hunger*, 2nd ed. (Downers Grove, IL: InterVarsity Press, 1984), pp. 75ff. David Chilton responds in *Productive Christians in an Age of Guilt Manipulators: A Biblical Response to Ronald J. Sider*, third revised edition (Tyler, TX: Institute for Christian Economics, 1985), pp. 79ff.
24. In answer to claims that certain Biblical texts do teach economic equalitarianism, see Chapter Five.
25. Aristotle, *Nicomachean Ethics*, V.iii, in J. A. K. Thomson, trans., *The Ethics of Aristotle: The Nicomachean Ethics*, rev. Hugh Tredennick (New York: Penguin, 1976), pp. 177f.
26. On the role of Old Testament Law in the Christian life and civil society, see "Appendix One: Methodological Note on the Use of Biblical Law."
27. A thorough study of the relationship of all of the Ten Commandments to economics is Gary North's *The Sinai Strategy: Economics and the Ten Commandments* (Tyler, TX: Institute for Christian Economics, 1986).
28. See Chapter Five for further discussion of Biblical support for private property.
29. See Chapters Eleven through Thirteen for a discussion of infringements of property rights.
30. Kirk, *A Program for Conservatives*, pp. 171, 172.
31. *Ibid.*, p. 178.
32. In Chapters Seven through Nine below we will encounter again the fact that attempts to enforce economic equality of condition—or even to control an economy by the coercive power of the State—necessarily lead to tyranny.
33. Russell Kirk, *Enemies of the Permanent Things* (New Rochelle, NY: Arlington House, 1969), p. 287.

CHAPTER FIVE: *Does Justice Demand Equality?*

1. Cited by Albert Henry Newman in "Communism," in Samuel Jackson Macauley, *et al.*, eds., *The New Schaff-Herzog Encyclopedia of Religious Knowledge*, fifteen vols. (Grand Rapids, MI: Baker, [1907] 1977), Vol. 3, p. 183. The article is a helpful survey of commu-

nistic ideas in church history.

2. I am using "communistic" here to designate groups and teachings that favor economic equality. I will capitalize "Communist" to refer to groups, governments, political parties, and teachings specifically related to Karl Marx and V. I. Lenin.

3. For an analysis of the communistic teachings of the Anabaptists, see Chilton, *Productive Christians in an Age of Guilt Manipulators,* Appendix Two, "Socialism, The Anabaptist Heresy," pp. 321ff.

4. The Adonai Shomo in Massachusetts (founded in 1861); the Altruist Community of Sulphur Springs, Missouri (late 1800s); the Amana Society of Amana, Iowa (started in the 1840s); the Church Triumphant, Koreshanity, of Estero, Florida (early 1900s); the Ephrata Community of Lancaster County, Pennsylvania (started in 1732); the Harmony Society of Pennsylvania (started in 1803); Icaria and New Icaria of Texas (started in 1848 by French immigrants); the Perfectionists of the Oneida Community of New York (founded in 1848); the Separatists of Tuscarawas County, Ohio (founded 1817-1819); and the Shakers or Millenial Church (which came to America in 1774 from England and settled in Watervliet, New York). See "Communism" in *The New Schaff-Herzog Encyclopedia of Religious Knowledge,* Vol. 3, pp. 182ff, for the histories and specific tenets of these groups.

5. We will argue in Chapters Seven through Nine below that force is the only means of avoiding the inequalities that naturally result from the free choices and actions of men.

6. See Chilton, *Productive Christians in an Age of Guilt Manipulators,* Appendix Three, and the articles "Anabaptists" and "Communism" in *The New Schaff-Herzog Encyclopedia of Religious Knowledge,* Vol. 1, pp. 161ff, and Vol. 3, pp. 182ff.

7. The liberation theology movement has a strong strain of equalitarianism, but the treatment here will focus more on evangelical writers—with the exceptions of Jose Miranda and Gustavo Gutierrez. For analysis of liberation theology, see Ronald H. Nash, ed., *Liberation Theology* (Grand Rapids: Baker, 1988), and Michael Novak, *Will It Liberate? Questions about Liberation Theology* (New York: Paulist Press, 1986), and James V. Schall, *Liberation Theology in Latin America* (San Francisco: Ignatius Press, 1982).

8. Sider never defines "justice" explicitly in *Rich Christians in an Age of Hunger.* His usage indicates that, at least in economic contexts, he takes it as nearly synonymous with equality of condition, contrary to the definition in Chapter Four above.

9. Sider, *Rich Christians in an Age of Hunger,* p. 91.

10. Francis Brown, S. R. Driver, and Charles Briggs, eds., *A Hebrew and English Lexicon of the Old Testament,* trans. Edward Robinson (Oxford: Clarendon Press, 1978), p. 1030, parentheses original.

11. In agreement see the *KJV.* The *NIV's* "cancel debts" is a sad instance of locking a dubious interpretation into a translation.

12. Brown, Driver, and Briggs, *Hebrew and English Lexicon,* p. 1030.

13. Albert Barnes, *Barnes' Notes on the Old Testament,* sixteen vols. (Grand Rapids, MI: Baker, 1976 rpt.), Vol. 3, p. 300.

14. C. F. Keil and Franz Delitzsch, *Commentary on the Old*

Testament , ten vols. (Grand Rapids, MI: Eerdmans, 1976), Vol. 1, Part 3, pp. 369f.

15. Keil and Delitzsch, *Commentary*, Vol. 1, Pt. 3, p. 370. Cf. Peter C. Craigie, *The Book of Deuteronomy* (Grand Rapids, MI: Eerdmans, 1976), pp. 236f.

16. Meredith G. Kline, *Deuteronomy*, in Charles F. Pfeiffer and Everett F. Harrison, eds., *The Wycliffe Bible Commentary* (Chicago: Moody Press, [1962] 1974), p. 175.

17. See Daryl S. Borgquist, *Toward a Biblical Theology of the Poor* (La Mirada, CA: Talbot Theological Seminary, unpublished thesis for Master of Theological Studies, 1983), p. 53.

18. "The sabbatical release of debts was an institutionalized mechanism for preventing an ever-growing gap between rich and poor." Sider, *Rich Christians in an Age of Hunger*, p. 91.

19. Gustavo Gutierrez, in *A Theology of Liberation: History, Politics and Salvation*, trans. and ed. Caridad Inda and John Eagleson (Maryknoll, New York: Orbis, 1973), p. 294, also mistakenly holds that the sabbatical law required cancellation rather than postponement of debts.

20. See the discussions of social, commutative, and distributive justice in Chapter Four.

21. Borgquist, *Toward a Biblical Theology of the Poor*, p. 56.

22. Waldron Scott, *Bring Forth Justice* (Grand Rapids, MI: Eerdmans, 1980), p. 56.

23. Here and throughout his book Sider (unconsciously?) assumes that poverty is unnatural and plenty is natural. We will see in Chapter Thirteen that the opposite is the case.

24. Sider, *Rich Christians in an Age of Hunger*, p. 80.

25. *Ibid.*, p. 81.

26. Normally someone would sell himself into indentured servanthood to pay off previous loans, but other circumstances—like a merchant's sudden loss of a large shipment on consignment—might also have occasioned it.

27. On God's rejection of equality by promising to bless the obedient with prosperity and to curse the disobedient with poverty, see, e.g., Deuteronomy 15:4, 5; Genesis 24:35; 26:12-14; 30:43; 41:41-45; Job 1:1-3; Daniel 2:48; 5:29; 6:1-3; Psalm 1:1-3; Proverbs 22:16; 22:22, 23; Lamentations 5:2, 3. Cf. Borgquist, *Toward a Biblical Theology of the Poor*, p. 51.

28. A document of the International Consultation on Simple Lifestyle at Hoddesdon, England, March 17-21, 1980. Co-chairmen of the consultation were Ronald Sider and John R. W. Stott. The full document is reprinted in Waldron Scott's *Bring Forth Justice* as Appendix B.

29. Cited in Scott, *Bring Forth Justice*, p. 283.

30. Some Christian equalitarians respond that these O.T. laws are inapplicable under the N.T. Aside from the fact that such a position flies in the face of Jesus' statement that He came not to abolish but to fulfill the Law (Matthew 5:17-19), the position is also inconsistent, since the same writers eagerly appeal to the sabbatical and jubilee laws.

31. The Bible requires charitable giving only to the poor—the actually destitute, not those with income below a set percentage of a society's aver-

age. See Daryl S. Borgquist, *Toward a Biblical Theology of the Poor.*

32. Though the word "justice" never appears in the contexts; note that his claim contrasts with the emphasis on love in the *Evangelical Commitment to Simple Lifestyle.*

33. Scott, *Bring Forth Justice,* p. 108; emphasis added.

34. Arthur G. Gish, *Living in Christian Community* (Scottdale, PA, and Kitchener, Ontario: Herald Press, 1979), p. 70; brackets added.

35. This was not the view of earlier radical Anabaptists Thomas Münzer, Jan Matthijs, and Jan Bokelson (John of Leyden), who in Münster used lethal force to establish their brand of communism—which ultimately included community of wives. See Chilton, *Productive Christians in an Age of Guilt Manipulators,* pp. 330ff.

36. Gish, *Living in Christian Community,* p. 70, citing Eberhard Arnold, *Inner Land* (Rifton, New York: Plough Publishing House, 1976), pp. 402f, brackets and emphasis added. Plough is the publishing arm of the communistic Bruderhof movement.

37. Gish, *Living in Christian Community,* p. 70.

38. For excellent analyses of liberation theology see Ronald Nash, ed., *Liberation Theology* (Grand Rapids: Baker,1988).

39. Gutierrez, *A Theology of Liberation,* p. 265.

40. This is the translation Gutierrez cites. The *NASB* has, "And do not neglect doing good and sharing; for with such sacrifices God is pleased."

41. Jose Porfirio Miranda, *Communism in the Bible,* trans. Robert R. Barr (Maryknoll, New York: Orbis, 1982), p. 7; emphases added on the word "communism" in both occurrences. Miranda argues for full-fledged Marxist Communism.

42. The texts don't warrant this clause. Better would have been, "freely gave away some private possessions." It was individual possessions, not the principle of private property, that were given away, not abandoned.

43. Sider, *Rich Christians in an Age of Hunger,* p. 90.

44. This is an example of the iterative (customary) imperfect. See A. T. Robertson, *Word Pictures in the New Testament,* six vols. (Nashville: Broadman, 1930), Vol. 3, p. 39.

45. Cf. Sider, *Rich Christians in an Age of Hunger,* p. 90. See also Peter H. Davids, "New Testament Foundations for Living More Simply," in Ronald Sider, ed., *Living More Simply* (Downers Grove, IL: InterVarsity Press, 1980), p. 46.

46. Sider, *Rich Christians in an Age of Hunger,* p. 90.

47. *Ibid.,* p. 96.

48. *Ibid.,* p. 98.

49. Cf. John Calvin, *New Testament Commentaries,* twelve vols., trans. T. A. Smail, eds. D. W. Torrance and T. F. Torrance (Grand Rapids, MI: Eerdmans, 1976), Vol. 10, p. 113.

50. R. C. H. Lenski, *The Interpretation of I and II Corinthians* (Minneapolis, MN: Augsburg, 1963), pp. 1145-1147, brackets added.

51. Note that justice can be compelled, and injustice punished by human authority, while love cannot be compelled and lack of love cannot be punished by human authority.

52. Smith, regenerate or not, was a theist, not a deist. His moral philosophy was firmly rooted in Christian theology, complete with belief in

Heaven, Hell, and redemption.
53. Adam Smith, *The Theory of Moral Sentiments*, II.ii.3 (Indianapolis: Liberty Press/Liberty Classics, 1977 rpt.), pp. 166, 167.

CHAPTER SIX: Working Harder

1. "Natural resources" are distinct from "raw materials" in that some-one knows how to use them, particularly how to convert them into some other form that serves a human interest. See Sowell, *Economics: Analysis and Issues*, pp. 65ff.
2. The "work ethic" derived from Scripture by John Calvin in the six-teenth century contributed mightily to the increased willingness of people in all social classes to work hard. See Rosenberg and Birdzell, *How the West Grew Rich*, p. 130.
3. On God's enabling later generations to build on the work of their forebears as an aspect of the Biblical Covenant, see Gary North, *The Sinai Strategy*, pp. 40-50.
4. For a chronicle of this process, see Rosenberg and Birdzell, *How the West Grew Rich, passim*.
5. See George Gilder, *Wealth and Poverty* (New York: Bantam Books, 1982), pp. 87ff.
6. *Ibid.*, p. 87.
7. The next verse, "A faithful man will abound with blessings, but he who makes haste to be rich will not go unpunished" (Proverbs 28:20) parallels this one. Conscientious work is a sign of faithfulness. True spirituality is practicality in God's world.
8. The gates of a city were where much business was transacted and elders gathered to hear disputes and render judgment. See C. Warren, "Gate," in James Hastings, *et al.*, eds., *A Dictionary of the Bible*, six vols. (New York: Charles Scribner's Sons, 1906), Vol. 2, pp. 110-113.
9. See Gilder, *Wealth and Poverty*, pp. 130ff.
10. Chilton, *Productive Christians in an Age of Guilt Manipulators*, p. 139.
11. Herbert Schlossberg, *Idols for Destruction: Christian Faith and Its Confrontation with American Society* (Nashville, TN: Thomas Nelson, 1983), pp. 51f (cf. pp. 53, 55, 58, 70, 74, 78, 97, 106), citing Max Scheler, *Ressentiment* (Glencoe, IL: Free Press, 1961), p. 52.
12. Chapters Twelve and Thirteen discuss public policies that remove incentives to work and so encourage the poor to avoid the one chief means of growing out of poverty.
13. Chapters Fourteen through Sixteen discuss evangelism and disciple-ship.

CHAPTER SEVEN: Working Smarter

1. Frank H. Thompson, "Wisdom," in Carl F. H. Henry, ed., *Baker's Dictionary of Christian Ethics* (Grand Rapids, MI: Baker Book House, 1973), p. 710.
2. See Rosenberg and Birdzell, *How the West Grew Rich*, Chapter Seven, "Technology, Trusts, and Marketable Stock," and Chapter Eight, "The Link between Science and Wealth."

3. For definition and discussion of this concept, see the section "Division of Labor" later in this chapter.
4. U.S. Department of Commerce, Bureau of the Census, *Statistical Abstract of the United States, 1984* (Washington, D.C.: U.S. Government Printing Office, 1984), p. 649, Table 1134.
5. In Chapter Eight below we will consider the wisdom of various valuing and pricing mechanisms; in Chapters Nine and Ten the wisdom of money and fiscal policy; in Chapters Twelve and Thirteen the wisdom of of various kinds of economic regulations.
6. We focus here on private planning by individuals, families, and businesses. In Chapter Eight we examine how the market—millions of buyers and sellers making choices—facilitates large-scale planning, and contrast it with central planning.
7. Helpful personal budgeting materials are available from Christian Financial Concepts, Route 5, Box 130, Dahlonega, GA, 30533.
8. Adam Smith, *An Inquiry into the Nature and Causes of the Wealth of Nations*, Book I, Chapter i, ed. Edwin Cannan (Chicago: University of Chicago Press, 1976), Vol. 1, pp. 8, 9.
9. This criticism is common to Marxism. See Rosenberg and Birdzell, *How the West Grew Rich*, pp. 180-182.
10. See Chilton, *Productive Christians in an Age of Guilt Manipulators*, pp. 291ff, and Leonard E. Read, *Anything That's Peaceful: The Case for the Free Market* (Irvington, New York: Foundation for Economic Education, 1964). See Chapters Eleven through Thirteen below.
11. We can view this from the opposite perspective. Workers buy jobs, bidding job prices (not wages but sacrifices made to get jobs) up by promising greater productivity or accepting lower wages. Employers sell jobs, bidding job prices down by promising higher wages, better working conditions, etc.
12. On the economic effects of minimum wage laws, see Chapter Twelve.
13. On the relationship of supply and demand to pricing see Sowell, *Economics: Analysis and Issues*, Chapters Two through Five, and Nash, *Poverty and Wealth*, pp. 30-32. We will discuss supply and demand pricing further in Chapter Eight and competition further in the next section.
14. In essence, the criticism answered here assumes the labor theory of value. We will see what that is, and why it is mistaken, in Chapter Eight.
15. For a similar illustration, see Sowell, *Economics: Analysis and Issues*, p. 243, Tables 14-1, 14-2, and 14-3.
16. *Ibid.*, pp. 242, 243.
17. A violent solution is use of political force to limit competition and so improve one's trading position. Domestically, that is done with things like unions, licensing, employment quotas, and minimum wage laws. Internationally, it is done with tariffs and import quotas. See Chapters Twelve and Thirteen below.
18. Political restraints on the economy imply violence because they can only be effective under the threat of violence and, if defied, by fulfilling the threat. See Ludwig von Mises, *Socialism: An Economic and Sociological Analysis*, 2nd ed., trans. J. Kahane (London: Jonathan

Cape, 1969 rpt.), Chapter Three.

19. For an example of proper concern coupled with improper suggested solutions, see Sider, *Rich Christians in an Age of Hunger*, pp. 130ff.

20. See von Mises, *Socialism: An Economic and Sociological Analysis*, p. 227.

21. *Ibid.*, p. 235.

22. For examples and refutations of economic arguments for protectionism, see Henry Hazlitt, *Economics in One Lesson* (Westport, CT: Arlington House, 1979), Chapters Eleven, Twelve, and Fourteen, and Frederic Bastiat, *The Law* (Irvington, New York: Foundation for Economic Education, 1974).

23. It could be argued that weakening its economy would tempt it to turn to violence to achieve its ends. But this is properly a political, not an economic, consideration.

24. Sowell, *Economics: Analysis and Issues*, pp. 27, 28.

25. Gish, *Living in Christian Community*, p. 54.

26. See Chapter Eight for discussion of the operation of the law of supply and demand on prices.

27. Nash, *Poverty and Wealth*, p. 73.

28. See Chilton, *Productive Christians in an Age of Guilt Manipulators*, pp. 286-297; Read, *Anything That's Peaceful*, *passim*; and Friedrich A. Hayek, *The Constitution of Liberty* (South Bend, IN: Gateway Editions, 1972 rpt.), Chapter Nine, "Coercion and the State."

29. The so-called "robber barons" of the late nineteenth century, who have given free market, or capitalist, economics a bad name, actually resorted repeatedly to state coercion to protect themselves from competition. See R. W. Grant, *The Incredible Bread Machine*, rev. and ed. Susan Love Brown, *et al.* (San Diego, CA: World Research, Inc., [1966] 1974), Chapter One.

30. Nash, *Poverty and Wealth*, p. 74.

31. Sowell, *Economics: Analysis and Issues*, p. 28. And high profit percentages will—except in the case of legally protected or natural monopolies (in which costs of operation are naturally so high as to limit participation to one or two businesses)—always attract new entries into the market.

32. Properly understood, however, this is not a criticism of profits alone, but of the freedom of choice inherent to a market economy. It is a rejection of the idea that, with the exceptions of fraud, theft, and violence, people ought to be free to do as they please. See Chapters Four, Five, and Eleven through Thirteen.

33. Chilton, *Productive Christians in an Age of Guilt Manipulators*, p. 182. The point of *laissez faire* economics is not anarchy, which is libertinism, but liberty within the bounds of law. See Chapter Eleven below.

34. Gilder, *Wealth and Poverty*, p. 30.

35. Neither can we save more than we earn in profits, which is another reason to recognize that earning a profit is a good thing.

36. See Edward C. Banfield, *The Unheavenly City Revisited* (Boston: Little, Brown and Co., 1974); Nash, *Poverty and Wealth*, pp. 173, 174; and Chilton, *Productive Christians*, pp. 221-223.

37. For a thorough study of the principle that the righteous will, by

God's judgment, inherit the wealth of the wicked, see Gary North, *Inherit the Earth: Biblical Principles for Economics* (Ft. Worth, TX: Dominion Press, 1987), Chapter Five, "Inheriting the World."

38. Similar passages include Genesis 4:12; Nehemiah 13:17,18; Job 27:13-23; Psalms 34:8-15; 92:5-8; Proverbs 13:11,25; Isaiah 1:19-23; 59:1-9; 65:11-14; Jeremiah 6:12-13,19; 27:3-5; Hosea 4:1-3; Amos 4:6-13; Micah 5:15; Haggai 1:3-11; Zechariah 7:13-14; Malachi 3:5; Revelation 18:7-17.

CHAPTER EIGHT: Value and Price

1. Unless they're rare ancient pins highly valued by museums. Then they're valued for their *scarcity,* a concept we'll encounter more shortly.

2. Augustine, *Expositions on the Book of Psalms,* in Philip Schaff, ed., *A Select Library of the Nicene and Post-Nicene Fathers of the Christian Church,* First Series, fourteen vols., trans. A. Cleveland Coxe (Grand Rapids, MI: Eerdmans, 1979), Vol. VIII, p. 341.

3 Salvation, of course, is free to us, but it is not absolutely free. Christ paid for it by suffering on the Cross as our substitute to bear the penalty for sin. See Matthew 20:28.

4. Scarcity is not the same as shortage. "A shortage may develop where the ratio of the good to population is unchanged or is even higher than before. The shortage indicates that not as much is offered for sale as is demanded *at that price.*" Sowell, *Economics: Analysis and Issues,* p. 30.

5. *Ibid.,* p. 2.

6. One might trade an item of which one had greater excess of possession over need for one of which he would have less excess of possession over need if he foresaw an opportunity to exchange the latter profitably for an item in which he presently had an excess of need over possession.

7. See Nash, *Poverty and Wealth,* pp. 54, 71f. Compare Andrew Kirk, *The Good News of the Kingdom Coming* (Downers Grove, IL: InterVarsity Press, 1985), p. 82, who thinks one person's gain must come at another's loss.

8. See Chapter Seven.

9. Sider, in *Rich Christians in an Age of Hunger,* pp. 151ff, makes precisely this mistake in charges of unfair profits. Cf. Chilton, *Productive Christians in an Age of Guilt Manipulators,* pp. 123ff, for an able refutation.

10. Sowell, *Economics: Analysis and Issues,* p. 23.

11. *Ibid.,* pp. 23ff. See Eugen von Böhm-Bawerk, *Capital and Interest,* three vols. in one, trans. George D. Huncke and Hans F. Sennholz (South Holland, IL: Libertarian Press, 1959), Vol. 2, p. 235.

12. Sowell, *Economics: Analysis and Issues,* pp. 19ff.

13. *Ibid.,* p. 35.

14. Böhm-Bawerk, *Capital and Interest,* Vol. 2, pp. 139, 423 n. 15.

15. *Ibid.,* Vol. 2, p. 143.

16. *Ibid.,* Vol. 2, pp. 121-256.

17. Carl Landauer, "Böhm-Bawerk, Eugen von," in *Encyclopedia*

Britannica, twenty-four vols. (Chicago and London: Encyclopedia Britannica, Inc., William Benton, Publisher, 1969), Vol. 3, pp. 855f.
18. Böhm-Bawerk, *Capital and Interest,* Vol. 2, p. 143.
19. *Ibid.*
20. *Ibid.,* Vol. 2, p. 245: ". . . it is sufficiently accurate, for purposes of the great numbers involved in a market economy, to state that market price *is determined by the valuation figure of the last buyer.*"
21. *Ibid.,* Vol. 2, p. 150.
22. Cf. Chapter Twelve, where we consider government-regulated maximum and minimum prices.
23. For more in-depth discussion of the effects—and morality—of legislated price controls, see Chapter Twelve.
24. See Chapters Twelve and Thirteen for more on price and production controls.
25. Sider, *Rich Christians in an Age of Hunger,* pp. 155-158.
26. von Mises, *Socialism: An Economic and Sociological Analysis,* pp. 132ff. Marx discounted the contribution of capital (buildings, tools, transportation systems, etc.) to production by alleging that all capital is simply the stored value of earlier labor.
27. ". . . the price of a commodity, and therefore also of labour, is equal to its cost of production." Karl Marx and Friedrich Engels, *The Communist Manifesto,* in *Harold J. Laski on the Communist Manifesto* (New York: New American Library, 1982), p. 139.
28. von Mises, *Socialism: An Economic and Sociological Analysis,* p. 133, citing Marx, *Das Kapital.*
29. *Ibid.,* p. 134.
30. This idea actually rests on the labor theory of value, presuming that civil government is best qualified to determine the value of labor used in producing any good.
31. William E. Diehl, in "The Guided-Market System," and John Gladwin, in "Centralist Economics," present and defend varieties of this theory. Their essays are included in Robert G. Clouse, ed., *Wealth and Poverty: Four Christian Views* (Downers Grove, IL: InterVarsity Press, 1984).
32. Cf. Chapter Twelve.
33. Von Mises argued this point with devastating force in his chapter "The Organization of Production Under Socialism," in *Socialism: An Economic and Sociological Analysis.* See especially Section 2, "Economic calculation in the socialist community," pp. 131ff.
34. Some socialists argue that planners could set their nation's prices by market prices elsewhere. This admits defeat: they depend on market prices to establish their own. It also means their prices won't reflect their community's different conditions, and so will still cause shortages and surpluses.
35. Nash, *Poverty and Wealth,* p. 82.
36. No other explanation for the landowner's willingness to pay higher wages makes sense, and the parable would have been persuasive to its hearers only if the occurrences it assumed were in fact common.
37. The parable does presuppose these underlying moral principles, for without them its point that complaint against God's sovereign grace is unwarranted would not follow in the course of Jesus' argument.

See my "A Note on Interpreting Parables" in *A Stranger in the Land: Wealth, Poverty, and the Sovereignty of God* (Los Angeles: International College: unpublished Master's thesis, 1983, available from the author), pp. 292ff. See also the discussions of parabolic interpretation by Leslie C. Allen (*The Books of Joel, Obadiah, Jonah, and Micah* [Grand Rapids, MI: Eerdmans, 1976], p. 178), A. Berkeley Mickelsen (*Interpreting the Bible* [Grand Rapids, MI: Eerdmans, 1974], pp. 213, 219, 229), C. H. Peisker ("Parable," in Colin Brown, ed., *New International Dictionary of New Testament Theology*, three vols. [Grand Rapids: Zondervan, 1976], Vol. 2, p. 747), and G. Heinrici ("Parables of Jesus Christ," in Samuel Macauley Jackson, ed., *The New Schaff-Herzog Encyclopedia of Religious Knowledge*, Vol. 8, p. 346). R. C. H. Lenski advises, ". . . we must remember that none of these resemblances is merely accidental, the invention of a versatile mind; also and especially that it is not the heavenly that is patterned after the earthly, but the reverse." *The Interpretation of St. Matthew's Gospel* (Minneapolis: Augsburg, 1943), p. 524.

38. See Chapters Eleven through Thirteen for discussion of property rights and infringements.

39. See the discussion of envy in Chapter Six.

CHAPTER NINE: *Stewardship and Money*

1. For a discussion of tithing see Chapter Sixteen.

2. We discussed the dominion mandate briefly in Chapter Two. For more on this, see Gary North, *The Sinai Strategy*.

3. Two helpful books on giving are Howard L. Dayton, Jr., *Your Money: Frustration or Freedom?* (Wheaton, IL: Tyndale House, 1971), and Edward J. Hales and J. Alan Youngren, *Your Money/Their Ministry: A Guide to Responsible Christian Giving* (Grand Rapids, MI: Eerdmans, 1981).

4. We will discuss giving in Chapters Fifteen and Sixteen.

5. The fairly precise market value of money holds under normal circumstances. Shortly we will consider some situations in which the value of money becomes so imprecise that parties to an exchange lose much of their ability to know its market value. This can have disastrous consequences.

6. Jacques Ellul, *Money & Power* (Downers Grove, IL: InterVarsity Press, 1984), cited in *Christianity Today*, Sept. 7, 1984, p. 30. Nash, in *Poverty and Wealth*, pp. 156ff, gives a devastating critique of Ellul's odd notions.

7. The subject is covered in every first level economics textbook and in most encyclopedia articles on money. E.g., Sowell, *Economics: Analysis and Issues*, Chapter Twelve, and Charles R. Whittlesey, "Money," in *Encyclopedia Britannica* (1969 ed.), Vol. 15, pp. 701f.

8. Whittlesey, "Money," *Encyclopedia Britannica* (1969 ed.), Vol. 15, p. 701.

9. Gary North, *Honest Money*, p. 13. North's book is a valuable study of Biblical principles related to money and monetary policy.

10. *Ibid.*, p. 22.

11. See Chapter One above and Nash, *Poverty and Wealth*, Chapter Fifteen.
12. This assumes a graduated income tax, which presently the United States has. A flat rate tax would alleviate this—but only this—ill effect of inflation.
13. In the five years ending in December 1923, the German Reichsbank issued 496.5 quintillion marks, each worth only one trillionth of its 1914 gold value and 1/42 billionth of an American penny. See Hans Sennholz, "Hyperinflation in Germany," *The Freeman*, October 1970, pp. 598ff.
14. At 5 percent annual inflation, prices double in about 15 years; at 10 percent, in about 8.5 years; at 13.5 percent (the 1980 U.S. rate), in 6.5 years. Prices triple at 10 percent in 12.5 years, quadruple in 15.5 years, and quintuple in 18 years. The 1940 U.S. dollar had the market purchasing power of 7.33 1983 dollars.
15. For a 1983 income to match the market purchasing power of a $10,000 annual income in 1940, it would have to be $73,260. And even then it wouldn't actually match the 1940 value because a larger proportion of it would be taken in taxes.
16. Consequently inflation tempts many people to finance purchases on credit, contrary to the Bible's warnings against debt. See Proverbs 22:7; Romans 13:8.
17. Consequently inflation drives up interest rates on loans because lenders hope to protect themselves against inflationary loss.
18. This is part of why it is difficult to persuade people to stop pressuring governments to increase money supplies. Debtors see inflation as an easy way out. They don't often realize that they are, in effect, stealing from creditors the difference in value between money loaned and money paid back.
19. Friedrich A. Hayek, in *Unemployment and Monetary Policy: Government as Generator of the "Business Cycle"* (San Francisco, CA: Cato Institute, 1979), p. 13, argues that it is necessary to increase the *rate* of inflation constantly to stave off the bust that must follow every boom.
20. This phenomenon, unemployment following inflation, is sometimes referred to as the "business cycle" or "boom and bust" cycle. Notice that it is caused solely by increased money supply—not by the operation of the free market but by civil government's interference in it, distorting its function.
21. See Hayek, *Unemployment and Monetary Policy*, p. 30.
22. Precisely this combination of events, though on a slightly smaller scale, would have followed execution of Senator George McGovern's plan, when running for President in 1972, to give every American a check for $2,000. With per capita income at the time hovering around $4,700, the gift would have spawned almost immediate 42 percent inflation. Politicians often fail to see the economic consequences of vote-buying schemes.
23. This thesis, now widely accepted by economists, is argued powerfully by Nobel prize-winning economist Friedrich A. Hayek in the three essays that make up his *Unemployment and Monetary Policy*.
24. *Ibid.*, pp. 8ff.

25. *Ibid.*, pp. 11-14.
26. *Ibid.*, p. 13.
27. *Ibid.*, p. 30.
28. Shortages will be in more essential goods, and surpluses in less essential, because inflation causes consumers to purchase more non-essential goods relative to essential goods. Producers follow their cue, then lag behind in responding when consumers realize their money's loss in value.
29. "Controls, and possibly dictatorship, follow inflation as day follows night." Lawrence Fertig, "Right Premise—Wrong Conclusion," *The Freeman*, Vol. 17, No. 1 (January 1967), p. 15. Fertig analyzes how inflation causes market confusion and, in turn, increased government control.
30. See Andrew Dickson White, *Fiat Money Inflation in France* (Irvington, New York: Foundation for Economic Education, [1914] 1959).
31. Compare Sennholz's "Hyperinflation in Germany" with Hans Kohn, "National Socialism," *Encyclopedia Britannica* (1969 ed.), Vol. 16, pp. 93ff, especially the middle paragraph of p. 93, col. 2.
32. See Chapters Seven and Eight for criticisms of socialism. For devastating economic and sociological critiques, see von Mises, *Socialism: An Economic and Sociological Analysis*, and Leszek Kolakowski, *Main Currents of Marxism: Its Origins, Growth and Dissolution*, three vols., trans. P. S. Falla (Oxford and New York: Oxford University Press, 1978).
33. Cited in Fertig, "Right Premise—Wrong Conclusion," p. 17.
34. Remember that we understand by "Kingdom of God" not solely numbers of souls saved and discipled but equally the expansion and intensification of man's dominion over the earth—his rule and development of it such that it serves man and glorifies God (Genesis 1:28).

CHAPTER TEN: *Sound Money for Good Stewardship*

1. Inflation is popularly mistaken for rising prices. Rising prices are an *effect* of inflation. Inflation causes prices to rise because money is less scarce; i.e., its supply rises relative to the goods for which it is exchanged. Hence its value must fall—i.e., prices must rise.
2. Recall that an optional definition of money is that it is the most marketable commodity in a given economy.
3. The Federal Reserve System, a private corporation, prints America's currency, not the Treasury Department.
4. This criticism should not be confused with promotion of the view that the Federal Reserve Act was the result of a conspiracy of major banking interests, a view I reject. For a thorough critique of that theory, see Wendell R. Bird, *Conspiracy Theory and the Federal Reserve Act* (unpublished thesis, Department of History, Vanderbilt University, 1975).
5. Brown, Driver, and Briggs, *Hebrew and English Lexicon*, p. 765.
6. North, *Honest Money*, p. 67. North's whole analysis of inflation as governmental counterfeiting is compelling Biblically, logically, and economically.
7. See the Federal Reserve System's book *The Federal Reserve System:*

Purposes and Functions (1963).

8. For a description of the system, see Sowell, *Economics: Analysis and Issues*, pp. 207ff. For a critical analysis, see North, *Honest Money*, pp. 80-90.

9. Making a strict dichotomy between wisdom and ethics is itself highly questionable from a Biblical standpoint. The opposite of wisdom is foolishness. God holds us responsible for gaining wisdom; refusing to do so is sin. Thus the Book of Proverbs consistently says that foolishness is sinful.

10. We observed instances of this in discussing the use of land and indentured labor as collateral in connection with the jubilee law. See Chapters Three and Five above.

11. Compare North, *Honest Money*, p. 81.

12. *Ibid.*, pp. 108f.

13. The parable of the talents (Matthew 25:14-30) clearly implies that such risk avoidance is bad stewardship, equivalent to burying money in the ground. God intends His people to serve others with money, either by giving it away or by investing it in productive enterprises.

14. Or perhaps earlier with a penalty to offset the remaining balance of the outstanding loan that was funded by the deposit.

15. This is similar to the way certificate of deposit accounts function today. We're not talking about a radically new way of banking, but about preventing one form of banking that is economically destructive.

16. Unless that body operates as a real insurance program, charging premiums to insure deposits. But private insurance companies probably could do the same job more efficiently, spurred to avoid bad risks by hopes for profits and fears of losses—hopes and fears governmental bodies lack.

17. North, *Honest Money*, p. 108.

18. Newly printed paper currency functions as money simply because civil government declares it legal tender—requiring people to accept it in exchange or be punished. This is called "fiat money" because it depends on a decree, the word "fiat" meaning "let it be."

19. See pages 139-141 above.

20. It would also rest on the Ninth Commandment by prohibiting the fraudulent practice of securing multiple loans with the same collateral, which happens in fractional reserve banking.

21. North, *Honest Money*, p. 103.

22. Marx and Engels, *Manifesto of the Communist Party*, in Laski, ed., *The Communist Manifesto*, p. 158.

23. This is because politicians benefit from the *appearance* of prosperity even if it is not real, so they inflate currency and hope the painful readjustments come after they're out of office.

24. See North, *Honest Money*, pp. 106f.

25. *Ibid.*, pp. 107f.

26. Hayek, *Unemployment and Monetary Policy*, p. 36.

27. Lewis, *The Abolition of Man*, p. 86.

28. This is not to imply that all—or even most—bad buying choices are engendered by inflation. Most probably stem from greed, discontent, and impatience. We must not externalize the cause of sin.

29. This is not to imply that inflationary sins are the only ones for

which God might punish our society, or that they are the only ones for which the punishment could be a ruined economy. God could punish us that way for permitting abortion or for any number of reasons.

30. This would follow historical precedent, as we saw in the cases of France and Germany.

CHAPTER ELEVEN: *Stewardship and Limited Government*

1. Note the term *"civil* government." This is to distinguish the institution of the state from the governing institutions of individual, family, and church, each of which is a government ordained by God. See Abraham Kuyper, *Christianity as a Life-System: The Witness of a World-View* (Memphis, TN: Christian Studies Center, 1980), pp. 37ff. Henceforth in this and later chapters the term "government," when it stands alone, will refer to civil government unless clearly distinguished by the context.

2. This is not the place for an in-depth study of the nature and functions of civil government. For a list of helpful works on the subject, see "Appendix Two: Bibliography on a Christian Philosophy of Civil Government."

3. See Kuyper, *Christianity as a Life-System*, pp. 37ff for a discussion of the idea of sphere sovereignty among the three fundamental spheres of government—civil, ecclesiastical, and individual.

4. Calvin, *Institutes of the Christian Religion*, IV. xx. 4; Vol. 2, p. 1490.

5. The good reputation one might get by being praised by government could itself have significant economic value, however.

6. On the deterrent effect of capital punishment, see Ernest van den Haag, "Death and Deterrence," *National Review*, Vol. 38 No. 4 (March 14, 1986), pp. 44, 61. Punishment must be justified on the basis of a just deserts understanding of justice. But it also has a beneficial deterrent side effect.

7. This text does not support situation ethics, which teaches that we can violate the Law for the sake of love. The Greek word for "fulfillment," *pleroma*, will not bear that sense. It means the opposite: the *pleroma* of something is its fullness, its complement, its whole substance. See E. Calvin Beisner, *A Biblical and Philosophical Critique of Situation Ethics* (unpublished term paper, University of Southern California, Department of Religion, 1977). Also see the commentaries on Romans 13:8-10 by Albert Barnes, John Calvin, Charles Hodge, R. C. H. Lenski, Martin Luther, H. C. G. Moule, John Murray, and A. T. Robertson, and J. B. Lightfoot, "On the Meaning of *pleroma*," in *Saint Paul's Epistles to the Colossians and to Philemon* (Grand Rapids, MI: Zondervan, [1879] 1974), pp. 257-273. The great commandments tell us to love God and man. The Law gives us the pattern of love.

8. Notice that Jesus treats the Commandments in this way in Matthew 5:21-48, acknowledging the minimum requirement set forth in the negative command, then showing the positive principle underlying it.

9. See the quotations from Smith's *Theory of Moral Sentiments* near the end of Chapter Five.

10. Robin Hood did not make his victims any more loving to the poor

merely by putting their goods in the hands of the poor.

11. This means that the Eighth Commandment, against theft, prohibits state-sponsored, coercive programs to transfer income to the poor. For some analysis of the failure of such programs, see Chapter Twelve. For answers to arguments against private property, see Chapter Five.

12. I am addressing here the question of self-sacrifice in an economic sense—giving things of value to others. I am not addressing the question of whether government has legitimate authority to compel military service. I understand the two questions to deal with different issues.

13. Gary DeMar and Colonel Doner, eds., *The Christian World View of Government* (Mountain View, CA: Coalition on Revival, 1986), Affirmation #16.

14. I understand preservation of peace against foreign and domestic oppressors to be an aspect of restraining and punishing injustice.

15. See Chapter Five.

16. The Tenth Commandment, against coveting, cannot be enforced by civil government—or by anyone but God, who alone knows the hearts of men. But neither should coveting be *encouraged*, as it is when government urges people to be discontent with their economic condition.

17. Biblical Law permits killing as punishment for capital crimes (Genesis 9:6; Numbers 31:7, 8; 1 Peter 2:13, 14) and in self-defense (Exodus 22:2). See Robert E. Farnell III, "Homicide," in Carl F.H. Henry, ed., *Baker's Dictionary of Christian Ethics* (Grand Rapids, MI: Baker, 1973), p. 294.

18. Some consumer safety laws are actually counterproductive. For instance, some medical drugs prohibited in the United States because of side effects are used effectively elsewhere because doctors realize that the harm from not using them is greater than that from using them. For a brief history of the Food and Drug Administration and the unintended consequences of its regulations (higher drug prices, longer development times, unavailability of clearly beneficial drugs in the U.S. that are available elsewhere), see Milton and Rose Friedman, *Free to Choose* (New York: Avon, 1980), pp. 193-200. The Friedmans' chapter, "Who Protects the Consumer?", is excellent reading on the pitfalls of much "consumer protection" legislation.

19. Some states no longer have laws prohibiting adultery, but a Biblical understanding of civil government indicates that they ought to.

20. Children cannot be required to obey their parents when doing so would require violating God's Law (Acts 5:29). Hence government must not enforce illegitimate parental authority.

21. "Once a family is headed by a woman, it is almost impossible for it to greatly raise its income even if the woman is highly educated and trained and she hires day-care or domestic help. Her family responsibilities and distractions tend to prevent her from the kind of all-out commitment that is necessary for the full use of earning power. . . . The key to lower-class life in contemporary America is that unrelated individuals, as the census calls them, are so numerous and conspicuous that they set the tone for the entire community. . . . It is

love that changes the short horizons of youth and poverty into the long horizons of marriage and career. When marriages fail, the man often returns to the more primitive rhythms of singleness. On the average, his income drops by one-third and he shows a far higher propensity for drink, drugs, and crime. But when marriages in general hold firm and men in general love and support their children, Banfield's lower-class style changes into middle-class futurity." George Gilder, *Wealth and Poverty*, pp. 89f.

22. The consent must be both free and *informed*. If it results from fraud—a violation of the Ninth Commandment—it is not knowledgeable.
23. Calvin, *Institutes*, IV.xx.3; Vol. 2, p. 1488.
24. On the great antiquity of property rights and their importance to societal development, especially liberty, see Gottfried Dietze, *In Defense of Property* (Baltimore: Johns Hopkins Press, [1963] 1975), pp. 48-63.
25. The landowner is symbolic of God in this parable, and thus cannot have done anything unjust.
26. Armen A. Alchian and William R. Allen, *University Economics: Elements of Inquiry*, 3rd ed. (Belmont, CA: Wadsworth, 1972), p. 142. Cited in North, *Sinai Strategy*, pp. 169f.
27. "Congress shall make no law respecting an establishment of religion, or prohibiting the free exercise thereof; or abridging the freedom of speech or of the press; or the right of the people peaceably to assemble and to petition the Government for a redress of grievances." First Amendment to the U.S. Constitution. Compare with the Fifth Amendment, cited below. The Fifth Amendment protects the life and property that underlie the freedoms protected in the First.
28. Property and liberty are not singular rights, but complex combinations of rights. The discussion of the American Founding Fathers' understandings of these terms in McDonald's *Novus Ordo Seclorum*, pp. 9-55, helps greatly to show why various rights are dependent on each other. Dietze's chapter "Property, Freedom and Civil Rights," in his *In Defense of Property*, is a lucid explanation of the interdependence of various personal and civil rights with property rights.
29. Such laws clearly infringe on property rights when they are applied *ex post facto*. They are more defensible otherwise, though I argue in Chapter Thirteen that even then they are suspect in terms of Biblical ethics.
30. For example, on June 26, 1987, the U.S. Supreme Court ruled in *Nollan v. California Coastal Commission* that the State of California "had to compensate owners of an oceanfront home for requiring them to grant public access to their beach as a condition for getting a building permit." See Charlotte Low, "Property Owners Get More Shelter," *Insight*, September 28, 1987, pp. 8-14, and Richard A. Epstein, *Takings: Private Property and the Power of Eminent Domain* (Cambridge, MA: Harvard University Press, 1985).
31. In "bait-and-switch," a company advertises a product that it doesn't have—or hides—to attract buyers, then uses high-pressure sales tactics to get them to buy a more expensive product.

32. Inflation, like any other debasement of a commodity, is in principle *fraud* first, *theft* second. Thus it is *theft by fraud*.
33. This is not the proper place to address the question to what extent civil government may rightly enforce the First through Fourth Commandments. In my view, ecclesiastical government, not civil, has authority to enforce those, insofar as they may be enforced at all.
34. This is done, for instance, in many public school textbooks. See *Douglas T. Smith, et al., v. Board of School Commissioners of Mobile County, et al.,* U.S. Dist. Court, Southern District of Alabama, Southern Division, Decision of Judge W. Brevard Hand, Appendix N, sub-Appendix B, pp. 1-3.
35. J. Barton Payne, "Property," in Henry, ed., *Baker's Dictionary of Christian Ethics*, p. 542.
36. R. C. Sproul, *Ethics and the Christian: Right and Wrong in Today's World* (Wheaton, IL: Tyndale House, 1983), p. 63. The Biblical gleaning law (Deuteronomy 23:24, 25; cf. Ruth 2:3-12; Matthew 12:1) is not a counterexample to this principle, for it rests on the principle that the produce of a field is not solely the property of the farmer who raises it, but also—and primarily—God's, since He owns the land and gives the rain and sun to make crops grow. For civil government to fabricate its own laws of a similar nature, however, is for it to assert its ultimate ownership analogous to—and instead of—God's.
37. "This view of theft and protection is not in conformity to either modern socialism or modern libertarianism. In the first system (socialism), the State collects the tithe for itself, and many times God's tithe, to be used for purposes specified by bureaucratic and political bodies. In the second system (libertarianism), all coercion against private property is defined as theft, including taxation itself (in some libertarian systems). Nevertheless, the Bible's standards are the valid ones, and the Bible is clear: *there is no absolute sovereignty in any person or institution.* Unquestionably, there are limits on the use of private property. But these limits are minimal." North, *Sinai Strategy*, p. 159.
38. See "King," *Encyclopedia Britannica* (1969 ed.), Vol. 13, pp. 360-362.
39. "Samuel Rutherford, in his 1664 (sic) book *Lex Rex*, wrote that law is king, and when kings and governors disobey the law Christians may disobey them." Marvin Olasky, *Prodigal Press: The Anti-Christian Bias of the American News Media* (Westchester, IL: Crossway, 1988), p. 115. (The actual date of *Lex Rex* was 1644.)
40. See Thomas Babington Macaulay, *The History of England from the Accession of James II*, five vols. (Chicago, New York, and San Francisco: Belford, Clarke & Co., 1889), Vol. 1, pp. 37-124.
41. The Magna Charta's protections extended almost exclusively to property, not to such things as trial by jury, *habeas corpus*, and other "chartered rights of the English" that later became recognized. See Dietze, *In Defense of Property*, pp. 54f.
42. McDonald, *Novus Ordo Seclorum*, pp. 24-28.
43. The saying, "The voice of the people is the voice of God" (**Vox populi, vox Dei**), though later used in positive contexts, originated in a letter from the Christian scholar Alcuin to the Emperor

Charlemagne ca. 800 A.D., in which he advised, "We would not listen to those who were wont to say the voice of the people is the voice of God, for the voice of the mob is near akin to madness." See Burton Stevenson, ed., *The Home Book of Quotations*, 10th ed. (New York: Dodd, Mead, 1967), p. 1480.

44. See Deuteronomy 1:9-18. Cf. McDonald, *Novus Ordo Seclorum*, Chapter III, "Systems of Political Theory," and Ralph Barton Perry, *Puritanism and Democracy* (New York: Vanguard, 1944).

45. See Alexis de Tocqueville, *Democracy in America*, two vols., ed. Phillips Bradley (New York: Random House, 1944), and Russell Kirk, *The Conservative Mind from Burke to Eliot*, 7th revised ed. (Chicago: Regnery, 1986), pp. 204-224.

46. John Stuart Mill, *Autobiography*, Chapter VI, in Charles W. Eliot, ed., *The Harvard Classics*, fifty vols. (N.Y.: P. F. Collier & Son, 1909), Vol. 25, p. 125. Mill's comment comes in the midst of his reflecting on Tocqueville's warnings against the tyrannical tendencies of democracy.

47. A classic argument against the use of government in violation of the Eighth Commandment is Frederic Bastiat's *The Law*, trans. Dean Russell (Irvington, New York: Foundation for Economic Education, [1850] 1974).

48. The sheer extent of governmental activity in the economy makes it difficult in some cases, and probably impossible in others, to avoid benefiting from some governmental forms of theft. For instance, it's easy—though financially costly—to refuse to accept AFDC or state or federal student grants or farm subsidies. But it's impossible to avoid benefiting from governmental transfers of wealth if one attends a public school (which is one argument for Christians' staying out of public schools) or uses a public library. For that matter, most hospitals, even private ones, have received some kinds of direct government funding. The trend toward governments taking on more and more functions once handled privately (e.g., municipal trash collection and ambulance service) only increases the difficulty. Enunciating the general principle that Christians should avoid becoming partners in legalized theft is simple enough. Putting it into practice—and identifying the precise lines of the permissible and the impermissible—is considerably more difficult. The passage in March 1988 of the Civil Rights Restoration Act, over President Ronald Reagan's veto, will make it even harder, since it greatly expands the intrusion of federal regulations in the private sector and codifies the effect of prior court decisions broadening the legal definition of federal aid to include payments to private institutions by recipients of government aid. There's room for plenty of individual discernment and, in the spirit of Romans 14:4-13, people should be slow to condemn one another for their respective choices. Nonetheless, Christians must begin to deal seriously with the problem of an ever-expanding governmental presence in what once were considered private activities.

49. "Theft and covetous yearnings cannot be justified by bringing government into the picture. There won't be much change until individuals begin to take Mosaic law seriously. Sennholz suggests that individuals should be informed of the nature and source of their Social

Security benefits. Every check should carry a stub that reveals the cumulative amount of benefits received as of that check. The shocking revelation that one has withdrawn $69,501.15 when he or she has contributed a paltry total of $817.15 would 'soon silence the most common defense: "I paid in."''' John Chamberlain, "Debts and Deficits," review of Hans Sennholz, *Debts and Deficits* (Spring Mills, PA: Libertarian Press, 1988), in *The Freeman*, Vol. 38, No. 3 (March 1988), pp. 118f. On the other hand, actuaries' forecasts of Social Security's coming bankruptcy—which may be delayed but not finally prevented—indicate that younger workers paying into the system today may never receive back what they pay in. The key problem is that Social Security recipients receive not what they've paid in, plus interest or dividends, but what current workers are paying in. This means that Social Security is an income transfer program, taking income from current workers to give it to current retirees. As such it violates the Eighth Commandment's prohibition of theft. This means no tinkering with the system will ever be able to solve its problems, since the system itself is contrary in principle to God's Law and hence cannot but have ill effects.

50. See Rousas John Rushdoony, *Law and Liberty* (Fairfax, VA: Thoburn Press, 1977).

CHAPTER TWELVE: *Stewardship and Economic Regulation: Price Controls*

1. Nevertheless, the Biblical doctrine that all of creation—physical and spiritual—is one implies that just acts will ultimately have good effects, and unjust acts will ultimately have bad effects (Galatians 6:10).

2. Williams, *The State Against Blacks*, p. 49.

3. Henry Hazlitt, *Economics in One Lesson* (Westport, CT: Arlington House, [1946] 1979), p. 17; emphasis original. The book is a valuable, clearly written case-by-case analysis of the unintended ill effects of many common economic regulations.

4. Inflation actually *causes* more unemployment than would occur without it. See Chapter Nine above.

5. We saw in Chapters Nine and Ten that a fourth type of economic regulation—manipulation of money supply through fiat inflation—both is unjust and has bad consequences. In addition, a fifth type—graduated (or progressive) taxation—is contrary to the Biblical principle of justice because it fails to meet the criterion of *impartiality*. Further, sound economic arguments can be made against graduated taxation in terms of: (1) Distortion of choices leading to unproductive allocation of resources: as income rises, earners are increasingly likely to "hide" it from taxation by investing in economically nonproductive enterprises and activities. (2) Barriers to economic progress: as lower-income earners reach tax rate thresholds, they face the paradox that an increase in income can be more than offset by an increase in tax rate, a situation to which many respond by choosing not to put forth the extra effort needed to climb the income scale. The scope of this book doesn't permit extensive analysis of taxation. Good economic analysis can be found in

Friedrich Hayek's *The Constitution of Liberty*, Chapter Twenty, "Taxation and Redistribution," and his "Progressive Taxation Reconsidered," in Mary Sennholz, ed., *On Freedom and Free Enterprise: Essays in Honor of Ludwig von Mises* (Princeton, NJ: D. Van Nostrand, 1956), pp. 265-284. Rushdoony, in *Institutes of Biblical Law*, pp. 281-284, argues that Scripture permits only two forms of tax: the poll (or head) tax, an equal sum for everyone (Exodus 30:11-16), and the tithe (Leviticus 27:32). He concludes that the poll tax goes to the state and the tithe to the church and the poor (p. 283). He argues that Scripture's insistence that the earth belongs to God (Exodus 9:29; Deuteronomy 10:14; Psalm 24:1; 1 Corinthians 10:26) implies that "... a land tax is not lawful. *A tax on the land is a tax against God and against His law-order*" (p. 283; emphasis original). Gary North, in *Inherit the Earth* (Ft. Worth, TX: Dominion Press, 1987), supports a flat rate tax by analogy with the tithe (p. 46), and warns that collection of as much as 10 percent of gross national product by the state is seen in Scripture as a judgment of God on sin (p. 148; cf. Genesis 47:24; 1 Samuel 8:15). In *Sinai Strategy* North presents economic arguments against both high and graduated income taxes (pp. 172-175).

6. See the discussion of these under the subhead "Protecting Rights" in Chapter Eleven above.

7. The benefits of regulations that result in increased scarcity of the products or goods affected will necessarily be such things as public health and safety.

8. This assumption rests on our understanding that the aim of good stewardship (economics) is to reduce the scarcity of goods and services for all people by the wise application of resources. This is part of what is implied in the dominion mandate of Genesis 1 and 2.

9. A proper understanding of the economic theory of value and price, rooted in the law of marginal utility and its extrapolation, the law of supply and demand, helps greatly in understanding the injustice of legal price controls. See the discussion of these principles in Chapter Eight.

10. See the discussion under the headings "Supply, Demand, and Marginal Utility," "Marginal Utility, Value, and Price," and "Implications of Marginal Utility Theory of Value and Price" in Chapter Eight above.

11. As a result, "black markets" develop, in which buyers and sellers ignore legal maximum prices for the sake of making exchanges possible.

12. William Tucker, "Where Do the Homeless Come From?," *National Review*, Vol. XXXIX, No. 18 (September 25, 1987), pp. 32-43.

13. It is important to remember that fewer units *available* does not mean the same thing as fewer units *in existence*. A shortage occurs when a lower ratio of units to buyers is *offered* on the market than are demanded by buyers at the legal maximum price.

14. See Chapter Eight above.

15. Meanwhile, people already renting when the control goes into effect benefit. Their possession of rental property is protected from the competition of others who might offer to pay more for it.

16. The free market mechanism also excludes some buyers and sellers,

of course—those who cannot afford to exchange at the equilibrium price set by the market. The point is that artificial maximum and minimum prices exclude *more* buyers and sellers than do market prices.

17. Many landlords are themselves far from rich. Such people own only a single small rental property, often heavily mortgaged. Yet the rent from it may be an important part of their income, which itself may be well below the national average.

18. Cf. Nash, *Poverty and Wealth*, p. 117.

19. Legal limits on interest rates, similarly, must cause shortages of credit. The Bible never limits interest *rates*. It prohibits interest on loans to the poor. See Gary North, "Stewardship, Investment, and Usury: Financing the Kingdom of God," in Rushdoony, *The Institutes of Biblical Law*.

20. This means that what were marginal units under market pricing are no longer marginal under minimum pricing. They're now off the margin. They're like the chunks of ice that have fallen from the edge (margin) of a glacier into the ocean: they're no longer marginal, they're lost.

21. See Richard B. McKenzie, *Economic Issues in Public Policies* (New York: McGraw-Hill, 1980), p. 28. Notice that this *minimum* price is argued for on the same basis as the *maximum* price considered under the example of rent control: without it consumers will suffer.

22. "In short, the control system only keeps a number of farmers in business who could not compete successfully in a free market. These farmers would be the ones pushed out [and into some other business—ECB] in the event the market were decontrolled." McKenzie, *Economic Issues*, p. 31.

23. ". . . under conditions that are otherwise identical, equal quantities of goods have quite unequal value for the rich and for the poor, that value being greater for the poor and smaller for the rich." Böhm-Bawerk, *Capital and Interest*, Vol. 2, p. 150.

24. The ill effect is hidden—really transferred to someone else—when the state buys the surplus milk and then *gives* it to people with low incomes. This "solution" still involves legalized theft because some people are taxed to pay for milk that is given to other people. This can't be justified on the grounds that it serves the poor at the expense of the rich (Exodus 23:2, 3). Further, the overall cost to society of getting that milk to its recipients is higher than it would be under market conditions because of intervening levels of bureaucracy.

25. "Minimum price controls over time tend to raise the price of milk above what would be charged in a free market, reduce the consumption of milk, and create market surpluses that must be handled by additional government actions." McKenzie, *Economic Issues*, p. 30.

26. The Ethiopian government, for instance, resold much of the food sent to it to buy arms, which it then used in its war against its own people.

27. See Peter T. Bauer, *Dissent on Development* ([1972] 1976) and *Reality and Rhetoric: Studies in the Economics of Development* (1984) (Cambridge, MA: Harvard University Press); Thomas Sowell, *Race and Economics* (New York: David McKay, 1975), pp. 195f;

Helmut Schoeck, *Envy: A Theory of Social Behaviour* (New York: Harcourt, Brace & World, 1970); Nash, *Poverty and Wealth*, pp. 190-193; Brian Griffiths, *The Creation of Wealth* (Downers Grove, IL: InterVarsity Press, 1985), p. 13; Chilton, *Productive Christians in an Age of Guilt Manipulators*, pp. 99-110.

28. We will discuss shortly the motives of those who lobbied for them. They probably differed significantly from those of legislators.

29. Because inflation is perceived as a way to fight unemployment—and works short-term—and minimum wage laws create unemployment, the two feed on each other. Inflation makes it more difficult to live on low incomes. That difficulty creates pressure for higher minimum wage laws. Those, in turn, create additional unemployment, which is fought by increased inflation to "prime the pump" of the economy, creating short-term expanded demand for labor but long-term displacement of labor because of misallocation of capital funds. The higher prices caused by the inflation make it still more difficult to live on low incomes. And so the vicious cycle continues. Only ending both inflation and minimum wage laws will break it.

30. Williams, *The State Against Blacks*, pp. 34f.

31. See *Ibid.*, Chapter Three, "Minimum Wage, Maximum Folly."

32. This happens despite laws against racial discrimination in hiring. People usually find ways to get around laws they don't like.

33. Figures and trends for blacks and whites aged eighteen to nineteen and twenty to twenty-four were similar. Williams, *The State Against Blacks*, p. 38. It could be argued that cultural factors (the breakdown of the black family and the resulting lack of self-discipline among many blacks, for instance) contributed significantly to the growing gap between black and white youth unemployment, but it appears that the unemployment trend preceded rather than followed the cultural factor trends.

34. Milton and Rose Friedman, *Free to Choose*, p. 227. Cf. Williams, *The State Against Blacks*, pp. 44ff.

35. Equal pay for equal work laws do not damage the economy as would "comparable worth" laws because the latter require massive government intrusion in the marketplace to assign specified "worths" to different jobs in various locations. We will have more to say about "comparable worth" shortly.

36. We focus on equal pay for equal work, but precisely the same analysis holds in principle against comparable worth laws. In their case, however, the argument is even more clear because they require equal pay for different jobs, for which the economic value can more readily be seen to differ.

37. A paradox is not an actually contradictory proposition (or set of propositions), but one that appears contradictory, unbelievable, or absurd but may be true in fact.

38. Remember that subjective economic value is distinct from objective moral value.

39. This is the law of diminishing returns.

40. This is because competition tends to result in a uniform price for a given good throughout the marketplace, other things being equal. See the discussion of this in the section "Competition and

Cooperation" in Chapter Eight.

41. "Despite a general consensus among today's public that people should be paid identically if they do identical work, this law is the first step toward handicapping the most disadvantaged group of workers." Williams, *The State Against Blacks*, p. 160, n. 11; cf. p. 106 on the fact that equal pay laws nearly eliminated blacks from employment in the railroad industry.

42. Equal pay for equal work laws have the same effect as price fixing. The latter, however, is illegal, viewed as collusion among sellers against buyers. The rationale of prohibiting price fixing is to permit competition to bring consumers goods and services at the lowest possible prices. Employers, however, are consumers of labor, just as housewives are consumers of laundry detergent. If housewives should be protected against price fixing on laundry detergent, there seems no reason why employers shouldn't be protected against price fixing on labor.

43. More competing buyers relative to sellers will push prices up; more competing sellers relative to buyers will push prices down. High competition of both buyers and sellers causes stable prices at the lowest level producers can afford. See the section "Competition and Cooperation" in Chapter Eight.

44. For additional analysis of price controls, see Williams, *The State Against Blacks*, Friedman and Friedman, *Free to Choose*, Milton Friedman, *Capitalism and Freedom* (Chicago: University of Chicago Press, 1968), Sowell, *Economics: Analysis and Issues*, and McKenzie, *Economic Issues*.

CHAPTER THIRTEEN: *Stewardship, Access Controls, and Subsidies*

1. Actually, the wide array of subsidies currently in effect in the United States and most Western nations results in transfers of wealth back and forth among a wide variety of segments of population.

2. Rights defined by the Ten Commandments, that is.

3. We'll meet a very different argument for licensure—protection of near-monopoly for the purpose of sustaining higher than market prices—shortly.

4. The enormously high prices of medical malpractice insurance certainly create a presumptive appearance that licensure has not succeeded in keeping incompetents out of that profession.

5. These and some sixty-five other occupations required licensing in one or another state in 1956. See Walter Gellhorn, *Individual Freedom and Governmental Restraints* (Baton Rouge: Louisiana State University Press, 1956). The list has grown since then.

6. Requiring registration of taxi services and posting of clear identification where passengers can see it can be defended as an assistance to law enforcement. It can make it easier for passengers who are robbed to identify drivers for police.

7. In the case of minimum wage laws, this was a revealing bit of information. It will be for licensing, too.

8. *Cui bono?* is a standard method of discovering who had *motive* for a crime. The Roman jurist Lucius Cassius Longinus asked, "*Cui bono*

fuerit?, Who stood to gain?" Cicero shortened the question to *Cui bono?*.

9. Friedman, *Capitalism and Freedom*, p. 140.
10. This occasions the problem of forged and inadequate licenses. According to Dr. Paul Vitz, professor of psychology at New York University (personal conversation, March 25, 1988), forgeries account for 2-3 percent of the medical licenses in the United States. Further, many medical licenses are based on training received in inadequate foreign medical schools. There simply is no evidence that the licensure requirement actually reduces the number of "quacks" in medicine or any other profession.
11. Friedman made the point well with respect to medical licensure, which, he said, renders average quality of medical services received low partly "by making it much more difficult for private individuals to collect from physicians for malpractice. One of the protections of the individual citizen against incompetence is protection against fraud and the ability to bring suit in the court against malpractice. Some suits are brought, and physicians complain a great deal about how much they have to pay for malpractice insurance. Yet suits for malpractice are fewer and less successful than they would be were it not for the watchful eye of the medical associations. It is not easy to get a physician to testify against a fellow physician when he faces the sanction of being denied the right to practice in an 'approved' hospital. The testimony generally has to come from members of panels set up by medical associations themselves, always, of course, in the alleged interest of the patients." *Capitalism and Freedom*, pp. 157f.
12. Friedman, *Capitalism and Freedom*, p. 153.
13. And this contingency is by no means proven for any licensed occupation.
14. "The members [of a licensed occupation] look solely at technical standards of performance, and argue in effect that we must have only first-rate physicians even if this means that some people get no medical service—though of course they never put it that way. Nonetheless, the view that people should get only the 'optimum' medical service always lead[s] to a restrictive policy, a policy that keeps down the number of physicians." Friedman, *Capitalism and Freedom*, p. 153.
15. A preferred option to licensing for many services is quality standards on end-product. Requiring inspection of electrical wiring, for instance, before payment can be made, would ensure safe wiring, but would still permit anyone to offer his services as an electrician.
16. This follows the model of Exodus 21:28f: "[I]f an ox gores a man or a woman to death, the ox shall surely be stoned and its flesh shall not be eaten; but the owner of the ox shall go unpunished. If, however, an ox was previously in the habit of goring, and its owner has been warned, yet he does not confine it, and it kills a man or a woman, the ox shall be stoned and its owner also shall be put to death." See verses 29-36 for further development of the distinction between civil and criminal liability in such cases.
17. On natural and legal monopolies, see Sowell, *Economics: Analysis and Issues*, Chapter Six, "Non-Competitive Product Markets," and

Chapter Seven, "Non-Competitive Factor Markets."
18. On labor unions, see Williams, *The State Against Blacks*, pp. 43-45, 69, 91-94, 99-102, 106-108, 119f; Friedman and Friedman, *Free to Choose*, pp. 218-232; Sowell, *Economics: Analysis and Issues*, 100f; McKenzie, *Economic Issues*, pp. 113, 120f, 131, 152.
19. On the effects of such laws see especially Williams, *The State Against Blacks*, Chapter Nine, "Interstate Commerce Commission Truck Regulation."
20. Doctors and lawyers, in particular, are restricted in how and where they can advertise.
21. Yale Brozen, *Advertising and Society* (New York: New York University Press, 1974); George Stigler, "The Economics of Information," *Journal of Political Economy*, LXIX (June 1961); David G. Tuerck, ed., *The Political Economy of Advertising* (Washington, D.C.: American Enterprise Institute, 1978).
22. Production quotas on domestic goods—e.g., agricultural products—have the same effects plus others. Clarence Carson, *The War on the Poor* (New Rochelle, New York: Arlington House, 1969), Chapter Four, "Farmers at Bay," and William Peterson, *The Great Farm Problem* (Chicago: Regnery, 1959).
23. See the sections "Comparative Advantage" and "Comparative Advantage, Free Trade, and National Security," in Chapter Seven.
24. Similar arguments hold against immigration and hiring quotas. Gary North, "Public Goods and Fear of Foreigners," *The Freeman*, March 1974; Thomas Sowell, *Ethnic America: A History* (New York: Basic Books, 1981) and *The Economics and Politics of Race* (New York: William Morrow, 1983).
25. "The Bible provides us with an example of 'spillover effects' [pollution] and what to do about them. If a man starts a fire on his property, and the fire spreads to his neighbor's property, the man who started the fire is responsible for compensating his neighbor for the latter's losses (Ex[odus] 22:6). Obviously, this invasion of property is *physical*, rather than merely competitive and economic in nature, and therefore the fire-starter is liable. The destruction of property in this instance is physical and immediate; the victim actually loses part of his crop. But what about noise pollution, where the man's house is not burned, but its market value drops as a result of his neighbor's noisy factory? This would seem to be covered by the case-law on fire, since sound waves are physical phenomena, just as sparks are. But when the loss is exclusively economic, *without physical invasion*, the Bible is silent: there is no law that would require the successful innovator to compensate those who lost money because of the introduction of new production techniques or new products. Alchian's analysis would seem to apply: 'Although private property rights protect private property from physical changes chosen by other people, no immunity is implied for the exchange value of one's property.'" North, *Sinai Strategy*, p. 171, citing Armen Alchian, "Some Economics of Property Rights," *Il Politico* (1965), reprinted in Alchian, *Economic Forces at Work* (Indianapolis: Liberty Press, 1977), p. 131. For legal and economic arguments against zoning, and a thorough study of the effects of

eliminating zoning laws, see Bernard H. Siegan, *Land Use Without Zoning* (Lexington, MA: Lexington, 1972).

26. Williams, *The State Against Blacks*, pp. 142-144.

27. It may seem strange to identify poverty as an "economic activity." We will see shortly why I have done so.

28. For precision's sake I am distinguishing subsidies from protectionist quotas and tariffs, and from minimum prices, though in fact they have the same economic effect. Subsidies involve direct transfers of money (or other commodities) from the state to the subsidized person or corporation; minimum prices, quotas, and tariffs bring more cash to the protected persons and businesses by artificially raising the prices consumers must pay for their products and services.

29. Not even by inflation, as we saw in Chapters Nine and Ten. Printing new money steals from others; it does not create new wealth.

30. The fact that subsidies are approved by a legislature does not make them right. See the section "Civil Government Is Not Above the Law," in Chapter Eleven. Taxation is appropriate only for proper functions of government, which do not include wealth transfers.

31. In Chapter Fourteen we will consider a Biblical definition of poverty and contrast it with current secular definitions. We will also see that not all poverty arises from people's free choices.

32. Except those who choose poverty for religious reasons.

33. This is true despite the fact that man, created in the image of God, is by nature a worker. The fall distorted that image. As a result, incentive normally is required to overcome the sinful tendency toward sloth.

34. This, like every other economic choice, is an application of the idea of *marginal utility*; see Chapter Seven.

35. Space permits quoting only a few of the many verses in Proverbs on the results of sloth and foolishness. The full force of the teaching comes only from reading the many verses on the subject together.

36. Proverbs does not teach that sloth and foolishness are the only causes of poverty. It recognizes others, some of which are not culpable. We will discuss the various causes of poverty in Chapter Fourteen.

37. Charles Murray, *Losing Ground: American Social Policy, 1950-1980* (New York: Basic Books, 1984).

38. *Ibid.*, pp. 56-58. Murray shows why no other plausible explanation for the reversal of progress is historically plausible. See pp. 58-66.

39. Murray's *Losing Ground* is an indispensable study of the impact of subsidies to the poor. Two other technical studies indicating the self-defeating nature of subsidies to the poor are Roger A. Freeman's *The Wayward Welfare State* (Stanford, CA: Hoover Institution Press/Stanford University, 1981) and A. Haeworth Robertson, *The Coming Revolution in Social Security* (Reston, VA: Reston Publishing Co./Prentice-Hall, 1981). An excellent history of self-defeating poverty relief programs undertaken by governments is Clarence B. Carson's *The War on the Poor*. An analysis of the development of American poverty subsidies against the backdrop of economic assumptions of the U.S. Constitution is Terry L. Anderson and Peter J. Hill's *The Birth of a Transfer Society* (Stanford, CA: Hoover Institution Press/Stanford University, 1980).

40. The municipal bonds frequently used to raise money for expensive professional sports stadiums are subsidies to team owners and players and to those who can afford to attend the events (usually not among the poorer people in a community). Not all subsidies—probably a minority of them—go to the poor.
41. Murray, *Losing Ground*, p. 233.

CHAPTER FOURTEEN: *The Nature and Causes of Poverty*

1. The financial picture is not of the exceptional welfare family, but of the average: "The figures indicate that the average welfare family of four received about $15,000 worth of subsidies in 1976 and close to $18,000 worth in 1979. These totals, which are real averages, not extreme cases, compare with an American median income of approximately $14,500 in 1976 and $16,500 in 1979, and annual minimum-wage earnings and benefits of about half the welfare level." Gilder, *Wealth and Poverty*, p. 136. Proportionately the picture is about the same today, though the absolute dollar amounts are higher due to inflation. Economist Herman Miller questions the legitimacy of calling such people "poor": "The term poverty may connote hunger, but this is not what is usually meant in discussions about poverty in America. Consider, for example, the facilities available to the poor. Runica County, Mississippi, is the poorest county in our poorest state. About eight out of every ten families in this county had incomes under $3,000 in 1960 [i.e., under the official poverty level—ECB] and most of them were poor by national standards; yet 52 percent owned television sets, 46 percent owned automobiles, and 37 percent owned washing machines. These families might have been deprived of hope and poor in spirit, but their material possessions, though low by American standards, would be the envy of the majority of mankind today." Miller, *Rich Man, Poor Man* (New York: Thomas Y. Crowell Co., 1971), pp. 110f.
2. Jean L. McKechnie, *et al.*, eds., *Webster's New Twentieth Century Dictionary of the English Language*, unabridged 2nd ed. (New York: Collins & World, 1977), pp. 1400, 1411.
3. Theodore Caplow, "Poverty," in *Encyclopedia Britannica* (1969 ed.), Vol. 18, p. 392.
4. William White Whitney, et al., eds., *The Century Dictionary: An Encyclopedic Lexicon of the English Language*, six vols. (New York: The Century Co., 1890), Vol. 4, p. 4660.
5. See *Statistical Abstract of the United States, 1982-83* (Washington, D.C.: U.S. Government Printing Office, 1983), Tables 718, 727, and page 417. It hardly needs pointing out that a relative definition automatically makes it almost impossible to reduce the rate of "poverty" in a given society.
6. See Gilder, *Wealth and Poverty*, p. 136.
7. The definition has a great deal to do with the magnitude of the problem. See the section "How Big Is the Problem?" in Chapter Fifteen.
8. Roland K. Harrison, "Poor," in Henry, ed., *Baker's Dictionary of Christian Ethics*, p. 515.
9. This does not mean that the Bible assumes that the rich never work. They may work, and many do work very hard.

10. It is common to translate *penes* "poor." If this is understood simply to mean "not rich," it may be unobjectionable. But if it implies destitution, it certainly is wrong. The noun comes from the verb *penamai*, "to work for one's living." A. T. Robertson, *Word Pictures in the New Testament*, six vols. (Nashville, TN: Broadman, 1931), Vol. 4, p. 249. As such it might better be translated, in its only occurrence in the N.T. (2 Corinthians 9:9),"laborer." See the discussion of that passage in Chapter Sixteen, note 3.

11. Note that we do not make the distinction between business owners and business employees. Most owners work themselves, many far more than their employees. The labor/capital distinction of Marxism is a vast overgeneralization and more often false than true.

12. All others—anyone able to do so—must work or go hungry (2 Thessalonians 3:10). It may be understood that a widow with young children might be unable to work sufficiently to support herself and them because much of her time is devoted to caring directly for them.

13. "From Xen[ophon] onwards *penes* refers to the man who cannot live from his property, but has to work with his hands. Hence the *penes* is not like the *ptochos*, who is poor enough to be a beggar and needs help. He is only relatively poor; the opposite of *penes* is *plousios*, wealthy. . . ." L. Coenen, *penes*, sub-article to "Poor," in Brown, ed., *The New International Dictionary of New Testament Theology*, Vol. 2, p. 820. "A far deeper depth of destitution is implied in [*ptocheia*] than in [*penia*]. . . . The [*penes*] may be so poor that he earns his bread by daily labour; but the [*ptochos*] is so poor that he only obtains his living by begging. . . . The [*penes*] has nothing superfluous, the [*ptochos*] nothing at all . . . ." R. C. Trench, *New Testament Synonyms* (Grand Rapids, MI: Eerdmans,[1880] 1976 rpt.), p. 129, cf. pp. 128-130. *Ptochos* ". . . signifies utter dependence on society." H. H. Esser, *ptochos*, sub-article to "Poor," in Brown, ed., *New International Dictionary of New Testament Theology*, Vol. 2, p. 821. Some finer distinctions may be made between these two classes of the poor, and there are several other words sometimes used in the New Testament, as well as several in the Old, to designate the "poor" in one or another of these two senses, and in additional senses having to do not with economic but with social, legal, or spiritual status. An excellent comparative study of all of the Hebrew and Greek Biblical words related to the poor is Daryl S. Borgquist's *Toward a Biblical Theology of the Poor*. Especially significant is his argument that the Septuagint frequently mistranslated key Hebrew terms, but that N.T. usage was governed more directly by the Hebrew O.T. than by the LXX. For the application of this distinction, see 2 Corinthians 9:8-10, discussed in Chapter Sixteen, note 3.

14. This does not mean that charitable giving is *forbidden* to anyone but the *ptochos*. It may be given to others to support a particular ministry, or simply out of spontaneous kindness.

15. A good introduction to the history of poverty is Henry Hazlitt's *The Conquest of Poverty* (New Rochelle, New York: Arlington House, 1973). See also Rosenberg and Birdzell, *How the West Grew Rich*, and Frederic Austin Ogg, *Economic Development of Modern Europe* (New York: Macmillan, 1918).

16. William Farr, "The Influence of Scarcities and of the High Prices of Wheat on the Mortality of the People of England," *Journal of the Royal Statistical Society*, February 16, 1846, Vol. IX, p. 158; cited in Hazlitt, *Conquest of Poverty*, p. 14.

17. A good summary of major famines in history is Reginald Passmore, "Famine," *Encyclopedia Britannica* (1969 ed.), Vol. 9, pp. 58f.

18. Ireland was at the time a one-crop, largely nonindustrialized nation.

19. Severe famines struck the U.S.S.R. in 1921 and 1932-1933. Passmore, "Famine," *Encyclopedia Britannica* (1969 ed.), Vol. 9, p. 58. They were engineered largely by the Communist rulers of the country. See Anton Antonov-Ovseyenko, *The Time of Stalin: Portrait of a Tyranny*, trans. George Saunders (New York: Harper & Row, 1981), p. 213; cf. pp. 56, 64-67, 307.

20. Passmore, "Famine," *Encyclopedia Britannica* (1969 ed.), Vol. 9, p. 58.

21. See Rosenberg and Birdzell, *How the West Grew Rich*, for a thorough study of the factors contributing to the economic development of the West—factors like hard work, free trade, division of labor, technological advances, and market prices.

22. Sproul, *Ethics and the Christian*, pp. 54-56.

23. See Chapter Eleven on the economic role of the state. Restitution must come from those who performed the injustice. The innocent must not be forced to pay for the crimes of the guilty. See Ezekiel 18 and E. Calvin Beisner, "The Lame Case for Affirmative Action," *World*, Vol. 2, No. 1, April 6, 1987, p. 8.

24. Judging proportions of each type is difficult, since many criteria are subjective. Amos G. Warner's unscientific study in the late 1800s indicated that 25 percent of American poor were so through laxness, shiftlessness, or drunkenness, the rest through misfortune. Charles Booth's more scientific contemporary analysis in London revealed low-wage or irregular employment as the principal cause of 62 percent, large families or illness of 23 percent, and drunkenness, overspending, and laziness of the remaining 15 percent. Caplow, "Poverty," *Encyclopedia Britannica* (1969 ed.), Vol. 18, p. 395.

25. Ronald Sider's assertion that God is "on the side of the poor!" dies the death of a thousand qualifications when he writes that ". . . there are several important things I do not mean. First, God is not biased. Second, material poverty is not a biblical ideal. Third, the poor and oppressed, just because they are poor and oppressed, are not thereby members of the church. . . . Fourth, God does not care more about the salvation of the poor than the salvation of the rich. Fifth, we dare not start with some ideologically interpreted context of oppression (for example, Marxist analysis) and then reinterpret Scripture from that ideological bias. Sixth, God does not overlook the sin of those who are poor because of sloth or alcoholism." Is there any sense left in which God really can be "on the side of the poor!"? Sider assures, "God, however, is not neutral. His freedom from bias does not mean that he maintains neutrality in the struggle for justice. [Note how "justice" sneaks in as if it had something to do with relative distributions of wealth. This is one of several Marxist categories that predetermine Sider's hermeneutic. Compare Chapter Five above.—ECB] He is indeed on the side of the poor! The Bible clearly and repeatedly

teaches that God is at work in history casting down the rich and exalting the poor because frequently the rich are wealthy precisely because they have oppressed the poor or have neglected to aid the needy." *Rich Christians in an Age of Hunger*, pp. 75f. The last sentence could just as well have been, "The Bible clearly and repeatedly teaches that God is at work in history judging the poor because of their sins and rewarding the wealthy because of their righteousness." Wealth and poverty are not the criteria of judgment, but righteousness and sin. For a devastating critique of Sider's idea that God is "on the side of the poor," see Chilton, *Productive Christians in an Age of Guilt Manipulators*, Chapter Four.

26. Carl F. H. Henry, *God Revelation, and Authority*, six vols. (Waco, TX: Word, 1976ff), Vol. 4, pp. 549f.

27. Borgquist, *Toward a Biblical Theology of the Poor*, p. 64.

28. Much poverty in America stems from or is magnified by government oppression in the form of wage and price controls, access controls, and subsidies (see Chapters Eleven through Thirteen). In addition, government's use of wealth transfer mechanisms—which violate the Eighth Commandment—implicates millions of Americans in theft by receiving. Though most of them probably are completely unaware of the oppression of which they are a part, they might still feel the oppression they suffer from the same kinds of structures.

29. See Borgquist, *Toward a Biblical Theology of the Poor*, pp. 61f.

30. See Chilton, *Productive Christians in an Age of Guilt Manipulators*, Chapter Five, "The Third World," and Chapter Six, "Foreign Aid."

31. Peter T. Bauer, *Dissent on Development* (Cambridge, MA: Harvard University Press, 1972), *Equality, the Third World, and Economic Development* (Harvard, 1981), and *Reality and Rhetoric: Studies in the Economics of Development* (Harvard, 1984). See especially the excerpt from *Equality, the Third World, and Economic Delusion*, "Western Guilt and Third World Poverty," in Franky Schaeffer, ed., *Is Capitalism Christian?* (Westchester, IL: Crossway, 1986), pp. 115ff. Adam Smith in *The Wealth of Nations*, Book IV, Chapter vii, Part iii, demonstrated that colonies ". . . have been a source of expence and not of revenue to their respective mother countries." See Cannan, ed., Vol. 2, p. 107.

32. See Max Weber, *The Protestant Ethic and the Spirit of Capitalism*, trans. Talcott Parsons (London: George Allen and Unwin, 1930).

33. "Since Judaism made Christianity possible and gave it the character of a religion essentially free from magic, it rendered an important service from the point of view of economic history. For the dominance of magic outside the sphere in which Christianity has prevailed is one of the most serious obstructions to the rationalization of economic life. Magic involves stereotyping of technology and economic relations." Max Weber, *General Economic History*, trans. Frank Knight (New York: Collier Books, 1961), p. 265; cited in Michael Novak, *The Spirit of Democratic Capitalism* (New York: American Enterprise Institute/Simon and Schuster, 1982), p. 374, n. 11. Novak's book is a broad study of the economic impact of the Christian worldview.

34. E. Stanley Jones, *The Christ of the Indian Road* (London: Hodder and

Stoughton, 1930), pp. 54f.

35. For detailed discussion of these ideals and their practical effects, see Rabindranath Maharaj, *Death of a Guru* (Philadelphia and New York: Holman, 1977).

36. Animism and spiritism, though typically estimated as the religions of only about 3 percent of the world's people, probably dominate far more people, since many backward people who profess Buddhist, Hindu, Shinto and even Roman Catholic faiths actually have animist or spiritist cosmologies.

37. Jones, *The Christ of the Indian Road*, pp. 52f. By giving India Christ, Jones emphatically did *not* mean superimposing Western culture on India. He greatly admired much Indian culture, but recognized that the false Indian worldview was necessarily economically unproductive.

38. See E. Calvin Beisner *A Stranger in the Land: Wealth, Poverty, and the Sovereignty of God*, p. 392, table in note 29.

39. Daniel J. O'Neil, "The Nations Rich and Poor: Four Theses in Search of More Facts," *This World*, Fall 1982, pp. 103-112.

40. See Beisner, *A Stranger in the Land: Wealth, Poverty, and the Sovereignty of God*, pp. 389-394, particularly the statistical tables on pp. 390-392.

41. Scripture reveals that God opposes those who oppose Him: Deuteronomy 4:23-28; 28:15-38; 2 Samuel 7:14; 1 Corinthians 3:10-15; Joshua 24:20; Judges 2:13f; Micah 5:15; Jeremiah 6:19; 8:12f; 14:1-10; Amos 1:3,6,9,11,13; 2:1,4,6; Zephaniah 1:12f; Psalm 16:4.

CHAPTER FIFTEEN: *How Churches Can Help the Poor*

1. See especially Chapters Eleven through Thirteen.

2. It might also be objected that civil government ought to be involved because poor relief is a matter of justice. It *is*, but not of the equalitarianism advocates of this argument normally have in mind; see Chapters Four and Five. If civil government confined itself to enforcing real justice (defined by Biblical Law), its ending of many economic regulations would do much to help the poor; see Chapters Eleven through Thirteen.

3. Some statistics in the following discussion are derived by extrapolation, an imprecise method, and will be noted as such in references. The point of all the statistics, however, is not to be precise but to have sound reasons for painting the overall picture as we do.

4. For criticisms of some such efforts, see the section on subsidies in Chapter Thirteen, and studies referenced there.

5. See *Statistical Abstract of the United States, 1984*, p. 444, Fig. 15.2; compare p. 475, Table 783.

6. Carolyn Lochhead, "Nowhere to Go, Always in Sight," *Insight on the News*, May 16, 1988, p. 10. Lochhead's three-part report on homelessness in that issue, with sidebars telling the stories of specific homeless people, is a poignant, yet objective and realistic, discussion of the problem of homelessness in America. She reports that from 30 to 40 percent of the homeless are mentally ill and that most other homeless people "often have histories of chronic unemployment, chronic poverty, family breakdown, illiteracy, welfare depen-

dency and crime. The vast majority are single males. Among homeless families, most are headed by urban welfare recipients, predomi-
nantly single mothers." Despite claims to the contrary by advocates
of the homeless, very few of the homeless are families of formerly
solid wage-earners laid off from jobs in industries hard hit by recent
changes in the American economy, she reports. "All Alone, with No
Home," *Insight on the News*, May 16, 1988, p. 13. George Grant, in
The Dispossessed: Homelessness in America (Ft. Worth, TX, and
Westchester, IL: Dominion Press/Crossway, 1986), pp. 28-31, reports
that the federal Department of Housing and Urban Development
estimates that homelessness is a chronic, permanent condition for
only about 250,000 Americans, while the Department of Health and
Human Services reports that three million are homeless. But the
HHS figure is based on advocates' guesses rather than hard data and
includes such shadow figures as the "hidden homeless" and the
"borderline homeless."

7. *Statistical Abstract of the United States, 1977*, pp. 51f, Table 74.
8. *Ibid.*
9. This assumption is actually conservative. Church attendance, with
its attendant good moral habits, tends to increase earnings. Per capita
income of church members, therefore, is, on the average, higher than
per capita income of non-church members.
10. *Statistical Abstract of the United States, 1977*, p. 419, Table 703.
11. *Ibid.*, p. 416.
12. Figures differ slightly for various years, and for the same year depending on sources' estimates (compare similar tables in the *Statistical
Abstract of the United States* for 1982-83 and 1984), but conclusions
remain roughly the same.
13. *Statistical Abstract of the United States, 1987*, p. 445, Table 750.
14. The average family money income shortfall is extrapolated from earlier trends. The known shortfall in 1979 was about 70 percent of
poverty level. (See *Statistical Abstract of the United States, 1984*, p.
477, Table 786, and p. 273, Table 449.) In other words, poor families'
money incomes were about 30 percent of poverty level in that year.
Official poverty level in 1985 was $10,989 for a family of four.
Assuming average money income for below-poverty level families
was about the same percentage of poverty level in 1985 as in 1979,
average below-poverty level family money income would have been
about $3,297, leaving a shortfall from poverty level of $7,692.
Multiplying the average shortfall times 7.2 million poor families renders the aggregate shortfall of $55.4 billion. Money income excludes
in-kind income (food stamps, public housing, free or reduced-cost
medical care and school lunches, etc.), which for average welfare
families was worth many thousands of dollars. See Chapter
Fourteen, note 2.
15. *Statistical Abstract of the United States, 1987*, p. 293, Table 480,
including federal expenditures of $100.2 billion on housing, food,
income security, health care, and social services, but excluding
Social Security and unemployment payments, and including state
expenditures of about $12.4 billion based on 1984 figures, see p. 431
of 1987 edition.

16. This assumes four church members per family and total church membership of 142 million. *Statistical Abstract of the United States, 1987*, pp. 51f, Table 74.
17. *Statistical Abstract of the United States, 1987*, p. 498, Table 844.
18. The tithe was practiced before Moses (Genesis 28:22), codified in the Law (Leviticus 27:30-33; Numbers 18:21-24; Deuteronomy 12:6, 7, 17, 19; 14:22-29; 26:12-15), and affirmed—not abolished or denied—by Jesus, who contrasted it with "the weightier provisions of the law: justice and mercy and faithfulness," indicating that it is a minimum rather than maximum or ordinary standard of giving, and adding, "these are the things you should have done without neglecting the others," implying that the tithe law was still morally binding (Matthew 23:23; Luke 11:42). While the N.T. nowhere rescinds the law of the tithe, it emphasizes "(1) the need for spontaneous generosity (Lk. 21:4; Acts 11:28-30; 2 Cor. 8:1-3, 7; 9:5-10; Eph. 4:28; 1 Tim. 6:18; Heb. 13:16; Jas. 2:15-16) in response to God's limitless giving (2 Cor. 8:8-9; 9:15; 1 Jn. 3:17); (2) the need for individual decision (1 Cor. 16:2; 2 Cor. 9:7; cf. Acts 11:29) apart from external pressure (2 Cor. 8:8; 9:5, 7); (3) the blessedness of giving (Acts 20:35); and (4) the consequence of giving as being the glory of God or Christ (2 Cor. 8:19; 9:12-13)." M. J. Harris, "*dekate*," subarticle to "Number," in Brown, ed., *New International Dictionary of New Testament Theology*, Vol. 2, p. 694. Each of these emphases can be found in the O.T. as well.
19. A conservative assumption, since church attendance tends to be accompanied by higher than average income earning.
20. This assumes tithing on post-tax income. Christian economist Gary North argues persuasively that taxes should be considered part of the cost of making a living and therefore be deducted from gross income before calculating the tithe. (See his newsletter *Dominion Strategies*, Vol. II, No. 1, January 1986.) Tithes would be higher on pre-tax income, and hence percentages of church families' *pre-tax* income needed to raise recipients to the poverty level would be lower. But the resulting figures are still around half of a full tithe.
21. Deuteronomy 14:28f tells us that the tithe of every third year—i.e., a third of total tithes—was to be used to support the Levites and the poor. See the discussion of the third-year tithe below. Clearly a third of American church-goers' tithes would be far more than sufficient to care for the Biblically defined poor of America, if half of their tithes would care for all of the governmentally defined poor, since the Biblical definition, as we have seen, would indicate that there are only about one tenth as many poor as the governmental definition indicates.
22. *Statistical Abstract of the United States, 1987*, pp. 54f, Table 78. The average American church member gave only about $275 in 1985, or about 1.98 percent of his pre-tax income or 2.33 percent of his post-tax income, assuming church members' per capita income was the same as the national average (compare p. 419, Table 703). Using different assumptions, John and Sylvia Ronsvalle estimate that average church members give 1.6 percent of their income to churches. See their *The Hidden Billions: The Potential of the Church in the U.S.A.* (Champaign, IL: C-4 Resources Inc., 1984), p. 67 and p. 142 n. 3.

23. Reference to a "list" indicates that Paul here has in mind limitations on the church's *systematic* charitable aid rather than on occasional aid in temporary emergencies. Many of the principles, however, are equally valid in either case.

24. One who refuses to provide for his children or disabled parents or grandparents "has denied the faith, and is worse than an unbeliever" (v. 8). Presumably he is to be excluded from Communion until he repents and expelled from fellowship if he persists in sin (Matthew 18:15-20; 1 Corinthians 5:1-5).

25. Also presumably, short-term support while the widow found a husband would be permitted so that she could continue to care for her children.

26. "Godliness," Greek *eusebeia*, is piety, godliness, or religion, and may be either sincere, as in vv. 3, 6, or a mere outward show, as apparently is the case in v. 5. Paul may be aiming his comments specifically at those who pretend Christianity to benefit from the churches' poor relief programs.

27. The amount people need for subsistence is considerably lower if they are taken into church families than if they are housed elsewhere.

28. This does not mean that our help should be *limited* to lifting them to subsistence. We may well want to give more, and can readily do so.

29. For a thorough analysis of the relationship between social and cultural attitudes, on the one hand, and economic prosperity, on the other, see Edward C. Banfield, *The Unheavenly City Revisited* (Boston: Little, Brown and Company, 1974).

30. Chilton, *Productive Christians in an Age of Guilt Manipulators*, p. 221.

31. Papers on the implications of the Christian worldview for various areas of life are available from The Coalition on Revival, 89 Pioneer Way, Mountain View, CA 94041. Subjects covered include: law, government, economics, business and professions, education, arts and media, medicine, science, psychology and counseling, family, evangelism, political action, helping the hurting, Christian college and seminary revitalization, pastoral renewal, Christian unity, and discipleship.

32. People interested in becoming financial counselors can get training from Christian Financial Concepts, Route 5, Box 130, Dahlonega, GA 30533.

33. Against this see Chapters Four and Five above.

34. There are "gray areas" related to this principle, however, and churches need to be sure to teach basic principles without inducing what might be false guilt over questionable matters (Romans 14). While accepting outright transfers of wealth by government seems clearly to violate the Eighth Commandment, other activities would not be so clearly condemned. Is it, for instance, wrong for a Christian to use a public library, a public recreational facility, or a publicly operated transportation system? Arguments can be made both ways, and it seems best to teach Biblical principles of justice like those described in Chapters Four, Five and Eleven; to leave believers free to apply those principles as they understand them; and to undertake the long-term work of replacing governmental provision of such services with private provision and influencing legislatures to end governmental

intrusions into the economy other than to enforce justice.

35. The chapter "Discovering and Identifying Needs," in George Grant's *Bringing in the Sheaves*, is an invaluable discussion of how to identify local needs through demographic study. Chapters Five through Thirteen in Grant's book suggest many practical, tested methods for churches to help the poor.

36. *Ibid.*, p. 80.

37. In agreement, see the discussion of 1 Timothy 5:9, 10, above.

38. "As a result, the apparatus of charity is kept simple. Accountability is enhanced, Flexibility is made possible. Local conditions are maximized. And personal attention is more likely." Grant, *Bringing in the Sheaves*, p. 81.

39. *Ibid.*, p. 82. In agreement, see the discussion of 1 Timothy 5:3-16 above.

40. John Naisbitt, *Megatrends* (New York: Warner Books, 1982), p. 153; cited in *Ibid.*, p. 81.

41. "On a busy day, manager D. L. Stone estimates that his bus boys [sic] throw away half a ton of food at the Wyatt's Cafeteria in suburban Dallas. At the Borden Dairy Plant in New Orleans, workers returning outdated milk from stores dump five tons of milk and other dairy products into tanks so they can be shipped to the Midwest to be used in animal food. At supermarkets throughout Des Moines, store managers say they throw out day-old bread and other food 'by the dumpster-full.' They say if it's of no value to the store, it's probably of no value to anyone. In the Rio Grande Valley, citrus farmers leave tons of unsaleable oranges and grapefruits to rot on the trees every year." Grant, *Bringing in the Sheaves*, p. 129.

42. "In Houston, Texas, executives of the Igloo Corporation teamed up with a local church charity to provide homeless families with ice chests, thermos jugs, and pure water containers. According to Igloo executive, Joe Decker, 'Most manufacturers of consumer goods have large supplies of unsaleable inventory. The items may be seconds, they may be outdated, or they may just be the wrong color. But, regardless, the stock must be disposed of somehow.' Most manufacturers destroy such inventory. 'If churches and other charities could organize a reputable and efficient distribution system,' he said, 'then I'm sure most of the waste would cease immediately and the goods could be had by those who probably need them the most.'" *Ibid.*, p. 128.

43. Community organizer Mitch Snyder, cited in *Ibid.*, p. 129.

44. Presumably the alien, orphan, and widow who might partake of the third-year tithe were in actual need; the alien, because he owned no land and so could not grow his own food, the orphan because he was too young to work, and the widow because she was too old or too burdened with caring for children.

45. See the discussion above of the magnitude of the problem of poverty in the United States.

46. Most people undervalue the capital investment needed to provide jobs. The cost—above wages and taxes—per employee work hour varies widely by industry in the United States. In 1979, for instance, average capital investment per employee work hour in selected industries were: public utilities, $167.09; petroleum, $69.60; commu-

nication, $67.06; transportation, $37.60; primary metals, $29.65; mining, $21.93; tobacco, $35.93; chemicals, $28.73; paper, $22.03; stone, clay, glass, $15.29; transportation equipment, $13.48; nonelectric machinery, $11.72; food, $13.06; services, $9.21; fabricated metals, $9.30; rubber and plastics, $8.96; finance and insurance, $10.56; lumber and wood, $7.64; instruments, $7.52; textiles, $9.43; electric machinery, $8.47; printing and publishing, $7.01; wholesale, retail trade, $7.33; construction, $3.39; furniture and fixtures, $5.02; leather, $3.58; apparel, $2.98. See *Statistical Abstract of the United States, 1982-83*, p. 539, Table 906. These hourly costs translate into annual costs per employee (above wages) of $6,198 at the low end of the scale and $347,547 at the high end. Investors who provide capital for business and industry do not reap where they have not sown.

47. Churches should be cautious about how they conduct such programs so long as minimum wage, overtime wage, child labor, and similar laws remain in effect. In a recent federal court case, District Judge Robert D. Potter found two firms operated by members of the Shiloh True Light Church of Christ near Charlotte, NC, in violation of child labor laws, ordered them to pay the U.S. Dept. of Labor's litigation costs and back wages to the under-age workers, and threatened fines for continued violation of the federal Fair Labor Standards Act. See Arthur H. Matthews, "Church Faces Fines for Child Labor 'Abuses,'" *World*, Vol. 2, No. 32 (February 1, 1988), pp. 6, 7, and "Shiloh Group Loses Case, But Not Its Spirit," *World*, Vol. 2, No. 39 (March 21, 1988), p. 11. Similar cases have been common in the past. They exemplify the way in which labor laws can curtail opportunity for poor and low-skilled workers to gain the experience necessary to climb the economic ladder.

48. Churches could also help by pressuring Congress to abolish the minimum wage and similar regulations that prohibit low-skilled workers from gaining experience necessary to earn higher wages. See Chapter Twelve for arguments that they are both unjust and economically destructive.

49. Grant, *Bringing in the Sheaves*, p. 86.

50. See Chapters Eleven and Thirteen above.

51. Like minimum wage laws, laws limiting the number of hours workers can be employed, prohibiting children from working, and requiring extra pay for overtime all diminish opportunities for low-skilled workers to learn and earn more.

52. See the discussion of minimum wages in Chapter Twelve and of licensure in Chapter Thirteen.

53. ". . . [M]ost people acquire work skills by working at a 'subnormal wage,' which amounts to the same thing as paying to learn. For example, inexperienced doctors (interns), during their training, work at wages which are a tiny fraction of that of trained doctors. . . . It is ironic, if not tragic, that low-skilled youths from poor families are denied an opportunity to get a start in life. This is exactly what happens when a high minimum wage forbids low-skilled workers to pay for job training in the form of a lower beginning wage." Williams, *The State Against Blacks*, p. 152, n. 3; cf. p. 153, n. 11. See the discussion of these laws in Chapter Twelve above.

54. See Gary North, "Public Goods and the Fear of Foreigners," *The Freeman* (March 1974). "Such restrictions, had they been passed into law and enforced prior to 1924, would have greatly reduced American economic growth. On the multiple cultural and economic contributions of several immigrant groups—Germans, Irish, Italians, Jews, Blacks, Puerto Ricans, Mexicans, and orientals—see Thomas Sowell, *Ethnic America: A History* (New York: Basic Books, 1981). . . . The political-economic problem today is twofold: 1) new immigrants in a democracy are soon allowed to vote, and 2) they become eligible for tax-financed 'welfare' programs. In the Old Testament, it took several generations for members of pagan cultures to achieve citizenship (Deut. 23:3-8), and there were very few publicly financed charities, the most notable being the third-year tithe (Deut. 14:28-29). Thus, mass democracy has violated a fundamental biblical principle—that time is needed for *ethical* acculturation of pagan immigrants—and the result of this transgression has been *xenophobia*: the fear of foreigners, especially immigrant newcomers." North, *The Sinai Strategy*, p. 100, n. 16.
55. See Chapters Nine and Ten above.
56. See Chapters Twelve and Thirteen above.
57. See Chapter Twelve above.
58. In inner cities, poor blacks frequently used to outbid middle-income whites for housing space by banding together and suggesting that landlords partition one brownstone into six apartments. Hence, "During the racially hostile times of the 1920s, 30s, and 40s, one could not prevent whole blocks and neighborhoods from going from white to black virtually overnight." Why not suburban areas? "Suburban areas, to a greater extent than cities, have highly restrictive zoning ordinances. There are laws that fix the minimum lot size, minimum floor space in the house, minimum distance to adjacent houses plus laws that restrict property use to a single family. The combined effect of these laws, independent of *de jure* or *de facto* racial discrimination, is to deny poor people the chance to outbid nonpoor people." Williams, *The State Against Blacks*, pp. 142f.
59. See Chapters Four, Five, and Eleven through Thirteen above.

CHAPTER SIXTEEN: *How Individuals and Families Can Help the Poor*

1. See, for example, Ronald Sider, *Rich Christians in an Age of Hunger.*
2. "Charity is personal, though not purely 'voluntary,' since biblical law commands it—but . . . those laws are not enforced by the state: the Bible mandates no civil penalties for failing to obey the charity laws." Chilton, *Productive Christians in an Age of Guilt Manipulators*, p. 8.
3. 2 Corinthians 9:8-10, a passage often misunderstood, makes a key and striking distinction between the *penes* and the *ptochos*. (For discussion of this distinction, see the section "Poverty Is Destitution," especially note 13, in Chapter Fourteen.) The *penes* are not destitute like the *ptochos*. Neither are they rich, like the *plousios*, but must work to earn a living. Verse 9 tells us that God "scattered abroad, He gave to the poor [*penes*]. . .," literally the laborers. What He gave was

seed to sow (v. 10), that from the harvest they might give liberally to the poor saints in Jerusalem. The poor in Jerusalem are not *penes* but *ptochos* (Romans 15:26)—truly destitute. Readers unaware of the distinction between the *penes* of 2 Corinthians 9:9 and the *ptochos* of Jerusalem might easily misunderstand Paul's argument to be, "God scattered abroad, He gave to the poor; you follow His example and do likewise." In itself that would be a good and legitimate argument, but it is not Paul's in this text. His actual argument in light of this distinction is, "God gave you laborers, the *penes*, seed to sow so that you might reap a harvest and have plenty to give to the truly poor, the *ptochos*. So don't misuse the harvest God has given you; instead, give liberally from it so that the poor in Jerusalem might have cause to thank God for giving you the seed in the first place." In the broader context of vv. 6-11, there is more to the argument: "Whoever sows sparingly reaps sparingly, and whoever sows abundantly reaps abundantly. God sowed abundantly in you and reaped abundantly in your salvation. You sow abundantly in the poor in Jerusalem and you will reap abundantly in righteousness." See the following commentaries on the passage: R. C. H. Lenski, *The Interpretation of St. Paul's First and Second Epistles to the Corinthians*, pp. 1167-1181; A. T. Robertson, *Word Pictures in the New Testament*, Vol. 4, pp. 248f; A. R. Fausset, in Robert Jamieson, A. R. Fausset, and David Brown, *A Commentary, Critical, Experimental, and Practical on the Old and New Testaments*, three vols. (Grand Rapids: Eerdmans, 1976 rpt.), Vol. 3, Pt. 2, p. 360.

4. Charitable giving should not be motivated by feelings of guilt over the fact that the giver happens to have more of the world's goods than the recipient. There is nothing unjust or sinful in either inequality or wealth.

5. See Chapters Six and Seven above.

6. See Chapter Fifteen, note 46 for a list of capital investments per employee work hour in selected industries.

7. He might, for instance, choose less profitable investments for the sake of greater security or to be of greater benefit to the poor.

8. For a discussion of the nature, function, and morality of profits, see Chapter Seven.

9. Some stock analysts specialize in helping Americans identify safe, profitable Third World investment opportunities. Often such investments employ—and hence support—more poor people per dollar than do domestic investments. Local investment advisors have access to such analysts.

10. 2 Thessalonians 3:8a carries a strong message against accepting handouts if someone is able to support himself. Not only does accepting handouts foster dependency instead of responsibility, but also it violates property rights when the handouts come from civil government. See Chapters Eleven and Thirteen above.

11. Leviticus 27:30-33; Numbers 18:21-24; Deuteronomy 12:6, 7, 17, 19; 14:22-29; 26:12-15; Matthew 23:23. See Chapter Fifteen, note 18, for a discussion of tithing as still binding under the New Testament and as a minimal rather than a maximal or normal standard of giving.

12. This is based on the principle of the third-year tithe (Deuteronomy

14:28f). See discussion of the third-year tithe in Chapter Fifteen. As noted there, far less than a third would be sufficient to care for America's poor. The rest could be given to poor in other countries.

13. Leviticus 19:9, 10; 23:22; Deuteronomy 24:19-22; 23:24, 25; Ruth 2:1-16; 1 Timothy 5—6. For a more thorough discussion of these principles, see the sections "The Standard of Contentment" and "The Gleaning Law" in Chapter Fifteen.

14. As demonstrated by the Christians in Jerusalem, fellow believers take priority over unbelievers in charitable activity: ". . . while we have opportunity, let us do good to all men, and especially to those who are of the household of the faith" (Galatians 6:10).

15. Theft is wrong even for the hungry, and though we can understand their weakness it cannot be excused: "Men do not despise a thief if he steals to satisfy himself when he is hungry; but when he is found, he must repay sevenfold; he must give all the substance of his house" (Proverbs 6:30, 31).

16. See Grant, *Bringing in the Sheaves*, pp. 58ff, for an argument that the primary function of deacons should be caring for the poor of the congregation and the community.

17. Grant's chapter "Discovering and Identifying Needs," in *Ibid.*, gives practical and comprehensive instructions on how to gather the information necessary for an effective ministry to the poor.

18. Grant suggests the following menu: four 16-ounce cans of vegetables, four 16-ounce cans of meat (tuna/chili), four 16-ounce cans of fruit, four 10-ounce cans of soup, one package each of noodles, dry beans, cereal, crackers, and powdered milk, one jar of peanut butter, and one family-size bar of bath soap. See his discussion of food pantries in Chapter Eleven of *Ibid.*

19. See Grant, *Ibid.*, pp. 79-82.

20. See Grant's discussion of job placement and training services churches can conduct in *Ibid.*, pp. 171-180.

21. Such a *commercial* loan could bear interest—though you would be free to make it at no interest, of course. It would not be regulated by the prohibition of interest on loans to the poor (Exodus 22:25; Leviticus 25:35-37; Luke 6:34, 35), for the "poor" to whom one could not lend on interest are specifically the *ani* (Hebrew in Exodus 22:25; see also Deuteronomy 15:11, which may be interpreted as prohibiting interest on charitable loans [Leviticus 25:35-37 uses a verb meaning "to slip" rather than one of the words for "poor"]), the "poorest and most dependent on others" (Borgquist, *Toward a Biblical Theology of the Poor*, p. 18). Thus they are equivalent to the *ptochos* of the N.T., the utterly destitute.

22. One sad fruit of outright gifts to those able but unwilling to work is that givers and receivers soon resent each other. The gleaning principle, in which givers and receivers cooperate, has the opposite effect. See the example of Ruth in the O.T.

23. See Chapter Two.

24. In Lk. 6:35 Jesus instructs believers to *"lend,* expecting nothing in return,*"* addressing not *giving* but *lending.* Upholding O.T. Law, Jesus forbids interest on charitable loans. One is to lend without expecting profit (which is otherwise permitted; Matthew 25:27; Luke

19:23), not without expecting repayment.

25. This does not mean that we *ought not* to give charitably to people who are not destitute and incapable of helping themselves. Our generosity should overflow to all people, but without creating dependency.

APPENDIX ONE: *Methodological Note on the Use of Biblical Law*

1. See Arthur Ivan Melvin, *Discovering Consensus on a Moral Valuing Standard: A Descriptive and Experimental Study of Century III's Valuing Analysis Process* (Evanston, IL: Northwestern University, unpublished dissertation for Ph.D. in Education, 1979; available from University Microfilms International, Ann Arbor, MI). Century III Foundation (P.O. Box 3762, Oak Brook, IL, 60521) conducts educational research and outstanding seminars in moral valuing that rest on the presupposition that the work of the Law is written on the heart of every man.

2. See C. S. Lewis, *The Abolition of Man* (New York: Macmillan, 1947).

3. Early American colonists cited specific O.T. texts to justify penalties for criminals. See *The Body of Liberties* (1641), the first code of laws established in New England, in Charles Eliot, ed., *The Harvard Classics*, fifty vols. (New York: P. F. Collier & Son, 1910), Vol. 43, pp. 70ff.

4. Major leaders are Rousas John Rushdoony, Gary North, Greg Bahnsen, James Jordan, and Ray Sutton. While I quote some of these authors here, my doing so does not imply that I endorse their whole system of thought. While I disagree with them on some points, some of their exegetical and ethical arguments are persuasive on others. It would have been intellectually dishonest to have reproduced their ideas without giving them credit. Much criticism of their thought in mainstream evangelical circles is, I think, based on misunderstanding and caricature.

5. Neither am I convinced that it is wrong. The exegetical and logical arguments for it deserve careful consideration. See Greg Bahnsen, *Theonomy in Christian Ethics* (Nutley, NJ: Craig Press, 1977).

6. Bahnsen, *Theonomy in Christian Ethics*, p. 34.

7. My approach then, while different from theonomy, is not logically exclusive of it.

SCRIPTURE INDEX

SUBJECT INDEX